THE CHARLTON STANDARD CATALOGUE OF

Volume One: General Issues
Third Edition

By
Pat Murray

Publisher:
W. K. Cross

The Charlton Press

TORONTO, ONTARIO • BIRMINGHAM, MICHIGAN

D0884810

Canadian Cataloguing in Publication Data

The National Library of Canada has catalogued this publication as follows:

Murray, Pat
    The Charlton standard catalogue of Wade

Biennial

3rd ed.
Previously published under title: Pre-war and more Wades.
Each issue published in 3 v.

ISSN 1203-4681
ISBN 0-88968-225-9 (v. 1) ISBN 088968-224-0 (v. 2)
ISBN 0-88968-226-7 (v. 3) ISBN 0-88968-237-2 (v. 4)

1. George Wade and Son - Catalogs. 2. Miniature pottery - England -
Catalogs. 3. Figurines - England - Catalogs. I. Title. II. Title: Pre-war and
more Wades.

NK8473.5.W33M8   738.8'2   C96-301353-X

The Charlton Press

Editorial Office
2040 Yonge Street, Suite 208, Toronto, Ontario M4S 1Z9
Telephone: (416) 488-1418 Fax: (416) 488-4656
Telephone: (800) 442-6042 Fax: (800) 442-1542
www.charltonpress.com e-mail: chpress@charltonpress.com

EDITORIAL TEAM

Editor	Eva Kovacs
Assistant Editor	Jean Dale
Graphic Technician	Davina Rowan

ACKNOWLEDGEMENTS

Many thanks to Derek Dawe and Ivan MacGee for their help in checking facts in parts of the manuscript; Ralph Brough, for his background information on Wade; Joy Damsell, for her assistance in answering our inquiries; Bill Walker, for his help regarding backstamps; Cynthia Risby and Jenny Wright, for their help in answering questions; and J. A. Stringer, for his assistance with Wade Ireland products.

Companies

We would like to thank the following individuals for supplying information and photographs concerning the Wade products that their companies commissioned:

Kate Peri, Executive Assistant, the Ford Motor Company New Zealand; Richard Blay, Manager, the Australian Guarantee Corporation; and Adele Hall and Jenny Wright, the International Wade Collectors Club.

Institutions

We are grateful to the following institutions for their research assistance:

Phillips Auctioneers and Valuers (U.K.); Daniel & Hulme Auctioneers (U.K.); the British Library (U.K.); and Stroud Public Library (Canada).

CONTRIBUTORS TO THE THIRD EDITION

Thanks also to the following collectors in Canada, England, New Zealand, Scotland and the U.S.A. for their photographs, measurements and backstamp information:

Gill Adams; Mary Andrews; Ernie Benjamin; Mr. Bentley; Sarah Bernotas; Trudi Blatchford; Valerie Bull; B. Bultz; John Carter; Peter Challenger; Peter and Lesley Chisholm; David Chown and Russell Schooley of C & S Collectables Direct; Father David Cox; Linda Cox (New Zealand); Andy and Christine Crowe; Jean Dale; Ben Dawson; Maria Deacon; Rachel Derby; Joyce and David Devilbis; Paula Doherty; Dick Ellis; Jean Ellison; David Elvin; Catherine Evans; Janet and Mike Evans of "Yesterdays"; Paul Farmer; Nancy Fronczac; Peggy Fyffe; G & G Collectables; Gordon and Pat (U.K.); Betty Hannigan; Al Halpern; Freda Harker (New Zealand); Charlie Harlan; Fatima and Vince Harvey; Joyce and Bob Hill; Val and Dave Holman; Pat and Connie Hoyle; Marian and Gareth Hunt; Lucy Hutchinson; Peg and Roger (Fred) Johnson; Ted Joiner; K & P Collectables; Patty Keenan; Adam Less; Jane and Tina Lister; Michael Lynch; Vera, Ian and Michelle MacKay; Margaret of "Rosetiques"; Lynne and David Maund; Alison Melcher; Scott and Kathy Meyer; Joe and Augusta Miller; Barbara Morgan; Gina and Jon Norridge; Lindsey Otter; Phyllis Palvio; P. and T. Partridge; Pat & Terry Collectables; Bruce Penny; June and Geoff Rance; Keeley Rich; Ginny Roberts; J. and B. Robinson (U.K.); Janet and Brian Robinson (New Zealand); Roy Senior; Philip Sharp; Nicholas Slater; Joyce and Leonard Steers; Trevor J. Stubbs; Mr. and Mrs. T. Swinhoe; T & A Collectables; D. Tindall; Duane and Jean Tranby; Joy and Art Turner; Kim and Derek Watson; Penny Webber; Harvey and Loris Westrom; Mr. and Mrs. Williams; Kim Williams; Sue Williams; Annie and Steve Windsor; Robert Wright; JoAnn Yadro; and Mary and Steve Yager.

Also, many thanks to all who helped with photographs and information but wish to remain anonymous.

A SPECIAL NOTE TO COLLECTORS

We welcome and appreciate comments or suggestions in regard to *The Charlton Standard Catalogue of Wade, Volume One*. If you would like to participate in pricing, please contact Jean Dale at The Charlton Press. To provide new information or corrections, please write to Pat Murray, Box 746, R.R. #2, Sroud, Ontario L0L 2MO, Canada.

HOW TO USE THIS CATALOGUE

The Listings

On the pages that follow, Wade models are listed, illustrated, described and priced.

The measurements of the models are given in millimetres. Items such as figurines, most animals and birds, tankards, decanters and water jugs are measured according to their height. For relatively flat objects — ashtrays, dishes, trays and the like — the measurement listed is the diameter of a round item, the side of a square, or the longest length of a rectangle or oval. For a few items, both height and width are provided.

Although the publisher has made every attempt to obtain and photograph all models listed, several pieces, naturally, have not come into the publisher's possession.

A Word on Pricing

The purpose of this catalogue is to give readers the most accurate, up-to-date retail prices for Wade models in the United States, Canada and the United Kingdom.

To accomplish this, The Charlton Press continues to access an international pricing panel of Wade experts who submit prices based on both dealer and collector retail-price activity, as well as current auction results in the U.S., Canadian, and U.K. markets. These market figures are carefully averaged to reflect accurate valuations for the Wade models listed herein in each of the three markets.

Please be aware that prices given in a particular currency are for models in that country only. The prices published herein have not been calculated using exchange rates; they have been determined solely by the supply and demand in the country in question.

A necessary word of caution: no pricing catalogue can or should be a fixed price list. This catalogue should be considered a guide only — one that shows the most current retail prices based on market demand in a particular region.

Current models, however, are priced differently: they are priced according to the manufacturer's suggested retail price in each of the three market regions. It should be noted that it is likely that dealer discounting from these prices will occur.

The prices published herein are for items in mint condition. The only exception is the prices for the cellulose figures, which are listed for models with a moderate degree of glaze flaking. Collectors are cautioned that a repaired or restored piece may be worth as little as 50 percent of the value of the same model in mint condition. Those collectors interested strictly in investment potential must avoid damaged items.

All relevant information must be known about an item to make a proper valuation. When comparing auction prices with catalogue prices, collectors and dealers should remember two important points. First, to compare "apples and apples," they must be sure that auction prices include a buyer's premium, if one is due. Prices realized for models in auction catalogues may not include this additional cost. Second, it may not be noted in the listing that an item has been restored or repaired and, as a result, the price will not be reflective of the price for the same piece in mint condition.

TABLE OF CONTENTS

INTRODUCTION

History

In the early 1930s, Wade consisted of three potteries — A. J. Wade Ltd., George Wade & Son Ltd. and Wade Heath and Co. Ltd. — with Wade Ulster (Ireland) being acquired in the mid-1940s. At first, the company mainly produced gas burners for domestic lighting, although a small amount of giftware was made as well. Later, Wade's chief output was insulating products, bobbins, thread guides and tiles. The company even made cone heads for guided missiles in the early 1960s.

At the onset of World War II, the government permitted the production of essential ceramics only. All giftware production came to an end, with parts of the potteries being used as emergency food stores for the duration of the war. Afterwards, the potteries were engaged in replacing the essential ceramics that had been destroyed by bombing. By the early 1950s, the George Wade pottery had begun producing small collectable figures and animals.

Between 1955 and 1969, Wade Heath and Co. Ltd. worked with Reginald Corfield (Sales) Ltd. of Redhill, Surrey (under the trademark of Regicor London), to produce a range of promotional and point-of-sale advertising ware. These earthenware products were produced by Wade Heath at its Royal Victoria Pottery in Burslem.

The Reginald Corfield sales force worked closely with the distilling, brewing and tobacco industries. Many original water jugs and ashtrays were created for specific clients and were retained as exclusive shapes for particular brands.

In 1958, the three English Wade potteries were restructured under the name Wade Potteries Ltd., later renamed Wade PLC. Wade (Ulster) Ltd. was renamed Wade Ireland in 1966.

The association with Reginald Corfield was discontinued in October 1969, and Wade Heath formed its own product, design and marketing company called Wade PDM ("PDM" stood for "point of sale, design and marketing"). This company specializes in advertising products for the distilling, brewing and tobacco industries, although its work is not limited to those areas. Wade PDM has become one of the leading suppliers of advertising products in the U.K.

In 1989, Wade PLC was taken over by Beauford PLC and renamed Wade Ceramics Ltd., which is still in operation today. Wade Ireland was renamed Seagoe Ceramics and continued to manufacture domestic tableware until 1993, when it reverted to the production of industrial ceramics.

The Production Process

The Wade potteries manufacture a particularly hard porcelain body that has been used in many different products. It consists of a mixture of ball clays, china clay, flint, feldspar, talc, and so on, some ingredients being imported from Sweden, Norway and Egypt. These materials are mixed in large vats of water, producing a thick sludge or "slip." The slip is passed into a filter to extract most of the water, leaving large flat "bats" of porcelain clay approximately two feet square and three inches thick. The clay bats are dried and then ground into dust ready for the forming process. Paraffin is added to the dust to assist in bonding and to serve as a lubricant to remove the formed pieces from the steel moulds. Once pressed into the required shape, the clay articles are allowed to dry and then all the press marks are removed by sponging and "fettling," the scraping-off of surplus clay with a sharp blade.

One or more ceramic colours are applied to the model, which is then sprayed with a clear glaze that, when fired, allows the colours underneath to show through. This process is known as underglaze decoration. On-glaze decoration — which includes enamelling, gilding and transfer printing — can also be done after the article has been glazed and fired.

Modellers

The following modellers have worked for Wade. We have listed below some of the different models that they designed.

HARPER, WILLIAM K., 1954 to 1962

Bard of Armagh
Irish Emigrant
Little Crooked Paddy
Little Mickey Mulligan
Molly Malone
Phil the Fluter
Star of County Down
Widda Cafferty

HOLMES, KEN, 1975 to the present

Dunbar Cake Decorators, wedding cake topper
The Great Priory of England and Wales,
    Knight Templar
Imperial Tobacco, St. Bruno Key Ring
J. W. Thornton delivery van money boxes
Lyons Tetley Tea Brew Gaffer items
Lyons Tetley Tea delivery van money boxes
My Fair Ladies
Sophisticated Ladies

LANG, FAUST, 1939

Brown Bear
Budgerigar on Branch
Budgerigars
Chamois Kid
Ermine
Grebe
Highland Stag
Horse
Capuchin on Tree
Panther
Parrot
Weasel

MASLANKOWSKI, ALAN, 1975

The Cheetah and Gazelle
The Connoisseur's Collection
University Treasures, Razorback Pigs
The World of Survival series

MELLOR, FREDERICK, 1979

Peter Thompson, The Thistle and the Rose
  Historical Chess Set

STABLER, PHOEBE, 1962 to 1963

Dan Murphy
Eileen Oge
Mother MacCree

SZEILOR, JOHN, late 1940s to early 1950s

Siamese Kittens
Begging Puppy

VAN HALLEN, JESSIE, 1930 to 1939

Lady figures
Large dog models

Insuring Your Models

As with any of your other valuables, making certain that your models are protected is very important. It is paramount that you display or store any porcelain items in a secure place, preferably one safely away from traffic in the home.

Your models are most likely covered under your basic homeowner's policy. There are generally three kinds of such policies: standard, broad and comprehensive. Each has its own specific deductible and terms.

Under a general policy, your models are considered part of the contents of your home and are covered for all of the perils covered under the contractual terms of your policy (fire, theft, water damage, and so on). However, since some models are extremely delicate, breakage is treated differently by most insurance companies. There is usually an extra premium attached to insure models against accidental breakage by or carelessness of the owner. This is sometimes referred to as a "fine arts" rider. You are advised to contact your insurance professional to get all the answers.

To help protect yourself, it is critical that you take inventory of your models and have colour photographs taken of all of your pieces. This is the surest method of clearly establishing, for the police and your insurance company, which items have been lost or destroyed. It is also the easiest way to establish the replacement value of the items.

Backstamps

Since the early 1950s, the George Wade pottery has used several types of impressed and embossed "Wade England" backstamps, which are incorporated into the mould. Transfer-printed backstamps were first used in the George Wade and Wade Heath potteries in 1953, and they are still in use today.

Wade has produced commissioned ware since 1955 through Wade Regicor and, later, Wade PDM. Several styles and colours of transfer-printed backstamps can be found with "Wade Regicor" and "Wade PDM" on them.

Wade Ireland used a wide variety of impressed and embossed marks in the 1950s, and reissued models produced using the original moulds still carried the 1950s backstamps. Because the colours remained the same, it is difficult to determine the age of some Wade Ireland models. Also in the 1950s, some figures had various types of ink-stamped "Wade Ireland" backstamps, which were used until 1991. Beginning in 1962, Wade Ireland began using transfer-printed backstamps.

For more information on backstamps, see the start of each chapter.

THE SURVIVAL SERIES

ADVERTISING PRODUCTS
1950 to the present

From 1953 to the present, Wade Ceramics has produced—through Wade Regicor then Wade PDM—a huge range of earthenware jugs, ashtrays and ancillary items for use as commissioned and advertising products, making it one of the leading suppliers of these items in the United Kingdom. The Royal Victoria, George Wade and Wade Ireland potteries all produced these models.

The items in this section were used to advertise various companies and products, with the exception of liquor advertising.

Advertising and commissioned products can be found — each in its separate section — under the headings of the sponsoring companies or brand names, which are listed alphabetically.

Please note that some dates in this section are approximate only, when no information on production start or end dates is available. They indicate the earliest and latest dates of the backstamps used; they do not imply that the product was made continuously during the range of dates.

BACKSTAMPS

Wade Regicor and Wade PDM Backstamps

Wade Regicor and Wade PDM transfer-printed backstamps are found in black, blue, yellow, white, green, red and gold. The colour of the backstamps varied in order to contrast with the base colour of the models. The dating of a product is not determined by the colour of the backstamp, but by its style.

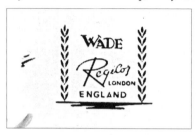

1953-1962: "Wade Regicor, London England" in between two upright rows of nine laurel-type leaves, large size (18 mm x 20 mm)

1962-1968: "Wade Regicor, London England" in between two upright rows of nine laurel-type leaves, small size (13 mm x 13 mm)

1968-1969: "Reginald Corfield Limited Redhill Surrey" printed in a circle, with "Wade Regicor England" printed through the circle

1969-1984: "Wade pdm England" printed in a circle (this was the first Wade PDM backstamp)

1984-1990: "Wade p d m England," with spaces between the letters *pdm*

1990-1996: "Wade P D M England" or "Wade P D M Made in England" within two red lines, one thick, the other thin

Private Backstamps

As well as the Wade Regicor and Wade PDM backstamps, many advertising and commissioned items produced from 1953 to the present are marked with some type of Wade England transfer print. Others are more elaborate and can be embossed or impressed. They can include details of the commissioning company and/or the occasion for which the product was created. Some companies have omitted a backstamp, believing that their name on the item was sufficient, and a few companies do not have their name on the product at all.

ACCESS BANKING

ASHTRAY, 1955-1962

This ashtray is decorated with a transfer print of a bank card.

Photograph not available at press time

Backstamp: "Wade Regicor, London England," laurel leaves, large size

No.	Description	Colourways	Shape/Size	U.S.$	Can.$	U.K.£
1.	Ashtray	Green; white/green print, lettering "Access Your Flexible Friend"	Oval/153	20.00	25.00	8.00

ALLIANCE FINANCE COMPANY

TYRE DISH 1936-A.F.C.-1961 WELLINGTON OCTOBER 19th 1961.

The Alliance Finance Company, based in Wellington New Zealand, provided finance for cars purchased from Ford dealers. In 1961 A.F.C. Celebrated their 25th anniversary. Approximately 200 of the Tyre dishes were produced for the proprietors of Ford franchises to keep for themselves or to give to respected customers. In 1972 the company changed its name to Australian Guarantee Corporation.

Tyre Dish

Backstamp: a "Moko Product by Wade England -Design Authenticated by the Veteran car Club of Great Britain"

No.	Description	Colourways	Shape/Size	U.S.$	Can.$	U.K.£
1.	1936-A.F.C.-1961	White dish; dark grey rim; black "Ford" "Wellington October 19th" print/lettering	125	15.00	20.00	10.00

BARRATT HOMES

ASHTRAY, 1984-1990

The print on this ashtray is of a helicopter flying over an oak tree.

Backstamp: "Wade p d m England"

No.	Description	Colourways	Shape/Size	U.S.$	Can.$	U.K.£
1.	Ashtray	Green; black print, lettering "Barratt"	Square/110	10.00	15.00	5.00

BENSON AND HEDGES CIGARETTES

ASHTRAY AND CIGARETTE LIGHTER, 1969-1984

Wade produced the hollow cube into which a lighter was fitted. The lettering is on the front of the cube.

Backstamp: A. "Wade pdm England"
B. "Wade Regicor London England 1962-1968" between two upright rows of laurel leaves, small size

No.	Description	Colourways	Shape/Size	U.S.$	Can.$	U.K.£
1.	Ashtray	Black/gold; gold lettering "Benson & Hedges Special Filter"	Rectangular/242	15.00	20.00	8.00
2.	Ashtray	White/red, gold label red/black lettering	230	25.00	30.00	15.00
3.	Lighter	Light brown; black lettering "Benson & Hedges"	Rectangular/114	25.00	30.00	12.00

BIRDS EYE WALL'S Ltd FROZEN FOODS

PINT TRADITIONAL TANKARD, FEBRUARY 1971

Come Home to Birds Eye Country, February 1971

Backstamp: Red printed "Wade England"

No.	Description	Colourways	Shape/Size	U.S.$	Can.$	U.K.£
1.	Tankard	Amber; black print of peas & lettering	125	10.00	15.00	8.00

BRITISH LEYLAND

STEERING WHEEL ASHTRAY, c.1969 - 1984

Backstamp: "Wade Pdm England"

No.	Description	Colourways	Shape/Size	U.S.$	Can.$	U.K.£
1.	Ashtray	Light blue	150	28.00	40.00	20.00
2.	Ashtray	Light blue	187	28.00	40.00	20.00

BRITISH OVERSEAS AIRWAYS CORPORATION

ASHTRAYS, JUGS AND TANKARDS, 1950-c.1970

B.O.A.C. (now known as British Airways) commissioned these products from Wade Heath through its association with Regicor. Seven items advertised B.O.A.C. and one advertised British Airways.

The round water jug has a recessed handle and an ice-check spout. When first produced the BOAC transfer prints were missing the . (full stop) between the initial letters; then, the full stop was added.

Ashtray

Water Jug

B.O.A.C. D.H. Comet 4

Tankards B.O.A.C. and BOAC

Backstamp: **A.** "Wade Regicor London England," laurel leaves, large size
B. "Wade Regicor London England," laurel leaves, small size
C. Transfer print "Wade PDM England"
D. "Reproduction by Wade of England in Collaboration with B.O.A.C."

No.	Description	Colourways	Shape/Size	U.S.$	Can.$	U.K.£
1.	Ashtray	Grey-blue; white print	Circular/142	30.00	35.00	15.00
2.	Ashtray	Blue/white; multiple red/blue British Airways	Circular/216	25.00	30.00	12.00
3.	Ashtray	Grey-blue; white B.O.A.C. print	Square/120	20.00	30.00	10.00
4.	Ashtray	Dark blue; white B.O.A.C. print	Square/140	20.00	30.00	10.00
5.	Ashtray	Grey-blue; white B.O.A.C. print clipped corners	Square/140	20.00	30.00	10.00
6.	Ashtray	Yellow-white; black lettering	105	35.00	45.00	20.00
7.	Water Jug	Grey-blue; white BOAC; black/white crest	133	40.00	45.00	20.00
8.	Water Jug	Grey-blue; white B.O.A.C.; black/white crest	133	40.00	45.00	20.00
9.	Tankard	Grey-blue tankard; white B.O.A.C. crest	½ pint/100	40.00	45.00	20.00
10.	Tankard	Grey-blue tankard; white B.O.A.C. crest	Pint/120	50.00	70.00	25.00
11.	Tankard	Grey-blue tankard; white BOAC crest	Pint/120	50.00	60.00	35.00
12.	Tankard	White tankard; black-grey-blue areoplane print D.H. Comet 4	Pint/120	35.00	45.00	25.00

BRITVIC SOFT DRINKS

ASHTRAY and WATER JUG, 1969-1984 to 1990-1996

The water jug has an ice check spout.

Backstamp: A. "Wade P D M Made in England" within two red lines
B. "Wade pdm England" (pdm joined 1969-84 to 1990-1996)
C. "Wade pdm Made in England" within two red lines (pdm separate 1990-1996)

No.	Description	Colourways	Shape/Size	U.S.$	Can.$	U.K.£
1	Ashtray	Black/orange; white lettering "Britvic"	Round/120	10.00	15.00	5.00
2.	Water Jug	Cobalt blue; gold rim / label; blue lettering	165	30.00	35.00	15.00

CAMEL CIGARETTES

SQUARE ASHTRAY, 1990-1996

Square Ashtray

Backstamp: Printed "Wade pdm Made in England" within two red lines (1990-1996)

No.	Description	Colourways	Shape/Size	U.S.$	Can.$	U.K.£
1.	Ashtray	Black tray; yellow/silver/blue Camel logo; silver & blue lettering "Genuine Taste Camel 1913 Genuine Nightlife"	165	22.00	28.00	14.00

CANADA DRY

ASHTRAY, 1955-1962

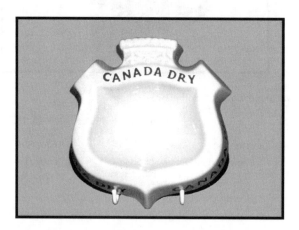

Backstamp: "Wade Regicor, London England," laurel leaves, large size

No.	Description	Colourways	Shape/Size	U.S.$	Can.$	U.K.£
1.	Ashtray	Pale blue; red lettering "Canada Dry Sparkling Drinks"	Shield/127	30.00	35.00	15.00
2.	Ashtray	Pale green; red and white lettering "Canada Dry Sparkling Drinks"	Shield/127	30.00	35.00	15.00

PEANUT DISH, 1955-1962

Photograph not available
at press time

Backstamp: "Wade Regicor London England" in laurel leaf frame, large size

No.	Description	Colourways	Shape/Size	U.S.$	Can.$	U.K.£
1.	Peanut Dish	Dark green/white dish; black lettering "Canada Dry Tonic"	18 x 20	38.00	50.00	15.00

CAPSTAN CIGARETTES

MENU HOLDER, c.LATE 1960s - 1970s

This advertising menu holder has a slot across the top in which a menu card was placed.

Backstamp: None

No.	Description	Colourways	Shape/Size	U.S.$	Can.$	U.K.£
1.	Menu Holder	White; gold/blue bands blue lettering	Pyramid/55	10.00	15.00	8.00

CARROLLS CIGARETTES

ASHTRAY, 1955-1962

Photograph not
available at press time

Backstamp: "Wade Regicor, London England," laurel leaves, large size

No.	Description	Colourways	Shape/Size	U.S.$	Can.$	U.K.£
1.	Ashtray	White; red/black lettering "Carrolls Virginia Cigarettes Number 1"	Oval/224	15.00	20.00	8.00

CASTELLA CIGARS

ASHTRAY, 1968 - 1969

Backstamp: Printed circular "Reginald Corfield Limited, Redhill Surrey," with "Regicor Wade England" through the circle (1968-1969)

No.	Description	Colourways	Shape/Size	U.S.$	Can.$	U.K.£
1.	Ashtray	White/red; black and white lettering "Enjoy a Castella Cigar"	Round/210	10.00	15.00	8.00

CAVALIER PANATELLAS

ASHTRAY, 1955-1962

Photograph not
available at press time

Backstamp: "Wade Regicor, London England," laurel leaves, large size

No.	Description	Colourways	Shape/Size	U.S.$	Can.$	U.K.£
1.	Ashtray	Light grey; red/black lettering "Cavalier Panatellas"	Oval/228	15.00	20.00	8.00

CORONA SOFT DRINKS

WATER JUG

Photograph not
available at press time

Backstamp: "Wade pdm England" (pdm joined 1969-1984)

No.	Description	Colourways	Shape/Size	U.S.$	Can.$	U.K.£
1.	Water Jug	Black; white lettering "Corona Soft Drinks"	Round/165	25.00	30.00	12.00

CREST HOTELS

ASHTRAYS, 1969-1990

Ashtray (1)

Ashtray (2)

Toothpick Holder (3)

Backstamp: A. "Wade pdm England"
B. "Wade p d m England"

No.	Description	Colourways	Shape/Size	U.S.$	Can.$	U.K.£
1.	Ashtray	Pale blue; black print, lettering "Crest Hotels"	Rect./210	15.00	20.00	8.00
2.	Ashtray	Maroon; gold print, lettering "Crest Hotels"	Rect./170	15.00	20.00	8.00
3.	Toothpick Holder	Maroon; gold print, lettering "Crest Hotels"	Unknown	12.00	15.00	6.00

CROSSE AND BLACKWELL

PLOUGHMAN'S PLATE, LATE 1980s

Wade produced this heavily embossed "Ploughman's Plate" as a promotional line for the British pickle company, Crosse and Blackwell. The plate has "Crosse and Blackwell" embossed on the top rim and "Branston, the Perfect Pickle for a Ploughman's" around the rim.

Ploughman's Plate

Backstamp: Black transfer print "Rockingham by Wade England"

No.	Description	Colourways	Size	U.S.$	Can.$	U.K.£
1.	Plate	Dark honey brown	225	30.00	35.00	15.00

DUNHILL CIGARETTES

ASHTRAYS AND WATER JUGS, 1968-1984

The water jugs are rectangular with ice-check spouts but there is also a tall round model.

Ashtray

Water Jug

Backstamp: **A.** "Reginald Corfield Limited, Redhill Surrey," "Wade Regicor England"
B. Transfer printed "Wade pdm England"
C. Printed "Wade Regicor England, Reginald Corfield, Redhill, Surrey"
D. Printed "Wade pdm England" (pdm joined 1969-1984)

No.	Description	Colourways	Shape/Size	U.S.$	Can.$	U.K.£
1.	Ashtray	Black; red label with gold lettering "Dunhill"	Square/177	15.00	20.00	8.00
2.	Ashtray	Black; gold rim, crest and lettering	Square/205	8.00	10.00	5.00
3.	Water Jug	Black; gold lettering "Dunhill International Cigarettes"	140	25.00	30.00	12.00
4.	Water Jug	Maroon; black lettering "Dunhill International Cigarettes"	146	25.00	30.00	12.00
5.	Water Jug	Black; red label; gold lettering "Dunhill"	171	25.00	30.00	12.00
6.	Water Jug	Black; maroon label; gold rim and lettering	Round/206	20.00	25.00	12.00

EDDIE STOBART LTD EXPRESS ROAD HAULAGE SPECIALIST

ROAD HAULAGE VEHICLE, 1998

Eddie Stobart Ltd. commissioned Wade Ceramics to produce a replica of one of their road haulage vehicles. The model was available to the Eddie Stobart Collectors club and was also available to Wade Collectors Club members in May 1998.

Backstamp: "Made Exclusively For Eddie Stobart Ltd by Wade Ceramics"

No.	Description	Colourways	Shape/Size	U.S.$	Can.$	U.K.£
1.	Lorry	Silver and green cab; green body/wheels; orange and white lettering	88 x 280	55.00	70.00	40.00

EMBASSY CIGARETTES

WATER JUG, 1969-1984

This water jug is square with an ice-check spout.

Embassy Regal, Today's Outstanding Value

Backstamp: "Wade pdm England"

No.	Description	Colourways	Size	U.S.$	Can.$	U.K.£
1.	Water Jug	Royal blue; white lettering "Embassy Regal"	146	30.00	35.00	15.00
2.	Water Jug	Royal blue; white lettering "Embassy Regal today's outstanding value"	150	30.00	35.00	15.00

EMBASSY HOTELS

ASHTRAY, 1984-1990

Photograph not available
at press time

Backstamp: "Wade p d m England"

No.	Description	Colourways	Shape/Size	U.S.$	Can.$	U.K.£
1	Ashtray	White; blue lettering "Embassy Hotels"	Round/120	8.00	10.00	3.00

555 CIGARETTES

ASHTRAY AND WATER JUG, 1955-1984

The ashtray has a large "555" in the center. The water jug is round with an ice-check spout and "555" is the only decoration.

Photograph not available
at press time

Backstamp: **A.** "Wade Regicor, London England," laurel leaves, large size
B. "Wade pdm England"

No.	Description	Colourways	Shape/Size	U.S.$	Can.$	U.K.£
1.	Ashtray	White; blue "555"	Round/140	15.00	20.00	8.00
2.	Water Jug	Dull blue; gold "555"	Round/165	25.00	30.00	12.00

FRANK WADE LTD

ASHTRAY

The Ploughshare Makers

Backstamp: Printed "Wade England"

No.	Description	Colourways	Shape/Size	U.S.$	Can.$	U.K.£
1.	Ashtray	Dark blue; white print and lettering	Square/140	6.00	8.00	4.00

GLOW WORM GAS FIRES

GLOW WORM PENCIL HOLDER, DATE UNKNOWN

This comical pencil holder was produced as a promotional item for Glow Worm Gas Fires and used in company offices and showrooms.

Backstamp: Unknown

No.	Description	Colourways	Size	U.S.$	Can.$	U.K.£
1.	Pencil holder	Pink worm; black gloves, golf bag; orange golf ball	101	70.00	90.00	42.00

GRANADA TELEVISION

ROVERS RETURN FLAN DISH, TEA CADDY AND TEAPOT

The tea caddy and teapot were produced for Granada Television studio tours as promotional items for its long-running British television series,"Coronation Street." The round jar has a transfer print of the Rovers Return Inn on the front as does the teapot.

Flan Dish

Backstamp: Unknown

No.	Description	Colourways	Size	U.S.$	Can.$	U.K.£
1.	Tea Caddy	White; green/brown/yellow print	185	40.00	45.00	20.00
2.	Teapot	Unknown	Unknown	40.00	45.00	20.00
3.	Flan Dish	White; green rim; green/brown/yellow print	Round/225	35.00	45.00	20.00
4.	Pie Dish	White; green rim; green/brown/yellow print	Rect/165	35.00	45.00	20.00
5.	Souffle Dish	White; green rim; green/brown/yellow	Round/145	35.00	45.00	20.00

GUINNESS PLC

NOVELTY MODELS, 1968

Wade produced 5,000 each of these four models in December 1968 for Guinness PLC. The four models were given to licensees and were not offered to the general public.

Backstamp: Raised "Guinness" on the front rim

No.	Description	Colourways	Size	U.S.$	Can.$	U.K.£
1,	Duke of Wellington	Brown/honey brown	90	155.00	180.00	90.00
2.	Mad Hatter	Brown/honey brown/greenish grey	85	155.00	180.00	90.00
3.	Sam Weller	Brown/honey brown	80	155.00	180.00	90.00
4.	Tweedle Dum and Tweedle Dee	Brown/honey brown	75	155.00	180.00	90.00

HARRISON LINE

MATCHBOOK AND TOOTHPICK HOLDERS

Produced for Harrison Line shippers, U.K.

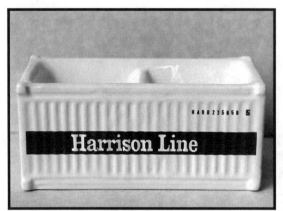

Matchbook Holder

Toothpick Holder

Backstamp: "Wade pdm England" (pdm separate 1984-1990)

No.	Description	Colourways	Shape/Size	U.S.$	Can.$	U.K.£
1.	Matchbook Holder (Container)	White; broad red band; white/black lettering	Unknown	12.00	15.00	8.00
2.	Toothpick Holder (Ships Funnel)	Black; broad white and red bands	Unknown	12.00	15.00	8.00

HARRODS OF KNIGHTSBRIDGE

TEAPOT, 1993

Backstamp: Black transfer print "Harrods Knightsbridge"

No.	Item	Description	Size	U.S.$	Can.$	U.K.£
1.	Teapot	White; multi-coloured print of store	135	100.00	145.00	55.00

HAYWOODS TOBACCONISTS

WATER JUG, 1955-1962

This round jug resembles the shape known as a "Dutch jug" and has been used by the Wade Heath Pottery in its range of tablewares since the early 1930s. It has an open spout.

Photographs not available
at press time

Backstamp: "Wade Regicor, London England," laurel leaves, large size

No.	Description	Colourways	Size	U.S.$	Can.$	U.K.£
1.	Water Jug	White; black lettering "Haywoods Wholesale Tobacconists Brighton"	140	50.00	70.00	25.00

I CAN'T BELIEVE IT'S NOT BUTTER

BUTTER DISH AND TOAST RACK, 1997 - MARCH 1998

A butter dish with an embossed design of cow faces, and a toast rack with a transfer printed design of a cow's face on the end were offered by the company. To obtain them, collectors had to send a cheque in the amount of £4.99 for the butter dish, and £3.99 for the toast rack plus two butter tub lids.

Butter Dish

Toast Rack

Backstamp: **A.** Embossed "I can't believe it's not Butter"
B. Gold printed "Wade England" with two lines

No.	Description	Colourways	Shape/Size	U.S.$	Can.$	U.K.£
1.	Butter Dish	Creamy yellow	140 x 173	15.00	20.00	8.00
2.	Toast Rack	Creamy yellow; multi-coloured print	78 x 160	10.00	12.00	6.00

IMPERIAL CHEMICAL INDUSTRIES (I.C.I.)

ATROMID-S MAN, 1967

The British pharmaceutical manufacturer Imperial Chemical Industries produced a drug called Atromid-S, which was used for weight reduction for patients at risk from heart disease. The Atromid-S Man depicts a person likely to suffer from heart disease, an overweight man sitting on a beer crate with a pint of beer in his hand. It was given by salesmen to general practitioners as a sales promotion. This model has been found in Germany named Regelan.

Backstamp: A. Raised "Wade England I.C.I." and "Atromid S"
B. Raised "Atromidin Wade England I.C.I."

No.	Description	Colourways	Size	U.S.$	Can.$	U.K.£
1.	Atromid-S Man	Dark blue all over	Small/80	90.00	130.00	45.00
2.	Atromid-S Man	Honey brown all over	Small/80	90.00	130.00	45.00
3.	Atromid-S Man	Black all over	Large/205		Rare	
4.	Atromid-S Man	Brown shirt, box; red trousers	Large/205		Rare	

IMPERIAL TOBACCO COMPANY LIMITED

ASHTRAY, CIGARETTE LIGHTER AND WATER JUG, 1969-1984

Backstamp: "Wade pdm England"

No.	Description	Colourways	Size	U.S.$	Can.$	U.K.£
1.	Ashtray	Maroon/deep red; gold lettering "Imperial International Filter Virginia"	115	15.00	20.00	8.00
2.	Cigarette Lighter	Maroon/red/gold; gold/black lettering "Imperial International Filter Virginia"	108	25.00	30.00	12.00
3.	Water Jug/ ice-check spout	Burgundy; red/gold lettering "Imperial International Filter Virginia"	153	25.00	30.00	12.00

ST. BRUNO KEY RING, 1986-1987

Backstamp: Unmarked

No.	Description	Colourways	Size	U.S.$	Can.$	U.K.£
1.	Key Ring	White; red-brown patches; yellow pouch	30	25.00	35.00	15.00

JOHN PLAYER CIGARETTES

ASHTRAY AND WATER JUGS, 1969-1984

The water jugs have ice-check spouts and are decorated with a print of the cigarette label.

Ashtray

Water Jug

Backstamp: "Wade pdm England" printed in a circle

No.	Description	Colourways	Shape/Size	U.S.$	Can.$	U.K.£
1.	Ashtray	Black; white print; gold lettering "John Player Special"	Square/195	15.00	20.00	8.00
2.	Ashtray	Black; gold crest; lines and lettering "Superkings"	Square/195	12.00	15.00	5.00
3.	Water Jug	Black; yellow/black print; gold lettering "John Player"	Rectangular/146	25.00	30.00	12.00
4.	Water Jug	Black; gold/yellow print and lettering "John Player Special" cigarette and packet print	Rectangular/153	25.00	30.00	12.00
5.	Water Jug	Black; gold lettering" John Player Special"	153	25.00	30.00	12.00

LAMBERT & BUTLER CIGARETTES

WATER JUG, 1969-1984

This rectangular water jug has an ice-check spout.

Backstamp: "Wade pdm England"

No.	Description	Colourways	Size	U.S.$	Can.$	U.K.£
1.	Water Jug	Black; white/red lettering "Lambert & Butler King Size"	153	30.00	35.00	15.00
2.	Water Jug	White; black/red lettering "L-B Kingsize"	153	25.00	30.00	12.00

LEGAL AND GENERAL ASSURANCE SOCIETY LTD.

ASHTRAYS, 1955-1969

Photograph not available
at press time

Backstamp: A. "Wade Regicor, London England," laurel leaves, large size
B. "Reginald Corfield Limited Redhill Surrey," "Wade Regicor England"

No.	Description	Colourways	Shape/Size	U.S.$	Can.$	U.K.£
1.	Ashtray	Blue; white lettering "Legal & General Assurance Society Limited"	Square/146	15.00	20.00	8.00
2.	Ashtray	Black; white lettering "Legal and General Assurance Society Ltd"	Square/140	15.00	20.00	8.00

LEGAL AND GENERAL PROPERTY LTD.

MILLBANK TOWER VASE, 1993

This oblong vase represents the Millbank Tower Building.

Backstamp: Dark blue print "An original Design for Legal and General Property Ltd by Wade England"

No.	Description	Colourways	Size	U.S.$	Can.$	U.K.£
1.	Tower	Grey/dark blue, white lettering	160	25.00	30.00	12.00

THE LICENCES AND GENERAL INSURANCE COMPANY LTD.

DISH, c.1950-c.1960

Photograph not available
at press time

Backstamp: Red transfer print "Wade England"

No.	Description	Colourways	Size	U.S.$	Can.$	U.K.£
1.	Dish	White; black print, lettering "The Licences and General Insurance Company Ltd"	Circular/110	8.00	10.00	3.00

LOFTHOUSE OF FLEETWOOD LTD.

FISHERMAN'S FRIEND TEAPOT

This teapot, commissioned by the manufacturer of Fisherman's Friend Throat Lozenges, is the same shape as that used for Wade's "English Life Conservatory Teapot," which was produced from 1988 to 1994.

Backstamp: Black and red transfer print "Made Exclusively for Lofthouse of Fleetwood Ltd by Wade England" and two red lines

No.	Description	Colourways	Size	U.S.$	Can.$	U.K.£
1.	Teapot	White; multi-coloured prints	114	50.00	70.00	30.00

LOUIS PATISSERIE

DISH

This round dish has a print of a bakers shop window and the words "Bakery Louis Patisserie, Hungarian Confectionery, Hampstead," with the telephone number.

Backstamp: "Wade pdm made in England" (pdm separate 1984-1990)

No.	Description	Colourways	Shape/Size	U.S.$	Can.$	U.K.£
1.	Dish	White; multi-coloured print	Round/110	12.00	15.00	4.00

LUCKY STRIKE CIGARETTES

ASHTRAYS, 1990-1995

Photograph not available
at press time

Backstamp: "Wade P D M Made in England"

No.	Description	Colourways	Shape/Size	U.S.$	Can.$	U.K.£
1.	Ashtray	White; red/black lettering "Lucky Strike"	Round/177	10.00	15.00	5.00
2.	Ashtray	Deep blue; red/black/white lettering "Lucky Strike"	Round/177	10.00	15.00	5.00
3.	Ashtray	Deep blue; red/black/white lettering "Lucky Strike"	Round/205	10.00	15.00	5.00

LYNNE'S IRISH MUSTARD

MUSTARD POT, c.1971 - 1976

This unusual brown glazed Irish Wade mustard pot was produced some time in the mid 1970s.

Lynne's Irish Mustard

Backstamp: Embossed "Made in Ireland Irish Porcelain Wade eire tire a dheanta"

No.	Description	Colourways	Shape/Size	U.S.$	Can.$	U.K.£
1.	Mustard Pot	Brown; gold print and lettering	50 x 75	50.00	65.00	25.00

MARLBORO CIGARETTES

ASHTRAYS, 1984-1995

Photograph not available at press time

Backstamp: A. "Wade p d m England"
B. "Wade P D M Made in England"

No.	Description	Colourways	Shape/Size	U.S.$	Can.$	U.K.£
1.	Ashtray	White; yellow/red lettering "Marlboro"	Hexagonal/190	15.00	20.00	8.00
2.	Ashtray	Black; red/white lettering "Marlboro"	Hexagonal/190	15.00	20.00	8.00
3.	Ashtray	White; red/black lettering "Marlboro"	Hexagonal/190	15.00	20.00	8.00

MARSTONS

CRUETS, c.1950-c.1960

Photograph not available at press time

Backstamp: Red printed "Wade England"

No.	Description	Colourways	Size	U.S.$	Can.$	U.K.£
1.	Pepper Pot	Beige; brown/black lettering "Marstons Good Food Quality and Value"	114	8.00	10.00	3.00
2.	Salt Cellar	Beige; brown/black lettering "Marstons Good Food Quality and Value"	114	8.00	10.00	3.00

MINSTER GINGER ALE

WATER JUG, 1962-1968

This water jug has a recessed handle and an open spout.

Minster Ginger Ale Water Jug

Backstamp: "Wade Regicor, London England," laurel leaves, small size

No.	Description	Colourways	Shape/Size	U.S.$	Can.$	U.K.£
1.	Water Jug	Black, white/gold lettering "Minster Ginger Ale"	Round/120	25.00	30.00	12.00

MONK CIVIL ENGINEERS

ASHTRAY

This rectangular ashtray was commissioned by Monk Civil Engineering. In the centre of the dish is a print of Spaghetti Junction with the words "Spaghetti Junction Motorway M6 and Gravelly Hill Interchange Connecting with the A38 and the Aston Expressway Birmingham. Constructed by Monk." Around the sides is printed "Monk Civil Engineers and Building Contractors."

Spaghetti Junction

Backstamp: Printed "Wade pdm England" (pdm joined 1969 - 1984)

No.	Description	Colourways	Size	U.S.$	Can.$	U.K.£
1.	Monk Ashtray	White: multi-coloured print and lettering	177 x 159	10.00	15.00	8.00

MONMOUTHSHIRE BUILDING SOCIETY

SQUIRREL WITH ACORN MONEY BOX, 1998

This cute squirrel, holding an acorn, was chosen by the Monmouthshire Building Society to encourage young savers under the age of 16 years to open accounts. Viewed as a long term promotion, the first production run was of 2,000 models. The model could only be obtained when the legal guardian of a child, with proof of identity of the child the account was being opened for, ie; birth certificate or passport, opened a savings account with the sum of £10.00. There was a choice of free gift when opening an account: the account holder could choose the "Squirrel Money Box," a back pack or sports bag. Printed on the front of the acorn is "Monmouthshire Building Society."

Backstamp: Unknown

No.	Description	Colourways	Size	U.S.$	Can.$	U.K.£
1.	Money Box	Tan brown	145 x 115	30.00	40.00	20.00

NATIONAL TRUST

TEAPOTS, 1989

Only two teapots are known to have been produced for the British National Trust. Two moulds from the English Life teapots were used. With the addition of new multi-coloured transfer prints, the "Flories Flowers Teapot" became the "Alfreston Lodge Teapot" and "The Conservatory Teapot" became the "Blaise Hamlet Cottage Teapot."

Photograph not available
at press time

Backstamp: Unknown

No.	Description	Colourways	Size	U.S.$	Can.$	U.K.£
1.	Alfreston Lodge	White; multi-coloured print	140	30.00	35.00	15.00
2.	Blaise Hamlet Cottage	White; multi-coloured print	135	30.00	35.00	15.00

NATIONAL WESTMINSTER BANK

MONEY BOXES

Mother Panda and Baby, 1989

Backstamp: Raised "Wade England"

No.	Description	Colourways	Size	U.S.$	Can.$	U.K.£
1.	Panda and Baby	Black/white	112	36.00	48.00	25.00

Pig Family, 1984 - 1998

A limited number of "Woody Money Boxes," glazed with 22-karat gold leaf were made exclusively for the board of directors of the National Westminster Bank.

Backstamp: A. Raised "Wade"
B. Raised "Wade England"

No.	Description	Colourways	Size	U.S.$	Can.$	U.K.£
1.	Woody (baby)	Pink; white nappy; silver/grey safety pin	135	22.00	30.00	12.00
2.	Woody (baby)	Gold	135	80.00	105.00	45.00
3.	Annabel (girl)	Pink; white blouse; green gym slip; blue bag	175	22.00	35.00	15.00
4.	Maxwell (boy)	Pink; red/white tie; blue trousers	180	80.00	105.00	45.00
5.	Lady Hillary (mother)	Pink; light blue blouse; navy skirt	185	46.00	61.00	30.00
6.	Sir Nathaniel Westminster (father)	Pink; black suit; red bow tie, rose	190	80.00	125.00	65.00

COUSIN WESLEY, 1998

National Westminster Bank launched its new "Children's Bond" account in February 1998. Cousin Wesley was available by opening a children's bond account for a child under the age of 16 years. To get Wesley meant an investment of £1,000.00 for five years in the child's name. Only 5,000 models of Wesley are known to have been produced.

Cousin Wesley Money Box, 1998

Backstamp: Unknown

No.	Description	Colourways	Shape/Size	U.S.$	Can.$	U.K.£
1.	Money Box	Pink pig; dark blue hat/pants; green shirt		225.00	250.00	125.00

MUG, 1987-1989

The Piggies 100 Club Mug was sent free of charge when the saver had £100.00 in their account for six months.

Backstamp: Red transfer print "Royal Victoria Pottery Wade Staffordshire England"

No.	Description	Colourways	Size	U.S.$	Can.$	U.K.£
1.	100s Club Piggy Mug	Pale grey; multi-coloured print	90	25.00	35.00	12.00

NELSON CIGARETTES

ASHTRAY, 1955-1962

Photograph not available
at press time

Backstamp: "Wade Regicor, London England," laurel leaves, large size

No.	Description	Colourways	Shape/Size	U.S.$	Can.$	U.K.£
1.	Ashtray	Pale blue; black lettering "Nelson Filter Tipped"	Oval/171	15.00	20.00	8.00

NESTLE

ASHBOURNE NATURAL WATER PEANUT BOWL, c.1984 - 1990

This round peanut bowl advertises Ashbourne Natural Water, a division of Nestle.

Backstamp: Printed "Wade pdm England" (pdm separated 1984-1990)

No.	Description	Colourways	Shape/Size	U.S.$	Can.$	U.K.£
1.	Bowl	White; red/white/blue Union Jack flags; blue lettering	95	10.00	15.00	6.00

PARKINSONS DONCASTER OLD FASHIONED HUMBUGS

ASHTRAY, 1955-1962

Photograph not available
at press time

Backstamp: "Wade Regicor, London England," laurel leaves, large size

No.	Description	Colourways	Shape/Size	U.S.$	Can.$	U.K.£
1.	Ashtray	White; red/black lettering "Parkinsons Doncaster Old Fashioned Humbugs"	Round/140	15.00	20.00	8.00

PEARS SOAP

SOAP DISH, 1987

This dish has pink flowers and a pink banner along two sides which proclaims "30 years of Miss Pears 1958 - 1987."

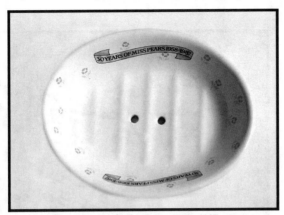

30 Years of Miss Pears 1958 - 1987

Backstamp: Red transfer print "Royal Victoria Pottery—Staffordshire Wade England"

No.	Description	Colourways	Size	U.S.$	Can.$	U.K.£
1.	Soap Dish	White; pink flowers and banners; gold lettering	20 x 145	15.00	20.00	8.00

PETER ENGLAND SHIRT MANUFACTURERS, ENGLAND

ASHTRAY, 1969-1984

This ashtray was modelled in the shape of a sitting cartoon-type lion, with the detailing in black. It was produced in a limited edition of 1,000.

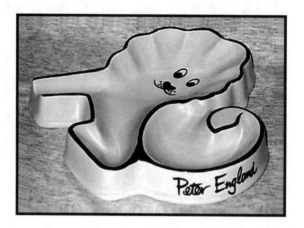

Backstamp: "Wade pdm England" printed in a circle

No.	Description	Colourways	Size	U.S.$	Can.$	U.K.£
1.	Ashtray	Bright yellow; black lettering "Peter England"	184	40.00	45.00	20.00

PETTER DIESEL ENGINES

DISH, 1953 - 1962

This dish was produced as a promotional item for Petter Engines of Staines, Middlesex, UK. Petter were noted for their diesel engines which were built for river boats, mostly pleasure craft.

"It Goes Much Better Powered by Petter"

Backstamp: Black transfer print "Wade Regicor England, Reginald Corfield, Redhill, Surrey" in laurel leaf frame, large size

No.	Description	Colourways	Shape/size	U.S.$	Can.$	U.K.£
1.	Dish	White dish; red and black logo; black lettering	18 x 20 mm	10.00	12.00	4.00

RANK FILM ORGANISATION

FRIED GREEN TOMATOES MONEY BOX, 1992

This tomato-shaped money box was produced for the Rank Film Organisation of England to promote its film, *Fried Green Tomatoes*. They were produced in a limited edition of 1,000.

Backstamp: Red print "Wade England"

No.	Description	Colourways	Size	U.S.$	Can.$	U.K.£
1.	Money Box	Pale green; dark green letters "Fried Green Tomatoes at the Whistle Stop Cafe"	135 x 155	358.00	475.00	200.00

READY MIXED CONCRETE UNITED KINGDOM LTD.

CARTOON DISHES, c.1960-1970

Cartoons by Ray Davis

These two sets of dishes are decorated with cartoons by Ray Davis. Set one has a black and white design on a white, square dish, while set two has cartoons that have multi-coloured prints on a white, triangular dish with a gold-lined rim. Only the first set of dishes is signed by Ray Davis.

Set One   Set Two

Backstamp: **A.** Red transfer print "Wade England," Set one
              B. Black transfer print "Wade England," Set two

No.	Description	Colourways	Size	U.S.$	Can.$	U.K.£
1.	Birds and Cement Mixer	Black cement mixer, birds (Set one)	106	10.00	15.00	5.00
2.	Birds and Cement Mixer	Orange cement mixer; black birds (Set two)	106	10.00	15.00	5.00
3.	Dice in Cement Mixer	Black cement mixer, dice (Set one)	106	10.00	15.00	5.00
4.	Dice in Cement Mixer	Orange cement mixer; yellow/white dice (Set two)	106	10.00	15.00	5.00
5.	Elephant Spraying Cement	Black cement mixer, dice (Set one)	106	10.00	15.00	5.00
6.	Elephant Spraying Cement	Orange cement mixer, white elephant (Set two)	106	10.00	15.00	5.00
7.	Golfer and Cement Mixer	Black cement mixer, golfer (Set one)	106	10.00	15.00	5.00
8.	Golfer and Cement Mixer	Orange cement mixer, golfer (Set two)	106	13.00	15.00	5.00

Cartoons by David Langdon

These cartoon dishes were signed by David Langdon. They have a multi-coloured print on a white dish with a gold-lined rim. The cartoons show Ready Mixed Cement being used to repair the Wonders of the World and special landscapes.

Great Wall of China

Pyramids of Egypt

Backstamp: A. Green transfer print "Wade PDM England"
B. Printed "Wade England"

No.	Description	Colourways	Size	U.S.$	Can.$	U.K.£
1.	Great Wall of China	Blue wall; red cement mixer	106	10.00	15.00	5.00
2.	Pyramids of Egypt	Blue/white pyramids; red cement mixer	106	10.00	15.00	5.00
3.	Moon Craters	White tray, multi-coloured print; red mixer	106	10.00	15.00	5.00
4.	Skyscraper	White tray; multi-coloured print; red mixer	106	10.00	15.00	5.00
5.	Volcano	White tray; multi-coloured print; red mixer	106	10.00	15.00	5.00

CIGARETTE BOX, c.1958

This cigarette box is decorated with a black-and-white transfer print of a Ready Mixed Concrete lorry with a large genie, wearing a bowler hat, floating from the mixer.

Photograph not available
at press time

Backstamp: Black ink stamp "Wade England"

No.	Description	Colourways	Size	U.S.$	Can.$	U.K.£
1.	Cigarette Box	Black base, print; white lid	50 x 125	40.00	55.00	20.00

REGINALD CORFIELD LTD.

DISHES, 1953 - 1962

This dish advertised Reginald Corfield's colour printing on metal. It is from the same mould as that used for Wade's 1953 "Coronation" Dish with the embossing changed. Inscribed around the rim in embossed letters is "Reginald Corfield Ltd - Colour Printing on Metal - Lombard Road, Merton SW 19." On the inside of the bowl is an inscribed quote from a speech Ralph Waldo Emerson made in 1871: "If a man can write a better book, preach a better sermon, or make a better Mouse trap than his neighbour, though he build his house in the Woods, the world will make a beaten path to his Door." The centre of the dish is inscribed with "Regicor - Regd - Trade Mark." In 1953 Wade Heath and Reginald Corfield Ltd. formed a partnership in advertising and promotional wares that lasted 16 years.

Backstamp: A. Embossed "Wade England"
B. Printed "Wade Regicor London England," in laurel leaf frame, large size

No.	Description	Colourways	Size	U.S.$	Can.$	U.K.£
1.	Dish	Light green; green lettering	120	30.00	35.00	15.00
2.	Dish, Advertising	White; black bands/lettering yellow background	134	20.00	30.00	15.00

ROBINSON WILLEY c.MID 1980s

TEAPOT

Commissioned by Robinson Willey Gas Appliance Manufacturers of Liverpool, England, this round 2-cup teapot has a small "gas flame" in the RW logo printed on the front. The name *Robinson Willey* is also on the teapot.

Backstamp: Circular red transfer printed "Royal Victoria Pottery Staffordshire Wade England"

No.	Description	Colourways	Size	U.S.$	Can.$	U.K.£
1.	Teapot	White; green/white logo; red lettering		30.00	40.00	20.00

ROSE'S LIME JUICE c.1969 - 1984

WATER JUG

This rectangular water jug has an ice check spout.

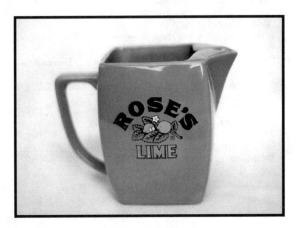

Backstamp: Red printed "Wade pdm England" (pdm joined 1969-1984)

No.	Description	Colourways	Size	U.S.$	Can.$	U.K.£
1.	Water jug	Lime green; yellow/green/white print; black and orange lettering	Rectangular/130	20.00	25.00	12.00

ROTHMANS CIGARETTES

ASHTRAYS, TANKARDS AND WATER JUG, 1969-1996

Tankard 5 has a transfer print on it of a Rothmans coach and horses. On the back is a history of the coach: "The Rothmans Coach, travels every day from Pall Mall through the West End of London along the Mall and Carlton Terrace. Rothmans still deliver their famous cigarettes to select Clubs and Embassies by coach and footman. This time honoured custom is a tradition of the House of Rothmans." Tankard 6 is decorated with a transfer print of the logo found on a Rothmans King Size Cigarette package.

Ashtray

Tankard

Waterjug

Backstamp: **A.** "Wade P D M Made in England"
B. "Wade pdm England"
C. Red printed "Wade PDM" (Between two red lines 1990-1996)
D. Transfer printed "Wade pdm England" (pdm joined 1969-1984)

No.	Description	Colourways	Shape/Size	U.S.$	Can.$	U.K.£
1.	Ashtray	Maroon; white lettering "Pall Mall"	Round/177	10.00	15.00	5.00
2.	Ashtray	White; blue/red/white lettering "Rothmans King Size"	Round/120	10.00	15.00	5.00
3.	Ashtray	White; gold rim; white/blue lettering "Rothmans King Size"	Rectangular/254	15.00	20.00	8.00
4.	Ashtray	Dark blue; gold rim; gold/red crest; gold/white lettering	Hexagonal/205	20.00	30.00	10.00
5.	Tankard	Amber; black print, lettering "Rothmans of Pall Mall"	Pint/115	25.00	30.00	12.00
6.	Tankard	White; blue/white/red print, lettering "Rothmans King Size"	Pint/115	25.00	30.00	12.00
7.	Tankard	Amber; red/white/black print; black lettering "Rothmans of Pall Mall"	Pint/115	25.00	30.00	12.00
8.	Water Jug Team Rothmans	White; red/gold/blue bands blue/white print and lettering	Round/135	20.00	30.00	15.00

S & M PHOTOLABELS 1987

T.V. PENCIL/POSY HOLDERS, 1987

An original box containing one of the T.V. Pencil holders shows an illustration of the Holder with a posy of flowers and pens/pencils and artists brushes. Printed on the side of the box is "Made exclusively for S & M Photolabels by Wade Stoke-on-Trent Staffordshire England." A leaflet explains how customers could have their own photograph placed in the television screen, either a personal photo or a business advertising photo, such as a restaurant or Public House.

"Box"

TV/Bear Cub Sleeping

Backstamp: Embossed "Wade (SM) England"

No.	Description	Colourways	Size	U.S.$	Can.$	U.K.£
1.	TV/Bear Cub Eating	Pearlised; gold knobs; brown/green print	90	22.50	30.00	15.00
2.	TV/Bear Cub Sleeping	Pearlised; gold knobs; brown/green print	90	22.50	30.00	15.00
3.	TV/Bear Cub Walking	Pearlised; gold knobs; brown/green print	90	22.50	30.00	15.00
4.	TV/Blank Screen	Off white	90	15.50	20.00	10.00
5.	The White Hart Pub	White; coloured print	90	25.00	30.00	15.00

SAFIR CIGARETTES

ASHTRAY, 1955-1962

Photograph not available
at press time

Backstamp: "Wade Regicor, London England," laurel leaves, large size

No.	Description	Colourways	Shape/Size	U.S.$	Can.$	U.K.£
1.	Ashtray	White; black lettering "Safir Filter Cigarettes"	Square/146	15.00	20.00	8.00

SENIOR SERVICE CIGARETTES

ASHTRAYS, 1962-1968

Photograph not available
at press time

Backstamp: "Wade Regicor, London England," laurel leaves, small size

No.	Description	Colourways	Shape/Size	U.S.$	Can.$	U.K.£
1.	Ashtray	Blue; white lettering "Senior Service"	Round/140	15.00	20.00	8.00
2.	Ashtray	Pale blue; black lettering "Senior Service Satisfy"	Round/140	15.00	20.00	8.00
3.	Ashtray	Blue; white lettering "Senior Service"	Triangular/242	15.00	20.00	8.00

7UP SOFT DRINKS

ASHTRAYS, 1955-1968

Backstamp: A. "Wade Regicor, London England," laurel leaves, large size
B. "Wade Regicor, London England," laurel leaves, small size

No.	Description	Colourways	Shape/Size	U.S.$	Can.$	U.K.£
1.	Ashtray	White; red/black lettering "7UP - Fresh up with Seven-Up The All Family Drink"	Square/146	15.00	20.00	8.00
2.	Ashtray	Pale green; multi-coloured lettering "7Up The All Family Drink"	Square/140	15.00	20.00	8.00

SHELL MEX AND BRITISH PETROLEUM

SHELL DISHES, 1953-1956

These shell-shaped dishes were printed with slogans associated with driving. It is believed that they were used as premiums at Shell petrol stations. For 1953 coronation dishes commissioned by Shell Mex and British Petroleum, see the section on commemorative items.

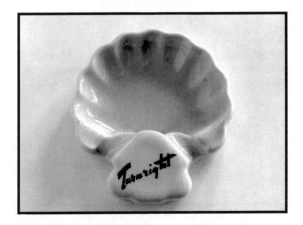

Backstamp: Gold transfer print "Wade England A," with raised "BCM/OWL"

No.	Description	Colourways	Size	U.S.$	Can.$	U.K.£
1.	"Keep Right"	Pale blue; gold print	85	20.00	20.00	8.00
2.	"Keep Left"	Pale pink; gold print	85	15.00	20.00	8.00
3.	"Turn Right"	Pale blue; gold print	85	15.00	20.00	8.00
4.	"Shell"	Pale green; gold print	85	15.00	20.00	8.00
5.	"Shell"	Pale green; gold print	85	15.00	20.00	8.00
6.	"Turn Right"	Yellow; black lettering	85	15.00	20.00	8.00

SILK CUT CIGARETTES

WATER JUG, 1969-1984

This water jug has an ice-catcher spout and is decorated with a transfer print of a label from the cigarette package.

Photograph not available
at press time

Backstamp: "Wade pdm England"

No.	Description	Colourways	Shape/Size	U.S.$	Can.$	U.K.£
1.	Water Jug	White; maroon print; gold lettering "Silk Cut"	Rect./146	25.00	30.00	12.00

SUPERKINGS CIGARETTES

WATER JUG, 1969-1990

These water jugs have ice-check spouts.

Photograph not
available at press time

Backstamp: "Wade pdm England"

No.	Description	Colourways	Shape/Size	U.S.$	Can.$	U.K.£
1.	Water Jug	Black; gold lettering "Superkings"	Rectangular/146	25.00	30.00	12.00
2.	Water Jug	Black; gold lettering "Superkings"	Rectangular/170	30.00	35.00	15.00

SYKES WARMINSTER

DISH c.1950s - 1960s

This dish with a print of a baby chick is advertising a company named "Sykes" of Warminster, who are believed to have been poultry breeders.

Backstamp: Red printed "Wade England"

No.	Description	Colourways	Size	U.S.$	Can.$	U.K.£
1.	Dish	White; red chick; black lettering	Square/140	10.00	15.00	6.00

TAYLORS MUSTARD

TANKARD, 1963

This half-pint Ulster Ware tankard is shape number I.P.1.

Backstamp: Impressed "Irish Porcelain" curved around shamrock leaf, "Made in Ireland" in straight line under shamrock

No.	Description	Colourways	Shape/Size	U.S.$	Can.$	U.K.£
1.	Tankard	Blue/grey; white lettering "1903 1963 Taylors"	½ pint/108	10.00	15.00	5.00

TIME LIFE INTERNATIONAL

CIGARETTE BOX, c.1965

The lid of this square cigarette box is decorated with a design of black letters, making up the name *Time Life*.

Photograph not available
at press time

Backstamp: Black print "Expressley Produced For Time Life International" and "Made in England By Wade, Stoke On Trent," with "Design By Alan Fletcher" on the underside of the lid

No.	Description	Colourways	Shape/Size	U.S.$	Can.$	U.K.£
1.	Cigarette Box	Black box; white/black lid	85 x 135	50.00	70.00	25.00

VALOR GAS

TEAPOT, 1990

The British company Valor Gas commissioned this teapot to celebrate their centenary year. The print on the front of the teapot shows an illustration of a "Victorian Jubilee" fireplace, and on the back is a print of a "Venetian" fireplace. The mould was taken from the *English Life* series "Antique Shop Teapot." The words "Valor Masters of the Living Flame" are printed on the lid. Only 1,000 of these teapots were produced.

Backstamp: Black print "Valor a limited edition of 1,000 by Wade" with No. of issue

No.	Description	Colourways	Size	U.S.$	Can.$	U.K.£
1.	Teapot	White; red/green prints	153	25.00	35.00	15.00

VAN HEUSEN SHIRTS

TANKARD, c.1970

Tankard (face)

Tankard (back)

Backstamp: "Wade pdm England"

No.	Item	Description	Size	U.S.$	Can.$	U.K.£
1.	Tankard	Pale grey; black print, lettering "... continuing the Craftsman's art"	Pint/115	25.00	35.00	15.00

VICEROY CIGARETTES

ASHTRAYS, 1962-1968

Photograph not available
at press time

Backstamp: "Wade Regicor, London England," laurel leaves, small size

No.	Description	Colourways	Shape/Size	U.S.$	Can.$	U.K.£
1.	Ashtray	White; black/red lettering "Viceroy Filter Tip"	Oval/171	15.00	20.00	8.00
2.	Ashtray	White; green lettering "Viceroy Filter Tip"	Round/140	15.00	20.00	8.00

WADE CERAMICS

COASTER AND PENCIL HOLDER, 1996 - 1997

The Pencil Holder and Coaster were promotional items presented to prospective customers. The inscription on the Pencil Holder reads "Wade Promotional Ceramics" and the pottery address, telephone and fax numbers. On the Coaster the inscription reads "Wade Ceramics Promotional, Point of Sale and Packaging Ceramics" with the pottery address, telephone and fax numbers.

Coaster

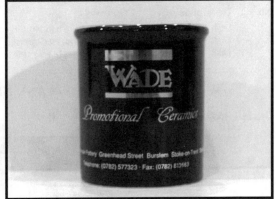

Pencil Holder

Backstamp: A. Red Printed "Wade pdm made in England" (pdm separate 1984 - 1996)
B. Brown printed "Wade England" between two lines (1997)

No.	Description	Colourways	Size	U.S.$	Can.$	U.K.£
1.	Coaster (1997)	White; red lettering	100	15.00	20.00	10.00
2.	Pencil Holder (1996)	Black; gold lettering	100	20.00	28.00	12.00

THE WESTBURY HOTEL, LONDON

DISH, c.1958

Backstamp: Red transfer "Wade England"

No.	Description	Colourways	Size	U.S.$	Can.$	U.K.£
1.	Dish	White; pale blue band; multi-coloured print	110	8.00	10.00	3.00
2.	Dish	White; red band; black print	110	8.00	10.00	3.00
3.	Dish	White; gold rim; black print	110	8.00	10.00	3.00

WINSOR AND NEWTON INKS LTD.

BRUSH AND INK STAND, c.1980

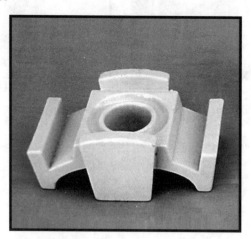

Backstamp: Blue transfer print "Wade Porcelain made in England"

No.	Description	Colourways	Size	U.S.$	Can.$	U.K.£
1.	Brush and Ink Stand	Cream	40 x 133	25.00	30.00	12.00

BRUSH POT, 1984

These round pots are decorated with a design of a flying griffin and the words "Winsor and Newtons Artists Brushes." They were produced as brush holders for Winsor and Newton inks and used in store displays.

Photograph not available
at press time

Backstamp: Unmarked

No.	Description	Colourways	Size	U.S.$	Can.$	U.K.£
1.	Brush Pot	Off white; black print	115	20.00	30.00	10.00

THE YORKSHIRE INSURANCE COMPANY LTD.

DISH, c.1950-c.1960

Backstamp: Red transfer print "Wade England"

No.	Description	Colourways	Shape/Size	U.S.$	Can.$	U.K.£
1.	Dish	White; red/gold print "Yorkshire 1824 The Yorkshire Insurance Company Ltd"	Round/110	8.00	10.00	4.50

ANIMALS

CELLULOSE MODELS c.1930-1939
HIGH GLOSS MODELS c1930-1979
FLAXMAN WARE 1935-1940
SERIES AND SETS 1975-1991

Wade animal models created from the early 1930s to 1939 and from the late 1940s up to the early 1950s are slip cast (hollow) and have a circular casting hole in the base. Beginning in the early 1950s, Wade produced some solid models, and afterwards all the models were solid.

The glazes used from the 1930s to the early 1950s are in delicate pastel and natural colours and are very different from the darker colours used from the late 1950s. Many of the models that were first produced in the early 1930s proved to be popular and were reissued in the late 1940s and early 1950s.

BACKSTAMPS

Handwritten Backstamps

Handwritten backstamps were used to mark models from 1930 to 1939.

Black handwritten, 1930-1939

Ink Stamps

Ink stamps were used from 1935 to 1953. The size of the mark has no relevance to the date; large ink stamps were used on models with large bases, small ink stamps on small bases. Many of the smaller models are unmarked.

Green ink stamp, 1940s-1953

Brown ink stamp, early 1940s-1953

Transfer Prints

Beginning in 1953 transfer prints were used.

Transfer print, 1953-late 1950s

W®RLD of SURVIVAL SERIES©
by
WADE OF ENGLAND
COPYRIGHT
SURVIVAL ANGLIA LIMITED
1976 ALL RIGHTS RESERVED

Transfer print, 1976-1982

CELLULOSE MODELS
c.1935-1939

The "Jack Russell Terrier" is sitting with his mouth open and his tongue out as though panting. There is an impressed Shape No. 334 on the base. For similar model see Flaxman Ware animals.

Alsatian, large size

Jack Russell Terrier

Seated Cat

Spaniel Puppy

Backstamp: **A.** Black handwritten "Wade Made in England"; black ink stamp of a leaping deer
B. Black handwritten "Wade," stamped "Made in England"; model name
C. Impressed "334"
D. Ink stamp "Wade England"

No.	Name	Description	Size	U.S.$	Can.$	U.K.£
1.	Alsatian	Mottled browns; red tongue	Small/115	125.00	150.00	65.00
2.	Alsatian	Mottled yellow/black; pink tongue	Large/255	475.00	630.00	275.00
3.	Alsatian	Black/tan; red tongue	Large/255	290.00	325.00	150.00
4.	Alsatian	Dark brown all over	Large/255	475.00	630.00	275.00
5.	Cat, seated	Black; white on chest; yellow eyes; pink nose and mouth	110	200.00	270.00	185.00
6.	Jack Russell Terrier	White; brown markings; pink tongue	95	85.00	115.00	55.00
7.	Scottie	Black	120	125.00	150.00	65.00
8.	Spaniel Puppy	Brown/black	85	135.00	165.00	80.00

HIGH-GLOSS MODELS
c.1930-c.1979

BEAR CUB, c.1935–c.1939

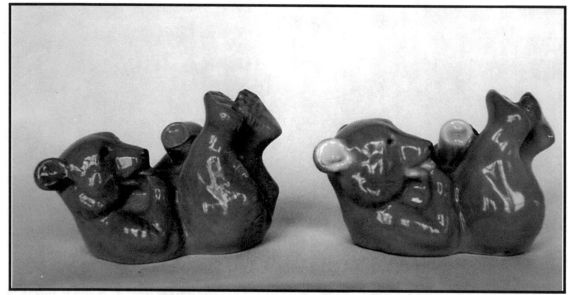

Bear Cub

Backstamp: Black handwritten "Wade England"

No.	Name	Colourways	Size	U.S.$	Can.$	U.K.£
1.	Bear Cub	Beige; white ears; white honey	50	125.00	155.00	80.00
2.	Bear Cub	Brown; white ears; yellow honey	50	95.00	135.00	50.00
3.	Bear Cub	Beige all over	50	95.00	135.00	50.00
4.	Bear Cub	White; pink ears; brown feet; yellow honey	50	125.00	155.00	80.00

BROWN BEAR, 1939

The "Brown Bear" was modelled by Faust Lang.

Backstamp: Blue handwritten "Wade England 1939 Brown Bear" and the incised signature of Faust Lang

No.	Name	Colourways	Size	U.S.$	Can.$	U.K.£
1.	Brown Bear	Beige; green/blue/grey rocky base	245	600.00	800.00	400.00

CALVES, c.1930-c.1948

First issued in the early 1930s, these models were reissued in the late 1940s and early 1950s. The reissues can be identified by the backstamp. The original price was 2/6d each.

Calf, eyes closed (2); Calf, eyes open (3)

Backstamp: **A.** Handwritten "Wade England"
B. Black ink stamp "Wade England"
C. Black ink stamp "Made in England"

No.	Name	Colourways	Size	U.S.$	Can.$	U.K.£
1.	Calf, standing	White/brown patches	65	125.00	160.00	85.00
2.	Calf, mooing, eyes closed	White/brown patches; pink ears; no mouth	45	125.00	160.00	85.00
3.	Calf, mooing, eyes open	White/brown patches; brown ears; black mouth	45	125.00	160.00	85.00

CAMEL, 1939

Photograph not available
at press time

Backstamp: Unknown

No.	Name	Colourways	Size	U.S.$	Can.$	U.K.£
1.	Camel	Light/dark brown	200		Extremely Rare	

CATS

ABC Cats, c.1930–c1955

The "ABC Cats" are identified by letters used by Wade in the sales catalogues. Only six cats are illustrated in the publication, but a seventh cat, which is looking at a dish, has been reported.

Originally issued circa 1930, these cats were so popular they were reissued during the late 1940s, and again from 1953 to circa 1955. The price for these models in the 1950s was 1/6d each.

Care must be taken when purchasing an unmarked cat, as many Japanese and German cats have been produced in very similar poses as the "ABC Cats." Whenever possible, compare such models with marked models first.

Cat A — Sitting cat with paws on ball, bow on left of neck
Cat B — Cat lying on its back, ball held in its front paws
Cat C — Sitting cat looking down at ball
Cat D — Sitting cat with paws on ball, bow on right of neck
Cat E — Drinking from dish of milk
Cat F — Cat on back with ball to mouth

Cat B, Cat A, Cat D, Cat E, Cat C

Backstamp: **A.** Black handwritten "Wade Made in England"
B. Brown ink stamp "Wade England"
C. Black transfer "Wade England"

No.	Name	Colourways	Size	U.S.$	Can.$	U.K.£
1.	Cat A	White/ginger cat; blue ribbon; yellow ball	38	125.00	160.00	85.00
2.	Cat A	White/grey cat; blue ribbon, ball	38	125.00	160.00	85.00
3.	Cat A	White/grey cat; blue ribbon; yellow ball	38	125.00	160.00	85.00
4.	Cat A	White/grey cat; yellow ribbon; blue ball	25	125.00	160.00	85.00
5.	Cat B	White/ginger cat; blue ribbon; yellow ball	27	125.00	160.00	85.00
6.	Cat B	White/grey cat; blue ribbon; ball	30	125.00	160.00	85.00
7.	Cat B	White/grey cat; yellow ribbon; blue ball	25	125.00	160.00	85.00
8.	Cat C	White/ginger cat; blue ribbon; yellow ball	40	125.00	160.00	85.00
9.	Cat C	White/grey cat; blue ribbon, ball	40	125.00	160.00	85.00
10.	Cat C	White/grey cat; blue ribbon; green ball	35	125.00	160.00	85.00
11.	Cat D	White/grey cat; blue ribbon, ball	40	125.00	160.00	85.00
12.	Cat D	White/grey cat; blue ribbon; green ball	40	125.00	160.00	85.00
13.	Cat D	White/grey cat; blue ribbon; red ball	40	125.00	160.00	85.00
14.	Cat E	White/grey cat; blue ribbon, dish	22	125.00	160.00	85.00
15.	Cat E	White/grey; cat yellow ribbon; grey dish	25	125.00	160.00	85.00
16.	Cat F	White/grey cat; blue ribbon, ball	25	125.00	160.00	85.00

Siamese Kittens, c.1948–c1953

Only four models in the "Siamese Kittens" set have been found to date. They were modelled by John Szeilor, who worked at the Wade Heath Royal Victoria Pottery in the late 1940s to the early 1950s, when he left to establish his own pottery, the Szeilor Studio Art Pottery. Some of the early Szeilor Studio figures have a great similarity to his Wade models and are now very collectable.

| Kitten, sitting, paw raised | Kitten, standing | Kitten, sleeping |

Backstamp: A. Black ink stamp "Wade England"
B. Black transfer stamp "Wade England"

No.	Name	Colourways	Size	U.S.$	Can.$	U.K.£
1.	Kitten, seated, paw down	Off white; grey markings; blue/black eyes	60	95.00	125.00	65.00
2.	Kitten, seated, paw raised	Off white; grey markings; blue/black eyes	60	95.00	125.00	65.00
3.	Kitten, standing	Off white; grey markings; blue/black eyes	45	95.00	125.00	65.00
4.	Kitten, sleeping	Off white; grey markings	35	95.00	125.00	65.00

CHAMOIS KID, 1939

The "Chamois Kid" was modelled by Faust Lang.

Backstamp: Blue handwritten "Wade England 1939 Chamois Kid" and the incised signature of Faust Lang

No.	Name	Colourways	Size	U.S.$	Can.$	U.K.£
1.	Chamois Kid	Honey/beige; green/blue rocky base	125	450.00	600.00	300.00

DOGS

Airedale, c.1935-1939

Photograph not available
at press time

No.	Name	Colourways	Size	U.S.$	Can.$	U.K.£
1.	Airedale	Brown/black	180 x 200		Rare	

Alsatian, c.1935-1939

Backstamp: Blue handwritten "Wade England"; model name

No.	Name	Colourways	Size	U.S.$	Can.$	U.K.£
1.	Alsatian, small	Dark grey/black; pink tongue	115	225.00	280.00	135.00

Borzoi, c.1935-1939

Photograph not available
at press time

No.	Name	Colourways	Size	U.S.$	Can.$	U.K.£
1.	Borzoi	White; black patches	300		Rare	

Bulldog, c.1948

The sitting bulldog wears a sailor cap with "H.M.S. Winnie" on the hat band.

Photograph not available
at press time

Backstamp: Black ink stamp "Wade Made in England"

No.	Name	Colourways	Size	U.S.$	Can.$	U.K.£
1.	H.M.S. Winnie	Beige; grey muzzle; white/blue sailor cap	100		Rare	

Dachshunds, c.1930

In these models a dachshund sits begging with its head turned slightly to the front, its tail curled around its front leg. The original price was 2/6d.

Dachshund

Dachshund Mustard Pot Posy Bowl

Backstamp: **A.** Black handwritten "Wade Made in England"
B. Black handwritten "Wade England"
C. Black handwritten "England"

No.	Name	Colourways	Size	U.S.$	Can.$	U.K.£
1.	Dachshund	Red-brown; white chest	80	98.00	130.00	48.00
2.	Dachshund	Beige all over	80	98.00	130.00	48.00
3.	Dachshund	Dark brown all over	80	98.00	130.00	48.00
4.	Dachshund	Beige; white flash on chest	80	98.00	130.00	48.00
5.	Dachshund	Dark/light brown	80	98.00	130.00	48.00

Derivatives

Dachshund Posy Bowls, c.1940

Sir George Wade's policy of creating new items by combining unsold stock from the George Wade Pottery and the Wade Heath Pottery produced many unusual and delightful "Stick-em-on-somethings." Unsold models were mounted on a new base with bramble-ware mustard pots or basket-weave egg cups to form posy bowls. The multi-coloured posy bowls usually have a moulded porcelain flower added to the bowl. Posy bowls in one colour with the added flower are rarely seen. All the posy bowls were produced in the Wade Heath Pottery.

Backstamp: Green-brown ink stamp "Wade England"

No.	Description	Colourways	Size	U.S.$	Can.$	U.K.£
1.	Mustard Pot	Dark brown dog; multi-coloured bowl, flower	90	90.00	130.00	45.00
2.	Mustard Pot	Matt green	90	75.00	95.00	40.00
3.	Mustard Pot	Matt cream	90	75.00	95.00	40.00
4.	Mustard Pot	Pale orange	90	75.00	95.00	40.00
5.	Egg Cup	Matt green	90	75.00	95.00	40.00

Dalmatian, c.1935-1939

Photograph not available
at press time

Backstamp: Blue handwritten "Wade England"; model name

No.	Name	Colourways	Size	U.S.$	Can.$	U.K.£
1.	Dalmatian	White/black	220		Rare	

English Setters, c.1930–c.1955

Backstamp: A. Black handwritten "Wade Made in England"
B. Black transfer "Wade England"

No.	Name	Colourways	Size	U.S.$	Can.$	U.K.£
1.	English Setter	White; orange patches	50	125.00	155.00	70.00
2.	English Setter	White; black patches	50	125.00	155.00	70.00

Puppies, c.1948–c.1953

Produced at the same time as the "Siamese Kittens" and also modelled by John Szeilor. Only three puppy models have been found to date.

| Puppy Begging | Puppy Seated | Puppy with Slipper |

Backstamp: **A.** Black hand painted "Wade"
B. Black transfer "Wade England"

No.	Name	Colourways	Size	U.S.$	Can.$	U.K.£
1.	Puppy Begging	White; beige ears; blue/black eyes; blue collar	60	130.00	175.00	95.00
2.	Puppy Seated	White; beige ears; blue/black eyes; blue collar	50	130.00	175.00	95.00
3.	Puppy with Slipper	White; beige ears, patch; black/blue eyes; blue slipper	45	130.00	175.00	95.00

Red Setter c.1930-1939

Photograph not available
at press time

No.	Name	Colourways	Size	U.S.$	Can.$	U.K.£
1.	Red Setter	Red-brown	150	200.00	275.00	100.00

Spaniel, 1935-1939

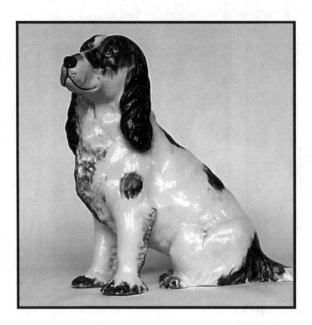

Backstamp: Black handwritten "Wade Made in England," red ink stamp of a leaping deer

No.	Name	Colourways	Size	U.S.$	Can.$	U.K.£
1.	Spaniel, seated	White; black markings, nose	135	350.00	400.00	175.00
2.	Spaniel, seated	White; brown markings; black nose	135	350.00	400.00	175.00

Spaniel, Seated on Round Base, 1945-1953

Photograph not available
at press time

Backstamp: Unmarked

No.	Name	Colourways	Size	U.S.$	Can.$	U.K.£
1.	Spaniel, seated on base	Honey/grey body; blue-grey ears; green base	75	50.00	70.00	25.00

Terriers, Begging, c.1935-c.1948

Terrier, begging

Terrier Egg Cup Posy Bowl

Backstamp: **A.** Black handwritten "Wade Made in England"
B. Black ink stamp "Wade England"

No.	Name	Colourways	Size	U.S.$	Can.$	U.K.£
1.	Terrier, begging	White; one black eye, ear	80	125.00	165.00	80.00
2.	Terrier, begging	White; light brown ear, eye, collar	80	125.00	165.00	80.00
3.	Terrier, begging	White; one black eye, ear	80	125.00	165.00	80.00
4.	Terrier, begging	White; two black ears; grey collar	80	125.00	165.00	80.00
5.	Terrier, begging	White; two black ears; brown collar	80	125.00	165.00	80.00

Terrier, Standing, 1935-1939

Photograph not available
at press time

No.	Description	Colourways	Size	U.S.$	Can.$	U.K.£
1.	Terrier, standing	White; brown/black patches	180		Extremely Rare	

Derivatives

Terrier Posy Bowls, c.1948–1953

These derivatives were made from the "Terriers, begging."

Backstamp: Green-brown ink stamp "Wade England"

No.	Description	Colourways	Size	U.S.$	Can.$	U.K.£
1.	Egg Cup	White dog; black ears; multi-coloured bowl	82	95.00	135.00	55.00
2.	Egg Cup	White dog; brown ears; multi-coloured bowl	82	95.00	135.00	55.00
3.	Mustard Pot	Green all over - reglazed	82	95.00	135.00	55.00

West Highland Terrier, c.1948

Photograph not available
at press time

No.	Name	Colourways	Size	U.S.$	Can.$	U.K.£
1.	West Highland Terrier	White; blue spots	50		Rare	

DONKEYS

Donkey Foals, c.1938-c.1953

Backstamp: A. Black handwritten "Wade England"
B. Black transfer "Wade Ireland"

No.	Name	Colourways	Size	U.S.$	Can.$	U.K.£
1.	Donkey Foal	Light grey; black mane	48 x 40	85.00	110.00	50.00
2.	Donkey Foal	Beige; black mane, tail tip	50 x 45	85.00	110.00	50.00

Donkeys with Baskets, 1965

The models of a small donkey with large baskets (panniers) on each side were produced by Wade Ireland for a short time in 1965. Some models have been found with the names of Irish towns hand painted on the baskets.

Donkey with Baskets

"Alexford" Donkey with Baskets

Backstamp: Ink stamp "Wade Ireland"

No.	Name	Colourways	Size	U.S.$	Can.$	U.K.£
1.	Donkey with Baskets	Grey/blue/green	95	55.00	75.00	35.00
2.	"Alexford" Donkey with Baskets	Grey/blue/green	95	55.00	75.00	35.00

ELEPHANT, c.1930, c.1950

The issues of the 1930s and 1950s can be identified by their backstamps. The original price of this model was 2/6d.

Backstamp: **A.** Black handwritten "Wade England," 1930s
B. Black transfer "Wade England," 1950s

No.	Name	Colourways	Size	U.S.$	Can.$	U.K.£
1.	Elephant	Pale grey; black eyes	50	125.00	160.00	65.00

ERMINE, 1939

The "Ermine," designed by Faust Lang, was made from the same mould as that used for the "Weasel."

Backstamp: Blue handwritten "Wade England 1939 Ermine"

No.	Name	Colourways	Size	U.S.$	Can.$	U.K.£
1.	Ermine	White; pink ears; black tail tip; blue-grey base	220 x 95	400.00	450.00	235.00

FAWNS, c.1938

These fawn models can be found in a variety of browns and greys. Most of the miniature models have no backstamps.

Fawn, facing right

Fawn, facing left

Backstamp: Black handwritten "Wade"

No.	Name	Colourways	Size	U.S.$	Can.$	U.K.£
1.	Fawn, facing right	Beige; light brown markings	Miniature/30	155.00	200.00	100.00
2.	Fawn, facing right	Beige; dark brown markings	Miniature/30	155.00	200.00	100.00
3.	Fawn, facing right	White; grey markings	Miniature/30	155.00	200.00	100.00
4.	Fawn, facing left	Off white; light brown markings	Small/61	155.00	200.00	100.00
5.	Fawn, facing left	Off white; grey/light brown markings	Small/61	155.00	200.00	100.00

Derivatives

For illustration of ashtray see page 131 "Kid Ashtray."

Fawn Ashtray

Photograph not available
at press time

No.	Description	Colourways	Size	U.S.$	Can.$	U.K.£
1.	Ashtray Fawn, facing right	Brown; yellow S-shaped ashtray	75 x 100	100.00	140.00	65.00

GIRAFFE, 1938

Photograph not available
at press time

No.	Name	Colourways	Size	U.S.$	Can.$	U.K.£
1.	Giraffe	Cream; beige markings	77	Extremely Rare		

GOATS, c.1930-c.1950

This set was first issued in the 1930s and was so popular that it was reissued in the 1940s and in the 1950s. The issues of the 1930s, 1940s and 1950s can be identified by their backstamps.

Goat

Kid

Backstamp: **A.** Black handwritten "Wade England"
B. Black ink stamp "Made in England"
C. Black transfer "Wade England"

No.	Name	Colourways	Size	U.S.$	Can.$	U.K.£
1.	Goat	Beige; creamy brown markings	55	120.00	150.00	75.00
2.	Goat	Off white; orange-brown markings	55	120.00	150.00	75.00
3.	Kid	Beige; creamy brown markings	45	100.00	135.00	65.00
4.	Kid	Off white; fawn markings	40	100.00	135.00	65.00

Derivatives

Kid Ashtray, c.early 1950s

This ashtray is one of Sir George Wade's famous "Stick-em-on-somethings." The S-shaped art deco ashtray has also been found with the Comic Rabbit (Little Laughing Bunny), and the Mini Bunnies mounted on the back rim. Note: Sylvac produced an almost identically shaped ashtray with small animals on, including "Kissing Bunnies." The Sylvac ashtray has an impressed registered Sylvac design number on the base which is different to the Wade design number.

Backstamp: Ink stamp "England 27631"

No.	Description	Colourways	Size	U.S.$	Can.$	U.K.£
1.	Kid Ashtray	White/beige kid; beige ashtray	102	125.00	150.00	75.00

HIPPOPOTAMUS, c.1930

Backstamp: Black handwritten "Wade England"

No.	Name	Colourways	Size	U.S.$	Can.$	U.K.£
1.	Hippopotamus	Light grey; brown eyes	50 x 90	140.00	165.00	75.00

HORSES

Foals, 1930-1950

| Foal, head back | Foal, head down |

Backstamp: **A.** Black handwritten "Wade England"
   B. Black transfer "Wade England"

No.	Name	Colourways	Size	U.S.$	Can.$	U.K.£
1.	Foal, head back	Beige; grey mane, tail	Large/65	90.00	130.00	65.00
2.	Foal, head back	White; grey mane, tail, hooves	Medium/55	90.00	130.00	65.00
3.	Foal, head back	Beige; grey mane, tail, hooves	Small/40	90.00	130.00	65.00
4.	Foal, head down	White; grey mane, tail, hooves	55	90.00	130.00	65.00
5.	Foal, head down	Beige; grey mane, tail, hooves	55	90.00	130.00	65.00

Foals, c.1948-1953

Foal, rear leg forward

Foal, rear legs parallel

Backstamp: Black ink stamp "Wade England"

No.	Name	Colourways	Size	U.S.$	Can.$	U.K.£
1.	Foal, rear leg forward	Light brown; black mane, tail; brown hooves	120	240.00	300.00	150.00
2.	Foal, rear leg forward	White; ginger mane, spots, tail, hooves	120	240.00	300.00	150.00
3.	Foal, rear leg forward	White; blue mane, spots, tail, hooves	120	240.00	300.00	150.00
4.	Foal, rear leg forward	Dark brown; black mane, tail, hooves	108	240.00	300.00	150.00
5.	Foal, rear legs parallel	White; pale blue mane, tail, hooves, spots	102	240.00	300.00	150.00
6.	Foal, rear legs parallel	Dark brown; black mane, tail, hooves	102	240.00	300.00	150.00

Horse, 1939

This is a Faust Lang model.

Backstamp: Blue handwritten "Wade England 1939 Horse" and the incised signature of Faust Lang

No.	Name	Colourways	Size	U.S.$	Can.$	U.K.£
1.	Horse	Brown; white socks; blue/green base	215	950.00	1,250.00	650.00
2.	Horse	Fawn brown; brown mane, tail; dark brown hooves; blue/green base	215	950.00	1,250.00	650.00

IBEX RAMS, c.1939–c.1953

Photograph not available
at press time

Backstamp: **A.** Black handwritten "Wade Made in England," c.1939
B. Black ink stamp "Wade Made in England," c.1948-1953

No.	Name	Colourways	Size	U.S.$	Can.$	U.K.£
1.	Ibex Ram	White; grey horns; green/beige rock base	80 x 65	140.00	165.00	75.00
2.	Ibex Ram	Cream/beige; dark grey horns; blue/grey rock base	80 x 65	140.00	165.00	75.00

LAMBS, 1930-c.1955

This set comprises three running lambs with long tails. The first two styles are very similar, but one lamb has its legs apart and the other has its legs closer together. Due to their delicate legs and tails, these models are easily damaged. Their original price was 2/6d each.

Lamb, Tail out (left) Lamb Tail in (right)

Backstamp: **A.** Black handwritten "Wade Made in England"
B. Black handwritten "Wade England"
C. Black handwritten "Wade"
D. Black ink stamp "Wade England"
E. Black transfer print "Wade England"

No.	Name	Colourways	Size	U.S.$	Can.$	U.K.£
1.	Lamb, tail in, legs apart	Dark brown; black/brown markings/ cream hooves	53	100.00	125.00	65.00
2.	Lamb, tail in, legs apart	Off white; grey markings and hooves	53	100.00	125.00	65.00
3.	Lamb, tail in, legs apart	Beige; cream markings and hooves	53	100.00	125.00	65.00
4.	Lamb, tail in, legs apart	Brown; cream markings; dark brown hooves	53	100.00	125.00	65.00
5.	Lamb, tail in, legs together	Beige; cream markings and hooves	53	100.00	125.00	65.00
6.	Lamb, tail out	Off white; grey markings and hooves	53	100.00	125.00	65.00
7.	Lamb, tail out	Beige; cream markings and hooves	53	100.00	125.00	65.00
8.	Lamb, tail out	Brown; cream markings; dark brown hooves	53	100.00	125.00	65.00

IF YOU WANT ALICE YOU MUST JOIN THE

"CLUB"

THE OFFICIAL INTERNATIONAL WADE COLLECTOR'S CLUB

Membership offers, besides the pleasure of sharing a hobby, such intangibles as greater appreciation of Wade collectables through initiation into techniques of designing, modelling and production. You can find out about inspired ideas that led to the creation of a new series of figurines — all ready to charm and capture the heart.

• ANNUAL MEMBERSHIP FIGURE

New each year, these exclusive annual membership figures become collector's items in their own right. "Alice" is the membership model for the 1999 year.

• MEMBERSHIP CERTIFICATE

Every new member receives a personalized membership certificate on joining.

• *WADE'S WORLD* MAGAZINE

This quarterly full-colour club magazine is packed with information on limited editions, club news, Wade fairs and events, and Wanted and For Sale adverts.

• CLUB LIMITED EDITIONS

Only club members can participate in purchasing the various club limited edition figures which are offered every year.

• ANNUAL MEMBERSHIP PIN

Each year a new collector's pin is included free with membership. The 1998 collector's pin was "The Wade Baby."

In the U.K.
Royal Works, Westport Road, Burslem
Stoke-on-Trent, ST6 4AP England
Tel.: 01782 255255 Fax.: 01782 575195
E-mail: club@wade.co.uk

In the U.S.
O.I.W.C.C.
3330 Cobb Parkway, Suite 17-333,
Acworth, Georgia 30101, USA
Tel.: 770 529 9908Fax.: 770 529 1515

http://www.wade.co.uk/wade

MEMBERSHIP OPTIONS

ANNUAL INDIVIDUAL MEMBERSHIP

(12 months from receipt of application)
UK Membership £20
Overseas Membership £25 or US $42

ANNUAL FAMILY MEMBERSHIP

(12 months from receipt of application)
UK Membership £68
Overseas Membership £82 or US $144

A family of four can enjoy full membership benefits. This is offered for up to four people; any additional family members will be charged at the full rate no reduction for families of less than four. All family membership's must enrol on one application form and all membership's will commence from the same month.

TWO-YEAR MEMBERSHIP

(24 months from receipt of application)
UK Membership £36
Overseas Membership £46 or US $78

Receive a special bonus price when you join for two years. You will receive your current years membership piece on receipt of your application and on the anniversary of your membership, you will automatically receive your second piece.

ENROL A FRIEND

The "Enrol a Friend" scheme is available when you introduce a new member for a one-year membership. Your friend will enjoy all the benefits of club membership plus you will both be sent a BONUS GIFT.

MEMBERSHIP APPLICATION FORM

Please enrol me/my family/my friend as a member(s):

Title . . . . First Name . . . . . . Last Name . . . .
Address . . . .
. . . .
. . . .
Post/Zip Code . . . . Telephone Number . . . .
❑ My cheque for . . . . made to payable to Wade Ceramics Limited is enclosed (cheques are accepted in pounds sterling and US dollars)
❑ Debit my credit/charge card ❑ Visa ❑Access ❑American Express for the sum of . . . .
Card No. ❑❑❑❑❑❑❑❑❑❑❑❑❑❑❑❑ Expiry ❑❑❑❑
Other 3 Family Names (for family membership): . . . .

Enrol a Friend and Both Receive a Bonus Gift

Title . . . . . First Name . . . . Last Name . . . .
Address . . . .
. . . .
. . . .
Postal/Zip Code . . . . Telephone Number . . . .
My Membership Number . . . .
Friend's Signature . . . . Date . . . .
I am/am not a member of the Jim Beam Bottle Club . . . . Number . . . .

Send to:

THE OFFICIAL INTERNATIONAL WADE COLLECTORS CLUB
Wade Ceramics Limited
Royal Works, Westport Road, Burslem, Stoke-on-Trent, ST6 4AP England
In UK: Tel.: 01782 255255   Fax.: 01782 575195
From Overseas: Tel.: 44 1782 255255 Fax.: 44 1782 575195

LIONS

Lion Cubs, 1939

This is a Faust Lang model.

Lion Cub with Paw Raised

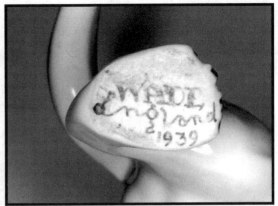

Backstamp of Lion Cub

Backstamp: Blue handwritten "Wade England 1939"

No.	Name	Colourways	Size	U.S.$	Can.$	U.K.£
1.	Lion Cub, paw raised	Brown; white tail tip	135	265.00	350.00	175.00
2.	Lion Cub, crouching	Brown; white tail tip	135	265.00	350.00	175.00

MONKEY

Seated Monkey, c.1930s

The seated monkey, his hand on his cheek, resembles a young "Capuchin" monkey and is finely detailed. He is one of two small monkeys produced by Wade in the 1930s.

Small Seated Monkey

Backstamp: Hand written "Wade Made in England"

No.	Description	Colourways	Size	U.S.$	Can.$	U.K.£
1.	Monkey seated hand on face	Light brown; creamy white markings	70	280.00	350.00	200.00
2.	Monkey seated arms by side	Light brown	35	95.00	130.00	65.00

Capuchin on Tree, 1939

This is a Faust Lang model.

Backstamp: Blue handwritten "Wade England 1939 Capuchin"

No.	Name	Colourways	Size	U.S.$	Can.$	U.K.£
1.	Capuchin	Pastel grey; pastel blue tree trunk blue/brown base	248	2,000.00	2,650.00	1,400.00

OTTER, 1939

Backstamp: Blue ink stamp "Wade England"

No.	Name	Colourways	Size	U.S.$	Can.$	U.K.£
1.	Otter	Brown; light brown paws	102 x 275	330.00	450.00	175.00

PANDA, BABY, c.1939

These small pandas are believed to have been produced at the same time as the popular "Panda" nursery ware sets.

Panda Sitting

Backstamp: **A.** Black handwritten "Baby Panda 2 Wade Made England"
B. Black hand written "Wade England"

No.	Name	Colourways	Size	U.S.$	Can.$	U.K.£
1.	Panda, walking	Black; white markings	40	110.00	150.00	75.00
2.	Panda, sitting	Black: white markings	50	110.00	150.00	75.00

PANDA, WAVING, c.1939
Shape No. 338

This model of a waving panda found in three sizes was produced at the same time as the Ming Ming "Panda" nursery ware sets (see *Standard Book of Wade Tablewares Vol. 3*), and is seen in Wadeheath advertising along with the nursery dishes. Produced in three sizes: large, medium and small. Shape No. 338.

Large and small Waving Pandas

Backstamp: Green ink stamp "Wade Heath England" The impressed shape No 338 has been found on the large size Pandas

No.	Description	Colourways	Size	U.S.$	Can.$	U.K.£
1.	Large Panda	Black and white	200	1,050.00	1,400.00	800.00
2.	Medium Panda	Black and white	165	675.00	800.00	450.00
3.	Small Panda	Black and white	153	400.00	500.00	200.00

PANTHER, 1939

The "Panther" was modelled by Faust Lang.

Backstamp: Blue handwritten "Wade England 1939 Panther" and the incised signature of Faust Lang

No.	Name	Colourways	Size	U.S.$	Can.$	U.K.£
1.	Panther	Light brown; blue eyes; green tree trunk base	215	750.00	1,000.00	500.00

POLAR BEAR, 1939

The "Polar Bear" was modelled by Faust Lang.

Backstamp: Blue handwritten "Wade England 1939 Polar Bear" and the incised signature of Faust Lang

No.	Name	Colourways	Size	U.S.$	Can.$	U.K.£
1.	Polar Bear	White; pink ears/mouth/blue base	195 x 290	1,500.00	2,000.00	1,000.00

RABBITS, c.1930 -c.1955

This series was first produced in the early 1930s, and due to its popularity, it was reissued in the late 1940s and again in the early 1950s. The reissued figures show very slight variations in colour and sizes.

The original price for the "Miniature Bunny" was 6d, the small "Double Bunnies" was 9d, the medium "Double Bunnies" sold for 1/-, and the large "Double Bunnies" cost 3/-.

Miniature, Double and Large Bunnies

Backstamp: **A.** Black handwritten "Wade Made in England"
B. Black ink stamp "Made in England"
C. Brown ink stamp "Wade England"
D. Black transfer "Wade England"

No.	Name	Colourways	Size	U.S.$	Can.$	U.K.£
1.	Bunny	White; light brown patches	Miniature/23	90.00	110.00	55.00
2.	Bunny	Brown; white patches	Miniature/23	90.00	110.00	55.00
3.	Bunny	White; light grey patches	Miniature/23	90.00	110.00	55.00
4.	Double Bunnies	White; grey patches	Small/21	100.00	125.00	60.00
5.	Double Bunnies	Brown; white patches	Small/21	100.00	125.00	60.00
6.	Double Bunnies	White; pale grey patches	Small/21	100.00	125.00	60.00
7.	Double Bunnies	White; grey patches	Medium/32	120.00	150.00	65.00
8.	Double Bunnies	White; grey patches	Large/45	125.00	145.00	75.00
9.	Double Bunnies	White; grey patches, ears	Large/45	125.00	145.00	75.00
10.	Double Bunnies	White; grey patches; pink ears	Large/45	125.00	145.00	75.00
11.	Double Bunnies	White; dark grey tail;	Large/45	125.00	145.00	75.00

SQUIRRELS, c.1930-c.1955

Both versions were first produced in the 1930s, the smaller model being reissued in the 1940s and 1950s, and the larger squirrel reissued in the 1940s. The original price for the "Squirrel, seated" was 1/-. The "Squirrel, lying" was recoloured and produced as a posy bowl.

Squirrel, Sitting   Squirrel, Lying

Backstamp: **A.** Black handwritten "Wade England"
B. Brown ink stamp "Wade England"
C. Black ink stamp "Wade England"
D. Black transfer "Wade England"

No.	Name	Colourways	Size	U.S.$	Can.$	U.K.£
1.	Squirrel, seated	Red-brown all over	40	100.00	125.00	65.00
2.	Squirrel, seated	Light brown; dark brown acorn	40	100.00	125.00	65.00
3.	Squirrel, seated	Light grey; white markings, brown claws	40	100.00	125.00	65.00
4.	Squirrel, seated	Light grey all over	40	100.00	125.00	65.00
5.	Squirrel, lying	Red-brown; black eyes; white back of tail; brown acorn	65	120.00	150.00	75.00
6.	Squirrel, lying	Beige; black eyes; white back of tail; green acorn	65	120.00	150.00	75.00

Derivative

Squirrel Posy Bowl, c.1948–1953

The multi-coloured "Squirrel Bramble Ware Mustard Pot Posy Bowl" was made from the model "Squirrel, lying" and had a moulded porcelain flower attached to it. All posy bowls were produced in the Wade Heath Pottery.

Photograph not available
at press time

Backstamp: Green-brown ink stamp "Wade England"

No.	Name	Colourways	Size	U.S.$	Can.$	U.K.£
1.	Mustard Pot	Red-brown squirrel; green/pink/yellow flower	70 x 97	85.00	110.00	55.00

STAG, 1939

The "Stag" was modelled by Faust Lang.

Backstamp: Blue handwritten "Wade England 1939 Highland Stag" and the incised signature of Faust Lang

No.	Name	Colourways	Size	U.S.$	Can.$	U.K.£
1.	Stag	Beige; blue/green rocky base	245	825.00	1,100.00	550.00

TORTOISES, c.1930

Backstamp: Black handwritten "Wade England"

No.	Name	Colourways	Size	U.S.$	Can.$	U.K.£
1.	Tortoise	Beige; blue grey patches on shell	55	145.00	180.00	70.00
2.	Tortoise	Fawn all over	55	145.00	180.00	70.00

WEASEL, 1939

The "Weasel" was modelled by Faust Lang. This mould was later used to make the model "Ermine."

Photograph not available
at press time

Backstamp: Blue handwritten "Wade Weasel designed in 1939 by Faust Lang"

No.	Name	Colourways	Size	U.S.$	Can.$	U.K.£
1.	Weasel	Fawn; black eyes; blue/green rock base	220	750.00	1,000.00	500.00

FLAXMAN WARE
1935-1940

The following models were made in the Wade Heath Pottery in Flaxman Ware matt glazes.

DOGS, 1935-1939

Alsatians, 1935-1939

The models of a resting Alsatian were produced with and without glass eyes.

Backstamp: **A.** Black ink stamp "Flaxman Ware Hand Made Pottery by Wadeheath England"
B. Black ink stamp "Flaxman Wade Heath England"
C. Impressed "British"

No.	Name	Colourways	Size	U.S.$	Can.$	U.K.£
1.	Alsatian, glass eyes	Green; black/yellow glass eyes	120	95.00	135.00	60.00
2.	Alsatian, glass eyes	Beige; black/yellow glass eyes	120	95.00	135.00	60.00
3.	Alsatian	Pale orange	120	90.00	120.00	50.00
4.	Alsatian	Orange	120	90.00	120.00	50.00
5.	Alsatian	Beige	120	90.00	120.00	50.00
6.	Alsatian	Green	120	90.00	120.00	50.00

Fox Terrier, c.1935-1937
Shape No. 528

This standing "Fox Terrier" with a smiling face has glass eyes. The Shape No. 528 is impressed on the stomach.

Backstamp: Black Ink Stamp "Flaxman Ware Hand Made Pottery by Wadeheath England" with impressed No. "528" (1935-1937)

No.	Description	Colourways	Size	U.S.$	Can.$	U.K.£
1.	Fox Terrier	Blue; black/yellow glass eyes	120	140.00	190.00	95.00

Long-Haired Dachshund, 1937-1939

Backstamp: Black ink stamp "Wadeheath Ware England"

No.	Name	Colourways	Size	U.S.$	Can.$	U.K.£
1.	Long-Haired Dachshund	Orange	95	125.00	150.00	65.00
2.	Long-Haired Dachshund	Pale green	80	125.00	150.00	65.00

Jack Russell Terrier
Shape No. 334

The terrier is sitting with his mouth open and his tongue out as though panting. For similar model with impressed Shape No. 334 on the base see "Cellulose" animals

Backstamp: Ink stamp "Wadeheath England"

No.	Description	Colourways	Size	U.S.$	Can.$	U.K.£
1.	Jack Russell Terrier	Green	101	85.00	115.00	60.00
2.	Jack Russell Terrier	Orange	101	85.00	115.00	60.00

Puppy in a Basket, 1937-1939

Backstamp: Black ink stamp "Flaxman Wade Heath England"

No.	Name	Colourways	Size	U.S.$	Can.$	U.K.£
1.	Puppy in a Basket	Orange	155	95.00	135.00	55.00

Scotties, 1937-1939
Shape No. 327

Scottie, Seated

Backstamp: A. Embossed "327" in a square
B. Black ink stamp "Flaxman Wade Heath England", impressed "327"

No.	Name	Colourways	Size	U.S.$	Can.$	U.K.£
1.	Scottie, seated	Brown	140	100.00	135.00	45.00
2.	Scottie, seated	Light brown	140	100.00	135.00	45.00
3.	Scottie, seated	Orange	140	100.00	135.00	45.00
4.	Scottie, seated	Light blue	140	100.00	135.00	45.00
5.	Scottie, seated	Light green	140	100.00	135.00	45.00
6.	Scottie, seated	Dark blue	140	100.00	135.00	45.00
7.	Scottie, walking	Unknown	115	—	—	—

Scotties, Crouching
Shape No. 527

This crouching Scottie has an elongated body and glass eyes.

Scottie, Crouching

Backstamp: Impressed "Made in England 527"

No.	Description	Colourways	Size	U.S.$	Can.$	U.K.3
1.	Crouching Scottie	Green	110 x 185	85.00	115.00	60.00

Terriers, 1935-1937
Shape No. 520

The seated terrier with one ear up and the other down has glass eyes. The Shape No. is impressed on the base of the black models.

Terrier, seated

Black Terrier, seated

Backstamp: **A.** Black ink stamp "Flaxman Ware Hand Made Pottery By Wadeheath England"
      B. Impressed "Made in England 520"

No.	Name	Colourways	Size	U.S.$	Can.$	U.K.£
1.	Terrier, seated	Beige; dark brown glass eyes	160	130.00	175.00	78.00
2.	Terrier, seated	Black; black glass eyes	165	130.00	175.00	78.00
3.	Terrier, seated	Blue; dark brown glass eyes	160	130.00	175.00	78.00
4.	Terrier, seated	Green	165	130.00	175.00	78.00
5.	Terrier, standing	Brown	125	130.00	175.00	78.00

PANTHER, 1937–1939

In this figure a slender, stylised panther is leaping over a rock base.

Photograph not available
at press time.

Backstamp: Black ink stamp "Flaxman Wade Heath England"

No.	Name	Colourways	Size	U.S.$	Can.$	U.K.£
1.	Panther	Matt orange	190		Rare	

RABBIT, CROUCHING, 1935-c.1940
Shape No. 337

The crouching rabbit has its ears apart and the Shape No. 337 impressed on the base.

Rabbit, crouching

Backstamp: Black ink stamp "Flaxman Wadeheath England," impressed "337"

No.	Name	Colourways	Size	U.S.$	Can.$	U.K.£
1.	Rabbit, crouching	Orange-brown; dark brown eyes	110 x 145	80.00	100.00	45.00

RABBIT, SEATED
Shape No. 305

The popular seated rabbits have been found in six sizes. A number of models have been found with the Shape No. 305 impressed on the bases. Unmarked Wade seated rabbits are very hard to separate from unmarked Sylvac rabbits, but on close inspection you will see that the lined pattern of the fur on the Wade rabbit runs downwards only and is sparse. The pattern on the fur of the Sylvac rabbits is lined and speckled and much more profuse. There is also a slight difference in the tails: the Wade rabbits have humps on the top and bottom of the tail; the Sylvac tail is squared. On smaller models and worn moulds the difference in the tail is very hard to detect.

Rabbits, seated

Backstamp: **A.** Black ink stamped "Flaxman Ware Hand Painted Pottery by Wadeheath England"
B. Black ink stamped "Flaxman Wadeheath England"
C. Black ink stamped "Made in England"
These models can also be found with no backstamp

No.	Name	Colourways	Size	U.S.$	Can.$	U.K.£
1.	Rabbit, seated	Light brown	Miniature/75 x 60	50.00	70.00	25.00
2.	Rabbit, seated	Light green	Miniature/75 x 60	50.00	70.00	25.00
3.	Rabbit, seated	Orange	Miniature/75 x 60	50.00	70.00	25.00
4.	Rabbit, seated	Brown	Small/105 x 88	60.00	80.00	30.00
5.	Rabbit, seated	Light brown	Small/105 x 88	60.00	80.00	30.00
6.	Rabbit, seated	Light green	Small/105 x 88	60.00	80.00	30.00
7.	Rabbit, seated	Orange	Small/105 x 88	60.00	80.00	30.00
8.	Rabbit, seated	Yellow	Small/105 x 88	60.00	80.00	30.00
9.	Rabbit, seated	Brown	Medium/135 x 115	70.00	90.00	35.00
10.	Rabbit, seated	Light brown	Medium/135 x 115	70.00	90.00	35.00
11.	Rabbit, seated	Green	Medium/135 x 115	70.00	90.00	35.00
12.	Rabbit, seated	Orange	Medium/135 x 115	70.00	90.00	35.00
13.	Rabbit, seated	Turquoise	Medium/135 x 115	70.00	90.00	35.00
14.	Rabbit, seated	Brown	Large/152 x 130	80.00	110.00	40.00
15.	Rabbit, seated	Light green	Large/152 x 130	80.00	110.00	40.00
16.	Rabbit, seated	Orange	Large/152 x 130	80.00	110.00	40.00
17.	Rabbit, seated	Blue	Large/165 x 135	80.00	110.00	40.00
18.	Rabbit, seated	Brown	Extra Large/190 x 160	80.00	110.00	40.00
19.	Rabbit, seated	Light green	Extra Large/190 x 160	80.00	110.00	40.00
20.	Rabbit, seated	Orange	Extra Large/190 x 160	80.00	110.00	40.00

Derivative

Matchbox Holder, 1937–1939

Backstamp: Black ink stamp "Wadeheath Ware England"

No.	Name	Colourways	Size	U.S.$	Can.$	U.K.£
1.	Matchbox Holder	Light green	105 x 85	110.00	150.00	75.00

SQUIRRELS
Shape No. 325

Backstamp: A. Impressed "Made in England 325"
B. Black ink stamp "Flaxman Ware Hand Made Pottery by Wadeheath England" impressed "325" (1935-1937)

No.	Name	Colourways	Size	U.S.$	Can.$	U.K.£
1.	Squirrel feeding	Light green	165 x 135	80.00	110.00	40.00
2.	Squirrel feeding	Light blue	165 x 135	80.00	110.00	40.00
3.	Squirrel feeding	Light brown	165 x 135	80.00	110.00	40.00
4.	Squirrel feeding	Off white; brown painted eyes	165 x 135	80.00	110.00	50.00
5.	Squirrel with Glass Eyes	Blue; brown glass eyes	180 x 150	125.00	140.00	65.00
6.	Squirrel with Glass Eyes	Light green	145 x 155	125.00	140.00	65.00

SERIES AND SETS
1975-1991

CHAMPIONSHIP DOGS, 1975–1981

Championship Dogs is a set of five dogs, all standing on green, oval bases. When produced, a bright orange label that reads "Wade England" was affixed to the base; some models still have them. This is the first issue of solid animals, except for the Whimsies. The original price was £2.65 per model.

Backstamp: Raised "Wade England"

No.	Name	Colourways	Size	U.S.$	Can.$	U.K.£
1.	Afghan Hound	Beige/white; light brown face, paws	85 x 90	80.00	110.00	40.00
2.	Cocker Spaniel	Beige/off white; black patches	80 x 90	95.00	135.00	50.00
3.	Collie	Honey/dark brown	85 x 85	95.00	135.00	50.00
4.	English Setter	Beige/off white; black patches	80 x 90	95.00	135.00	50.00
5.	Old English Sheepdog	Grey/white	85 x 90	95.00	135.00	50.00

THE WORLD OF SURVIVAL SERIES, 1976–1982

British Anglia Television's *World of Survival* film series has won world-wide acclaim. Naturalists and film makers have praised these documentaries featuring many endangered species. George Wade and Son Ltd. collaborated with Anglia Television to produce two sets of six models. The figures are perfect in every detail. They are slip cast and open cast (standing on their feet, not on a base). Produced in a biscuit porcelain, they are matt and rough to the touch and completely unlike any other Wade models.

Due to their expensive retail prices, necessitated by high production costs, only a limited number of models were released. Their original prices started from £45 to £65.

SET 1

African Elephant

American Bison

Polar Bear

Tiger

Backstamp: **A.** Black transfer print "World of Survival Series, by Wade of England. Copyright Survival Anglia Limited. 1976 All rights reserved"
B. White transfer print on brown label "World of Survival Series, by Wade of England. Copyright Survival Anglia Limited. 1976 All rights reserved"

No.	Name	Colourways	Size	U.S.$	Can.$	U.K.£
1.	African Elephant	Grey; white tusks	160 x 260	395.00	525.00	280.00
2.	African Lion	Biscuit brown; dark brown mane	110 x 200	395.00	525.00	250.00
3.	American Bison	Dark brown body; charcoal-grey mane	120 x 190	395.00	525.00	250.00
4.	Black Rhinoceros	Light grey; white horns	110 x 240	395.00	525.00	250.00
5.	Polar Bear	White; black eyes, nose	110 x 210	395.00	525.00	250.00
6.	Tiger	Orange/yellow/white/black	95 x 190	500.00	600.00	300.00

SET 2

African Cape Buffalo

American Brown Bear

American Cougar

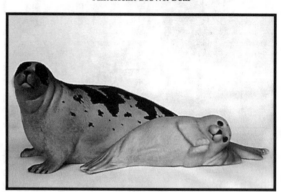
Harp Seal and Pup

Hippopotamus

Mountain Gorilla

Backstamp: Black transfer print "World of Survival Series, by Wade of England. Copyright Survival Anglia Limited. 1976 All rights reserved"

No.	Name	Colourways	Size	U.S.$	Can.$	U.K.£
1.	African Cape Buffalo	Dark brown; grey/white horns	170 x 240	500.00	600.00	300.00
2.	American Brown Bear	Dark brown; black nose	105 x 145	395.00	525.00	280.00
3.	American Cougar	Beige; dark grey muzzle	150 x 225	500.00	600.00	300.00
4.	Harp Seal and Pup	Off white; light grey/black markings	85 x 220	500.00	600.00	300.00
5.	Hippopotamus	Chocolate brown/pink; pink mouth	105 x 220	395.00	525.00	250.00
6.	Mountain Gorilla	Black body; silver grey mane; copper head	150 x 150	500.00	600.00	300.00

CHEETAH AND GAZELLE, 1991

Only five copies of the beautifully sculptured "Cheetah and Gazelle" are known to have been produced. This figure of a cheetah chasing a Grants gazelle was modelled by Alan Maslankowski and made of biscuit porcelain. Each model was sold with a signed and numbered limited-edition certificate. The original price direct from the Wade Pottery was £1,200.

Cheetah and Gazelle, front view

Cheetah and Gazelle, back view

Backstamp: The model is unmarked, but a gold-coloured metal plaque on the front of the wooden base is inscribed "Survival" with the model number

No.	Colourways	Size	U.S.$	Can.$	U.K.£
1.	Orange yellow/black cheetah; orange/white/black gazelle	240 x 200		Extremely rare	

WADE IRELAND WILDLIFE ANIMALS, c.1978

The exact name of this series is unknown. There are thought to be at least seven animals in this set produced by Wade Ireland during the late 1970s. Four known models are shown below; there is also the Walrus and two other models are reputed to be a lion and a rhinoceros. I would appreciate hearing from collectors who have the above mentioned models for inclusion in the next edition of this book. It is interesting to note that the Irish Wade Koala bear was reissued as the Dunstable UK Wade Show Model "The Australian Koala" in October 1997.

Baby Elephant

Chimpanzee Seated on Leafy Base

Koala Bear on Tree Stump

Polar Bear Seated Upright

Backstamp: Red and gold label "Wade Ireland"

No.	Description	Colourways	Size	U.S.$	Can.$	U.K.£
1.	Baby Elephant	Grey streaked body; small off white tusks	90	525.00	700.00	350.00
2.	Chimpanzee	Black and grey; brown eyes; off white face; grey/green base	115	850.00	1,100.00	500.00
3.	Koala Bear	Brown; dark brown nose/tree stump; dark green leaves	115	525.00	700.00	350.00
4.	Polar Bear	White; black nose	140	725.00	960.00	450.00
5.	Walrus	Mottled brown/black; white tusks	85	800.00	1,000.00	450.00

BIRDS

HIGH GLOSS MODELS c.1930 - c.1935
SETS AND SERIES 1978 to the present

Wade bird models created from the early 1930s to 1939 and from the late 1940s up to the early 1950s are slip cast. Beginning in the early 1950s, Wade produced some solid models, and afterwards all the models were solid.

The glazes used from the 1930s to the early 1950s are in delicate pastel and natural colours and are very different from the darker colours used from the late 1950s. Many of the models that were first produced in the early 1930s proved to be popular and were reissued in the late 1940s and early 1950s.

BACKSTAMPS

These bird models were produced in both the Wade Heath and the George Wade potteries, which accounts for the various backstamps used in the same time spans.

Handwritten Backstamps

Handwritten marks are found on models produced from the early 1930s to the 1940s.

Black handwritten, early 1930s-1940s

Blue handwritten, 1939-1940s

Blue handwritten, 1939-1940s

Ink Stamps

Ink stamps were used from the late 1940s to 1953.

The size of the mark has no relevance to the date; large ink stamps were used on models with large bases, small ink stamps on small bases. Many of the smaller models are unmarked

Black, brown or green ink stamp, late 1940s-1953

Transfer Prints

Transfer prints have been used from 1953 to the present.

Transfer print, 1978-1982

HIGH-GLOSS MODELS
c.1930-c.1955

BLUEBIRDS ON FLORAL NEST AND STUMP, c.1930s

These novelty bluebird models with floral bases, one on a nest, the other on a stump, were produced as a pair during the mid to late 1930s, and are believed to have been modelled by Jessie Van Hallen who worked for Wadeheath from 1930-1940. Jessie Van Hallen is well known to Wade collectors for her lady figurines, and she also modelled the Wade flowers, some of which have the same mottled moss and floral bases that are seen on the bluebird models. The "Flicker," a North American bird of the Woodpecker family, has been documented as modelled by Jessie Van Hallen; therefore it is possible that a few other birds were also modelled by Jessie during her ten years with Wade Heath.

Bluebird on Floral Nest

Bluebird on Floral Stump

Backstamp: **A.** Black handwritten "Wade 9 England No 123" sometimes found with the letter L added (possibly the painter's identifying initial
B. Black handwritten "Wade 9 England No 124" sometimes found with the letter L added (possibly the painter's identifying initial

No.	Name	Colourways	Size	U.S.$	Can.$	U.K.£
1.	Bluebird on nest	Blue/white/yellow bird; mottled brown maroon/yellow/pink/blue flowers	50 x 76	225.00	300.00	150.00
2.	Bluebird on stump	Blue/white/yellow bird; mottled brown maroon/yellow/pink/blue flowers	90	225.00	300.00	150.00

BUDGERIGARS, 1939-c.1955

The budgerigar figures listed on this page were modelled by Faust Lang and have a 1939/1941 date incised on the base. The original price for the "Budgerigar, Style One" was 10/-.

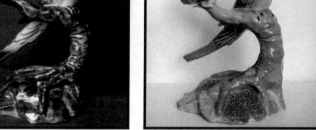

| Budgerigar, Style One | Bugerigar, Style Two | Budgerigars |

Backstamp: **A.** Blue handwritten "Wade England," date, name of model
B. Green-brown ink stamp "Wade England"
C. Black ink stamp "Wade England"

No.	Name	Colourways	Size	U.S.$	Can.$	U.K.£
1.	Budgerigar, Style One	Pale blue; yellow head; fawn branch, pale blue/green mottled base	190	250.00	325.00	150.00
2.	Budgerigar, Style One	Yellow; dark green tail, markings; dark brown stump; brown/green mottled base	190	250.00	325.00	150.00
3.	Budgerigar, Style One	Yellow; green wings, tail; dark brown stump; brown/green mottled base	190	250.00	325.00	150.00
4.	Budgerigar, Style Two	Pale green; black wing markings; light brown tree branch; dark blue flower; brown/green mottled base	175	250.00	300.00	125.00
5.	Budgerigar, Style Two	Pale blue /grey; yellow head; light green tree branch; pink flower; brown/green base	175	300.00	365.00	175.00
6.	Budgerigars	Yellow/blue/green bird; all green bird; fawn branch; pale blue/grey/green mottled base	195	300.00	365.00	185.00
7.	Budgerigars	Yellow bird with green tail; all green bird; fawn branch; pale blue/grey/green mottled base	195	300.00	365.00	185.00

CHICK, c.1940-1953

The "Chick, Version 3," is a reissue of the earlier models.

Backstamp: A. Brown handwritten "Wade Made in England"
B. Brown ink stamp "Wade England"

No.	Name	Colourways	Size	U.S.$	Can.$	U.K.£
1.	Chick	Pastel blue/grey; pink beak	55	270.00	350.00	175.00
2.	Chick	Light/dark grey; yellow eyes; pink beak	55	270.00	350.00	175.00
3.	Chick	Light/dark blue; black eyes; grey beak	55	300.00	400.00	215.00

COCKATOO, 1939-1955

This is a Faust Lang model. The original issue price for the "Cockatoo" was 5/9.

Cockatoo (No. 4)

Backstamp: A. Blue handwritten "Wade England," date, name of model
B. Green-brown ink stamp "Wade England"
C. Black ink stamp "Wade England"

No.	Name	Colourways	Size	U.S.$	Can.$	U.K.£
1.	Cockatoo	White; bright yellow crest; beige-pink eyes, beak	160	850.00	1,100.00	400.00
2.	Cockatoo	White; bright pink crest, beak, wing tips; yellow feet	160	850.00	1,100.00	400.00
3.	Cockatoo	White; bright pink crest, beak; grey wing tips; yellow feet	160	850.00	1,100.00	400.00
4.	Cockatoo	Grey; pale pink crest, beak; beige feet	160	850.00	1,100.00	400.00

COCKEREL, c.1940

Cockerel (No. 1)

Cockerel Mustard Pot (No. 2)

Backstamp: Black handwritten "Wade Made in England"

No.	Name	Colourways	Size	U.S.$	Can.$	U.K.£
1.	Cockerel	Off white; pink comb, eyes, beak, legs; pale green base	90	100.00	150.00	60.00

Derivatives

Cockerel Posy Bowls, c.1940

A single Cockerel model was mounted on a base with a bramble ware mustard pot to make a posy bowl.

Backstamp: Green-brown ink stamp Wade England

No.	Name	Colourways	Size	U.S.$	Can.$	U.K.£
1.	Cockerel Mustard Pot	Brown; pink comb, beak; multi-coloured tail; green/pink/yellow posy	95	68.00	90.00	45.00
2.	Cockerel Mustard Pot	Creamy beige/orange all over	95	68.00	90.00	45.00

DRAKE AND DADDY, c.1938-1953

The original price of this model was 2/6d.

Backstamp: A. Black handwritten "Wade England"
B. Brown ink stamp "Wade England"

No.	Name	Colourways	Size	U.S.$	Can.$	U.K.£
1.	Drake and Daddy	Daddy white/brown; blue head; pink beak, feet Drake white; grey wings; pink beak, feet	90	85.00	100.00	50.00
2.	Drake and Daddy	Daddy blue head; beige/white body; grey wings; yellow beak/feet Drake white; grey wings; yellow beak, feet	90	85.00	100.00	50.00

DUCKS, c.1932-1953

Duck, head forward, small; Duck, pecking, medium

Duck, head back; Duck, preening, medium

Backstamp: **A.** Black handwritten "Wade Made in England"
B. Black handwritten "Wade England"
C. Brown ink stamp "Wade England"
D. Black transfer "Wade England"

No.	Name	Colourways	Size	U.S.$	Can.$	U.K.£
1.	Duck, head forward	Beige/white; blue-grey head; dark grey wings; pink beak, feet; grey base	Large/90	90.00	120.00	45.00
2.	Duck, head forward	Beige/white; grey head; grey wings; pink beak, feet; grey base	Small/75	90.00	120.00	45.00
3.	Duck, head forward	White/beige; grey head; grey wings; pink beak, feet; white base	Small/75	90.00	120.00	45.00
4.	Duck, head forward	Beige/white; blue head; grey wings; yellow beak, feet; grey base	Small/75	90.00	120.00	45.00
5.	Duck, head forward	White; blue/green head, wings; yellow beak, feet; grey base	Small/70	90.00	120.00	45.00
6.	Duck, preening	Beige/white; blue/grey head; dark blue wings; pink beak, feet; grey base	Large/85	90.00	120.00	45.00
7.	Duck, preening	White /beige; grey head, wings; pink beak, feet; grey base	Medium/80	90.00	120.00	45.00
8.	Duck, preening	White/grey; grey blue head; blue/ green wings; yellow beak, feet; grey base	Medium/80	90.00	120.00	45.00
9.	Duck, preening	White; blue/green head, wings; yellow beak, feet; dark grey base	Small/70	90.00	120.00	45.00
10.	Duck, preening	White; light grey head, wings, base; yellow beak, feet	Small/70	90.00	120.00	45.00
11.	Duck, head back	White; grey head, wings; pink beak, feet; grey base	74	90.00	120.00	45.00
12.	Duck, head back	Beige/white; grey head; blue wings; yellow beak, feet; blue base	74	90.00	120.00	45.00
13.	Duck, head back	White; blue/green head, wings; yellow beak, feet; dark grey base	74	90.00	120.00	45.00
14.	Duck, pecking	White /light grey body, head; blue wings; pink feet, beak; white base	44	90.00	120.00	45.00
15.	Duck, pecking	Dark grey /white body, head; blue/ black wings; pink beak, feet; white base	44	90.00	120.00	45.00
16.	Duck, pecking	White; light grey head; deep blue wings, base; yellow beak, feet	44	90.00	120.00	45.00
17.	Duck, pecking	White/beige; grey blue head; blue wings; yellow beak, feet; grey base	44	90.00	120.00	45.00
18	Duck, pecking	White; blue/green head, wings; yellow beak, feet; grey base	44	90.00	120.00	45.00

Derivatives

Duck Posy Bowls, c.1948-1953

The multi-coloured posy bowls have a moulded porcelain flower attached to the rim of the bowl. One-colour posy bowls are rarely found with the added flower decoration.

Duck, pecking, Posy Bowl

Backstamp: Green-brown ink stamp "Wade England"

No.	Name	Colourways	Size	U.S.$	Can.$	U.K.£
1.	Duck, head forward	White; pale grey head, wings; yellow beak, feet; green/pink/yellow bowl	80	75.00	90.00	45.00
2.	Duck, preening	White; grey head, wings; yellow beak, feet; multi-coloured bowl	Medium/85	75.00	90.00	45.00
3.	Duck, preening	Pale yellow all over	Medium/85	75.00	90.00	45.00
4.	Duck, preening	Light green all over	Medium/85	75.00	90.00	45.00
5.	Duck, preening	Dark blue all over	Medium/85	75.00	90.00	45.00
6.	Duck, pecking	White; grey head, wings, yellow beak, feet; multi-coloured bowl	55	75.00	90.00	45.00
7.	Duck, pecking	Dark blue all over	55	75.00	90.00	45.00

Ducks, Open Wings, 1935-1953

All three ducks have open wings. The "Duck, preening" has turned its head over its back, beak open, as though preening a wing. The "Duck, head forward" has its head tilted, beak closed. The "Duck, head up" has its head up and its beak closed.

| Duck, head forward | Duck, head up |

Backstamp: **A.** Black handwritten "Wade England"
B. Black transfer "Wade England"

No.	Description	Colourways	Size	U.S.$	Can.$	U.K.£
1.	Duck, preening	White; light brown head, wings; pink feet	35	75.00	100.00	50.00
2.	Duck, preening	White; blue-grey head, wings; black beak; pink feet	35	75.00	100.00	50.00
3.	Duck, head forward	White; blue-grey head, wings; black beak; pink feet	45	75.00	100.00	50.00
4.	Duck, head up	White body; blue-grey head, wings; black beak; pale pink feet	45	75.00	100.00	50.00

FLICKER, c.late 1930s

Backstamp: Blue handwritten "Wade England Flicker"

No.	Name	Colourways	Size	U.S.$	Can.$	U.K.£
1.	Flicker	Off white; blue head, wings, tail; orange beak	115	145.00	185.00	95.00

GOLDFINCHES, 1946-1953

The original price of these models was 6/6d each.

Goldfinch, wings closed

Goldfinch, wings open

Backstamp: A. Green-brown ink stamp "Wade England"
B. Black ink stamp "Wade England"
C. Black ink stamp "Wade Made in England"
D. Black ink stamp "England"

No.	Name	Colourways	Size	U.S.$	Can.$	U.K.£
1.	Goldfinch, wings closed	Yellow; black wings, tail, head patch; brown beak; mottled green/brown tree branch	100	265.00	350.00	175.00
2.	Goldfinch, wings open	Yellow; black wings, tail, head patch; brown beak; mottled green/brown tree branch	100	265.00	350.00	175.00

GREBE, 1939

This is a Faust Lang model.

Backstamp: **A.** Blue handwritten "Wade England," date, name of model
B. Blue handwritten "Wade England," name of model

No.	Name	Colourways	Size	U.S.$	Can.$	U.K.£
1.	Grebe	White/grey; dark grey crest; yellow beak; blue fish; blue/green/white mottled base	235	850.00	1,300.00	650.00

HERON, 1946-1953

Backstamp: Green-brown ink stamp "Wade England"

No.	Name	Colourways	Size	U.S.$	Can.$	U.K.£
1.	Heron	Dark blue/grey; pink breast; orange legs; mottled brown/green tree stump, rock base	190	625.00	800.00	400.00

INDIAN RUNNER DUCKS, c.1932-1953

These three Indian Runner or Peking-type ducks were first produced in the early 1930s and reissued in the late 1940s to 1953. They have long thin bodies; the mother is looking down at her two ducklings, one with its head up the other with the head down. The original selling price was 9d for a set of three.

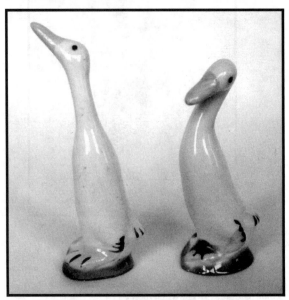

Duckling, head up, Duckling, head down

Backstamp: A. Black handwritten "Wade England"
B. Black transfer print "Wade England"

No.	Name	Colourways	Size	U.S.$	Can.$	U.K.£
1.	Mother Duck	Blue/grey/white; light brown head; yellow beak, feet; pale blue base	95	100.00	150.00	75.00
2.	Duckling, head down	White; yellow beak, feet; pale blue base	53	100.00	150.00	75.00
3.	Duckling, head up	White; yellow beak, feet; pale blue base	55	100.00	150.00	75.00

OWL, 1940

Backstamp: Black handwritten "Wade Made in England," date and name of model

No.	Name	Colourways	Size	U.S.$	Can.$	U.K.£
1.	Owl	Brown/white; black markings; pale blue log	146	300.00	400.00	200.00

PARROT, 1939

This is a Faust Lang model.

Backstamp: Blue handwritten "Wade England," date and name of model

No.	Name	Colourways	Size	U.S.$	Can.$	U.K.£
1.	Parrot on Stump	Blue head, wings; green body; peach face, breast; fawn stump	267	1,500.00	2,000.00	1,400.00

PELICAN, 1946-1953

The original price of this model was 6/6d.

Backstamp: A. Blue handwritten "Wade England," date and name of model
B. Green-brown ink stamp "Wade England"
C. Black ink stamp "Wade England"
D. Handwritten "Pelican Wade England 1939"

No.	Name	Colourways	Size	U.S.$	Can.$	U.K.£
1.	Pelican	White; bright yellow beak; pale green feather tips; brown/orange feet; black claws	170	550.00	800.00	400.00
2.	Pelican	White; yellow beak; brown feet; black claws	170	550.00	800.00	400.00
3.	Pelican	Pearl white with green feathering; yellow/black eyes and feet	170	550.00	800.00	400.00

PENGUIN

Backstamp: Handwritten "Wade England"

No.	Description	Colourways	Size	U.S.$	Can.$	U.K.£
1.	Penguin	Grey-blue/white; beige feet	65 x 40	160.00	210.00	100.00

SEAGULL ON ROCK, c.1948-1953

This rarely found model was produced in the late 1940s and reissued in 1953. The original price of the reissue was 3/-.

Backstamp: A. Black ink stamp "Wade Made in England"
              B. Black transfer "Wade England," 1953

No.	Name	Colourways	Size	U.S.$	Can.$	U.K.£
1.	Seagull	White; grey head; blue rock	40	125.00	165.00	80.00
2.	Seagull	Grey/white; pale blue rock	40	125.00	165.00	80.00

TOUCAN, 1946-1953

The original issue price for the "Toucan" was 10/-.

Photograph not available
at press time

Backstamp: A. Green-brown ink stamp "Wade England"
              B. Black ink stamp "Wade England"

No.	Name	Colourways	Size	U.S.$	Can.$	U.K.£
B-30	Toucan on Stump	White; dark grey head; black wings; orange beak; brown tree stump	175	375.00	500.00	250.00

WOODPECKER, 1939-1953

The original issue price for the "Woodpecker" was 10/-.

Woodpecker, 1939 Issue   **Woodpecker, 1946 - 1953 Issue**

Backstamp: A. Green-brown ink stamp "Wade England"
B. Black ink stamp "Wade England"
C. Blue ink handwritten stamp "Wade England Woodpecker"

No.	Name	Colourways	Size	U.S.$	Can.$	U.K.£
1.	Woodpecker	Off white; maroon head; grey-blue beak, feet; light green/brown wings, tail; green/brown trunk	175	260.00	350.00	165.00
2.	Woodpecker	Black and white; red patch on head and throat; blue/green trunk	184	400.00	530.00	250.00

THE CONNOISSEUR'S BIRD COLLECTION, 1978-1982

This series of 12 British birds was made in the same biscuit porcelain as that used for the *World of Survival* animals. The models are all slip cast and produced in their natural colours and settings. Their original retail prices ranged from £20 to £45. Set 1 was issued without plinths while Set 2 was issued with circular polished wooden plinths.

Set 1 Without Plinths

Goldcrest

Nuthatch

Robin

Wren

Backstamp: Black transfer "The Connoisseurs Collection by Wade of England," model name and number

No.	Description	Colourways	Size	U.S.$	Can.$	U.K.£
1.	Bullfinch	Black head; brown body; pink breast; yellow caterpillar	185	355.00	475.00	220.00
2.	Coaltit	Black/grey bird; green holly; red berries	145	355.00	475.00	220.00
3.	Goldcrest	Yellow stripe on head; off-white body; brown branch	135	355.00	475.00	220.00
4.	Nuthatch	Grey/white bird; yellow/brown log	125	355.00	475.00	220.00
5.	Robin	Brown body; red breast; orange mushrooms	125	355.00	475.00	220.00
6.	Wren	Brown bird; grey stones	115	355.00	475.00	220.00

Set 2 - With Plinths

Three of the illustrations are shown without their base due to adhesive failure over time.

Bearded Tit

Kingfisher

Woodpecker (on plinth)

Dipper

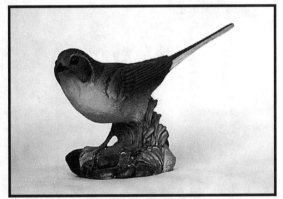
Yellow Wagtail

Backstamp: Stamped on metal disk set in base "The Connoisseurs Collection by Wade of England," model name and number

No.	Description	Colourways	Size	U.S.$	Can.$	U.K.£
1.	Bearded Tit	Reddish brown; grey head	165	355.00	475.00	220.00
2.	Dipper	Light brown/pale brown bird; grey pebbles	140	355.00	475.00	220.00
3.	Kingfisher	Blue/grey/white/orange; grey stump	180	355.00	475.00	220.00
4.	Redstart	Grey/black/reddish brown	180	355.00	475.00	220.00
5.	Woodpecker	Red/white/black/yellow; brown/yellow stump	165	355.00	475.00	220.00
6.	Yellow Wagtail	Pale yellow/grey/black; grey/brown pebbles	115	355.00	475.00	220.00

COMMEMORATIVE WARE
1935 to 1990

The Wade potteries, primarily Wadeheath, have issued a large line of commemoratives. In 1935 Wade began its range of commemorative ware with items marking the silver jubilee of King George V and Queen Mary. Since then Wade has issued commemoratives for coronations, the silver jubilee of Queen Elizabeth, royal birthdays, royal weddings and royal births, as well as for less regal occasions.

The models are listed according to the event they commemorate, which appear here in chronological order.

BACKSTAMPS

Ink Stamps

From 1935 to 1953, the backstamps used on commemorative items were black ink stamps that included the name Wadeheath. A green ink stamped "Wade England" was introduced on some of the 1953 coronation ware.

Black ink stamp, 1937

Green ink stamp, 1953

Embossed Stamps

Also beginning in 1953, the Wade backstamp was either embossed on the model or applied on a transfer print.

Embossed, 1981

Transfer Prints

Transfer print, 1981-1990

KING GEORGE V AND QUEEN MARY SILVER JUBILEE, 1935

To celebrate the silver jubilee of George V and Queen Mary in May 1935, Wadeheath produced a set of *Jubilee Ware*. These items have transfer prints of King George V and Queen Mary on the front.

Photograph not available
at press time

Backstamp: Black ink stamp "Wadeheath England" with a lion

No.	Description	Colourways	Shape/Size	U.S.$	Can.$	U.K.£
1.	Child's Beaker	Cream; multi-coloured print	75	95.00	135.00	50.00
2.	Child's Dish	Cream; multi-coloured print	165	95.00	135.00	50.00
3.	Cup	Cream; multi-coloured print	65	95.00	135.00	50.00
3.	Saucer	Cream; multi-coloured print	140	See above		
4.	Mug	Cream; multi-coloured print	Footed/135	120.00	150.00	60.00
5.	Plate	Cream; multi-coloured print	Octagonal/165	95.00	135.00	50.00

EDWARD VIII CORONATION, 1937

Wade produced a small amount of commemorative pottery for the coronation of King Edward VIII. Some of the pottery was adapted from miniature jug designs already in production at the Wade Heath Pottery. A limited supply of these jugs was produced with a multi-coloured transfer print of Edward on the front and a design of flags and a scroll with the words "Long May He Reign" on the back. With the abdication of Edward, the jugs were withdrawn from sale and the transfers replaced with those of George VI and Queen Elizabeth.

The jugs are miniature and come with short- and long-loop handles and a handle of three rings. They have V-shaped moulded spouts and bright orange and blue bands around their bases and handles. The loving cup has a musical box in the base, held in place by a wooden disc, which plays "God Save the King" when lifted. The words "Long May He Reign" are printed on a gold band across the front and "Coronation King Edward VIII May 12th 1937" is on the back.

Jug, long-loop handle

Jug, short-loop handle

Loving Cup, musical

Backstamp: A. Black ink stamp "Wadeheath Ware England" and impressed "88M"
B. Black ink stamp "Wadeheath Ware England" and impressed "106M"
C. Black ink stamp "Wadeheath England" with a lion and impressed "113M"
D. Black ink stamp "Wadeheath Ware England"

No	Description	Colourways	Size	U.S.$	Can.$	U.K.£
1.	Jug, long-loop handle	Cream; orange/blue bands; multi-coloured print	140	95.00	125.00	55.00
2.	Jug, short-loop handle	Cream; orange/blue bands; multi-coloured print	140	95.00	125.00	55.00
3.	Jug, three-rings handle	Cream; orange/blue bands; multi-coloured print	135	95.00	125.00	55.00
4.	Loving Cup, musical	Cream; red/white/blue striped handles; red/blue/green print	125	550.00	625.00	300.00

KING GEORGE VI AND QUEEN ELIZABETH CORONATION, 1937

To commemorate the coronation on May 12, 1937, Wade issued several new items as well as reissuing the Edward VIII commemorative ware by replacing the original transfer prints of Edward with prints of George VI and Queen Elizabeth.

BOWLS

This was a limited edition of approximately 250 bowls. They were issued in all-over glazes of royal blue, orange and light green. A signed, limited edition of 25 bowls was issued in white with gold edging.

Backstamp: **A.** Black ink stamp "Manufactured in England by Wadeheath and Co Ltd to Commemorate the Coronation of King George VI and Queen ElizabethMay 12th 1937. 'Long May They Reign'" and the signature of Robert R. Barlow

B. Black ink stamp "Wadeheath England" and a lion

No.	Description	Colourways	Size	U.S.$	Can.$	U.K.£
1.	Bowl	White and gold	110	550.00	625.00	300.00
2.	Bowl	Mottled orange	110	375.00	475.00	200.00
3.	Bowl	Light green	110	375.00	475.00	200.00
4.	Bowl	Royal blue	110	375.00	475.00	200.00

CHILDREN'S WARE

The beaker and dish are the same shapes as those used for the silver jubilee of George V. Both have a multi-coloured transfer print of George VI and Queen Elizabeth, but on the dish it is set inside a Canadian maple leaf.

Photograph not available
at press time

Backstamp: Black ink stamp "Wadeheath Ware England"

No.	Description	Colourways	Size	U.S.$	Can.$	U.K.£
1.	Beaker	White; multi-coloured print	75	65.00	80.00	35.00
2.	Dish	White; multi-coloured print	165	65.00	80.00	35.00

CORONATION NURSERY WARE

This unusual child's tea set was from the same mould as the Wadeheath Walt Disney children's tea sets. The boxed set comprised 12 pieces—four cups, four saucers, a teapot and lid, a milk jug and a sugar bowl. Each piece, except for the teapot lid, has a multi-coloured portrait on it of King George VI and Queen Elizabeth, surrounded by flags. There is a portrait of Princess Elizabeth on the milk jug and sugar bowl. The original box is blue, with a label that reads "Coronation Nursery Ware," along with portraits of the King and Queen.

Backstamp: Black transfer "Wadeheath England"

No.	Description	Colourways	Size	U.S.$	Can.$	U.K.£
1.	Cup and Saucer	Cream; multi-coloured print	48	70.00	90.00	40.00
2.	Milk Jug	Cream; multi-coloured print	49	30.00	40.00	20.00
3.	Sugar Bowl	Cream; multi-coloured print	37	30.00	40.00	20.00
4.	Teapot	Cream; multi-coloured print	83	70.00	90.00	40.00

JUGS, LOVING CUP, AND PLATE

The same three shapes used for the Edward VIII coronation jugs and loving cup were reused here, with the transfer prints changed to show King George VI and Queen Elizabeth. On the back of the jugs is a portrait of Princess Elizabeth. The "Coronation Musical Loving Cup" plays "God Save the King" and has the words "Long May They Reign'" on a gold band across the front and the initials GR on the back. The square-cornered plate is the same shape used for the silver jubilee of George V, with a dark red and gold transfer print of the profiles of George VI and Queen Elizabeth set in a gold laurel wreath.

Jug, three-ring handle; Jug, long-loop handle

Coronation Plate

Backstamp: **A.** Black ink stamp "Wadeheath England" and a lion
B. Black ink stamp "Wadeheath Ware England" and an impressed "88M"
C. Black ink stamp "Wadeheath England," a lion and an impressed "106M"
D. Black ink stamp "Wadeheath Ware England" and an impressed "106M"
E. Black ink stamp "Wadeheath England," a lion and an impressed "113M"
F. Black ink stamp "Wadeheath Ware"
G. Black ink stamp "Wadeheath Ware England"

No.	Description	Colourways	Shape/Size	U.S.$	Can.$	U.K.£
1.	Jug, short-loop handle	Cream; orange/blue bands; multi-coloured print	140	80.00	95.00	40.00
2.	Jug, long-loop handle	Cream; orange/blue bands; multi-coloured print	140	80.00	95.00	40.00
3.	Jug, three-ring handle	Cream; orange/blue bands; multi-coloured print	135	80.00	95.00	40.00
4.	Loving Cup, musical	Cream; red/white/blue striped handles; multi-coloured print	125	450.00	525.00	250.00
5.	Milk Jug	Cream; orange spout, handle; multi-coloured print	108	80.00	110.00	40.00
6.	Plate	Cream; multi-coloured print	Octagonal/155	95.00	135.00	50.00

QUEEN ELIZABETH II CORONATION, 1953

Commemorative items with multi-coloured transfer prints were produced by Wade England and Wade Ireland to celebrate the coronation of Queen Elizabeth II on June 2, 1953.

BEAKERS, CUPS AND SAUCERS

Child's Beaker   Regency Cup

Backstamp: A. Large green ink stamp "Wade England"
B. Small green ink stamp "Wade England"
C. Multi-coloured transfer print "Coronation of Her Majesty Queen Elizabeth II Wade England"

No.	Description	Colourways	Size	U.S.$	Can.$	U.K.£
1.	Child's Beaker	White; gold rim, multi-coloured print	72	70.00	90.00	35.00
2.	Child's Tea Plate	White; gold rim, multi-coloured print	170	70.00	90.00	35.00
3.	Cup, Regency	White; gold rim; multi-coloured print	67	70.00	90.00	35.00
4.	Saucer, Regency	White; gold rim; multi-coloured print	140	See above		
5.	Cup, plain	White; gold rim; multi-coloured print	72	70.00	90.00	35.00
6.	Saucer, plain	White; gold rim; multi-coloured print	140	See above		

JUGS

The round milk jug is the same jug as that produced for the 1937 coronation of King George and Queen Elizabeth, except that the transfer print is of Queen Elizabeth II.

Photograph not available
at press time

Backstamp: Large green ink stamp "Wade England"

No.	Description	Colourways	Size	U.S.$	Can.$	U.K.£
1.	Milk Jug	White; gold rim; multi-coloured print	108	70.00	90.00	35.00

PLATES AND TANKARD

Tea Plate

Wall Plate

Beer Mug

Backstamp: A. Large green ink stamp "Wade England"
B. Green ink stamp "Wade England"

Orb Cup and Saucer

Regency Tea Plate "Queen Elizabeth II"

No.	Description	Colourways	Size	U.S.$	Can.$	U.K.£
1.	Regency Tea Plate "Royal Coat of Arms"	White; multi-coloured print	170	40.00	55.00	20.00
2.	Regency Tea Plate "Queen Elizabeth II"	White; multi-coloured print	170	40.00	55.00	24.00
3.	Wall Plate	Maroon; white centre; gold edges; multi-coloured print	235	90.00	110.00	48.00
4.	Beer Mug	White; gold/red/blue bands; multi-coloured print	Pint/125	70.00	90.00	35.00
5.	Cup/saucer Orb-shaped "Queen Elizabeth II"	White; multi-coloured print	71/142	40.00	55.00	24.00

DISHES AND BOWLS

The "Coronation Dish" was a scaled-down replica of the 1937 "Coronation Bowl."

The "Coronation Fruit Bowl" has a fluted body and a multi-coloured transfer print of the coat of arms of Queen Elizabeth in the centre. The first "Coronation Dessert Bowl" has gold emblems around the rim and the royal coat of arms in the centre; the second has a fluted body and a portrait of Queen Elizabeth in the centre.

Dish

Backstamp: **A.** Raised "Wade England Coronation 1953"
B. Green transfer print "Wade England"
C. Small green ink stamp "Wade England"
D. Embossed "Coronation 1953" with embossed Hand and Owl (c.1950-1953)

No.	Description	Colourways	Size	U.S.$	Can.$	U.K.£
1.	Dish	Dark green	120	28.00	35.00	12.50
2.	Dish	Turquoise	120	28.00	35.00	12.50
3.	Dish	Beige	120	28.00	35.00	12.50
4.	Dish	Dark blue	120	28.00	35.00	12.50
5.	Dish	Honey brown	120	28.00	35.00	12.50
6.	Dish	Light green	120	28.00	35.00	12.50
7.	Dish	Blue	120	30.00	40.00	15.00
8.	Dish	Green	120	30.00	40.00	15.00
9.	Dish	Grey	120	30.00	40.00	15.00
10.	Fruit Bowl, fluted	White; gold rim; multi-coloured print	190	60.00	80.00	30.00
11.	Dessert Bowl	White; gold band; multi-coloured print	165	45.00	55.00	20.00
12.	Dessert Bowl, fluted	White; gold band, emblems; multi-coloured print	165	45.00	55.00	20.00

ULSTER WARE GOBLETS AND TANKARDS

In early 1953 Wade (Ulster) Ltd. produced a very limited range of coronation ware goblets and tankards. The enamelled decoration was known as "Coronation" and the design of crossed bands and raised dots was known as "Ulster Ware." The goblets were hand turned, so there are slight variations in sizes. The print on the front of the goblets is of the royal crest. Although the Ulster Ware design were in production for over thirty years, the "Coronation" colours were never used again.

Goblet

Royal Ulster Coat of Arms Goblet

Tankard

Backstamp: Impressed "Wade (Ulster) Ltd Porcelain"

No.	Description	Colourways	Size	U.S.$	Can.$	U.K.£
1.	Goblet	Ivory; yellow print	120	80.00	110.00	40.00
2.	Goblet	Grey/blue/green; yellow print	120	80.00	110.00	40.00
3.	Goblet, plain	Green/brown	120	45.00	55.00	25.00
4.	Goblet with Royal Ulster Coat of Arms	Green/brown	120	55.00	75.00	35.00
5.	Tankard	Orange/lilac; multi-coloured arms	Pint/118	70.00	90.00	35.00
6.	Tankard	Grey/blue; multi-coloured crest	Pint/118	50.00	70.00	25.00
7.	Tankard	Orange/grey; multi-coloured arms	½ pint/98	70.00	90.00	35.00
8.	Tankard	Grey/blue; multi-coloured crest	½ pint/98	50.00	70.00	25.00

1953 ADVERTISING COMMEMORATIVES

BURROWS AND STURGESS DISH

Commissioned by Burrows and Sturgess, which produced Spa Table Waters, this dish has "Burrows and Sturgess Ltd" embossed on the top rim and "Spa Table Waters" on the lower rim. In the centre is an embossed design of a shield and laurel wreath, with the initials *ER*. Encircling the dish are embossed animals and the embossed emblems and names of some of the members of the British Empire—a lion (Great Britain), kangaroo (Australia), kiwi (New Zealand), beaver (Canada), sea lion (Newfoundland), elephant (India) and springbok (South Africa).

Photograph not available
at press time

Backstamp: Raised "Wade England Coronation 1953" in hollow of base

No.	Description	Colourways	Size	U.S.$	Can.$	U.K.£
1.	Dish	Dark green	120	30.00	40.00	22.00
2.	Dish	Turquoise	120	30.00	40.00	22.00
3.	Dish	Mint green	120	30.00	40.00	22.00
4.	Dish	Amber brown	120	30.00	40.00	22.00

REGINALD CORFIELD LTD.

The water jug is a large round-bodied jug, with a portrait of Queen Elizabeth and June 2nd 1953 on it. Produced in collaboration with Reginald Corfield Ltd., it was intended for use in public houses. (This is the same style jug as that used for Trumans Beer.)

Photograph not available
at press time

Backstamp: Black transfer print "Wade Regicor England"

No.	Description	Colourways	Size	U.S.$	Can.$	U.K.£
1.	Water Jug	White; multi-coloured print	115	60.00	80.00	30.00

SHELL MEX AND BRITISH PETROLEUM DISH

This dish is the same as that for Burrows and Sturgess, with the words "Shell Mex and British Petroleum" added to the upper rim and "North Eastern Division" on the lower rim.

Photograph not available
at press time

Backstamp: Raised "Wade England 1953"

No.	Description	Colourways	Size	U.S.$	Can.$	U.K.£
1.	Dish	Dark green	120	20.00	30.00	12.00
2.	Dish	Maroon	120	20.00	30.00	12.00

TRUMAN'S - C&S ALES - WATNEYS

The same Dutch shape 1953 Coronation Commemorative jug (No 1) as produced for Truman's Beer was also produced with C & S X-L Ales on the back, and also with a Watneys barrel on the back.

Truman's Beer Jug, Front

Truman's Beer Jug, Back

C & S X-L Ales Jug

Backstamp: A. Black transfer print "Wade Regicor England"
B. Printed "Wade Regicor London England," in laurel leaf frame, large size (1953-1962)

No.	Description	Colourways	Size	U.S.$	Can.$	U.K.£
1.	Jug	White; gold rim; multi-coloured print; blue lettering	108	70.00	90.00	35.00
2.	Jug C&S Ales	White; gold rim; multi-coloured print on front, green lettering "C&S X-L Ales" on back	108	65.00	90.00	35.00
3.	Jug Watneys Barrel	White; gold rim; multi-coloured print	108	65.00	90.00	35.00

ROYAL VISIT REDBOURN WORKS, JUNE 1958

This traditional tankard has a print of Buckingham Palace on the front and is inscribed on the back "Presented as a memento of the visit of H.M. Queen Elizabeth and H.R.H. Prince Philip to Redbourn Works 27th June 1958" "RTB" (I would be grateful to anyone who can tell me what and where the Redbourn Works are).

Tankard, Front

Tankard, Back

Backstamp: Red printed "Wade England"

No.	Description	Colourways	Size	U.S.$	Can.$	U.K. £
1.	Traditional Tankard	Cream; multi-coloured print; black lettering	½ pint/91	25.00	38.00	16.00

LORD BADEN POWELL, 1957

PLATE

A plate with a portrait of Lord Baden Powell in the centre was produced in 1957 to commemorate the 50th anniversary of the first Scout camp on Brownsea Island, near Poole, in Dorset, England.

Photograph not available
at press time

Backstamp: Black transfer "Wade England"

No.	Description	Colourways	Size	U.S.$	Can.$	U.K.£
1.	Plate	White; multi-coloured print	155	50.00	70.00	25.00

FOUNDERS' DAY BELFAST, 1960

BUTTER PAT

The commissioner of this Butter Pat, Irish Shape No I.P. 619 is unknown.

Backstamp: Embossed "Irish Porcelain Made in Ireland"

No.	Description	Colourways	Size	U.S.$	Can.$	U.K. £
1.	Butter Pat	Grey blue; black lettering	120	8.00	10.00	4.00

RACING CAR SHOW, 1961

JACK BRABHAM RACING CAR DISH AND TANKARD

Produced to commemorate the 1961 Racing Car Show, this dish is from the same mould as the "Veteran Car Tire Dishes," with details of the champion racing car on the base.

Photograph not available
at press time

Backstamp: Black transfer print "Racing Car Show 1961 Jack Brabham Cooper Climax 1960 World Champions, Wade England"

No.	Description	Colourways	Size	U.S.$	Can.$	U.K.£
1.	Dish	White; grey rim; green car print	125	35.00	30.00	10.00
2.	Tankard	Amber; green print	½ pint/90	25.00	30.00	10.00

STOKE CITY FOOTBALL CLUB, 1963

CENTENARY TANKARD, 1963

Wade Heath was asked to produce this rare "Centenary Tankard" by the Stoke City Football Club talent scout Harry Were. It is believed that only fifty tankards were produced for presentation to the team and Stoke city staff. The tankard has the crest of the Stoke City Football Club on the front and is inscribed "Stoke City Football Club Centenary 1963." The reverse has the history of the club. On the base of the tankard are sixteen signatures of the Stoke team. Four of the signatures are those of the star players of that era, Sir Stanley Matthews and Dennis Violet and of the team manager Tony Waddington and team secretary W. Williams.

Tankard, Front

Tankard, Back

Tankard. Bottom

Backstamp: Black handwritten signatures

No.	Description	Colourways	Size	U.S.$	Can.$	U.K. £
1.	Tankard	Amber; red/black crest; black lettering	95	400.00	530.00	200.00

BASS, 1977

200TH ANNIVERSARY JUG

200TH ANNIVERSARY JUG

In 1977 Wade PDM produced a traditional-style water jug to commemorate the 200th anniversary of the building of the first brewery in Burton-upon-Trent by William Bass & Company. The jug is decorated with a print of the beer label and golden yellow prints of barley and hops.

200th Anniversary Water Jug, Front

200th Anniversary Water Jug, Back

200th Anniversay Water Jug, Bottom

Backstamp: Black print "This jug was produced in 1977 to celebrate the two hundred years that have passed since William Bass first brewed in Burton-upon-Trent—Supplied by Wade (PDM) Limited, England"

No.	Description	Colourways	Size	U.S.$	Can.$	U.K.£
1.	Jug	White; multi-coloured prints	160	65.00	80.00	40.00

NEWCASTLE BROWN ALE GOLDEN JUBILEE, 1977

TANKARD

This traditional shaped tankard was produced for Scottish and Newcastle Breweries LTD. On the back in gold letters is printed "To celebrate the 50th anniversary of Newcastle Brown Ale 1927-1977."

Backstamp: Black printed "A Limited Edition. Golden Jubilee. Newcastle Brown Ale. The Newcastle Breweries LTD. No 3869 by George Wade & Son LTD., Burslem, England"

No.	Description	Colourways	Size	U.S.$	Can.$	U.K. .£
1.	Tankard	Pinky brown; gold thumb rest and rims; gold/red/black beer label	Pint/100	50.00	70.00	35.00

SILVER JUBILEE OF QUEEN ELIZABETH II, 1977

Only a very limited quantity of commemorative ware was produced by Wade for the silver jubilee of Queen Elizabeth II on June 2, 1977.

The unusual "Silver Jubilee Beer Stein" has a pewter lid, which is lifted by pressing down on a thumb lever on the top of the handle. The tankard has a transfer print of Queen Elizabeth and Prince Philip on the front and the words "1952-1977 The Queen's Silver Jubilee."

The "Silver Jubilee Dish" is from the same mould as the 1953 "Coronation Dish." The centre design has been changed to show a crown and a scroll, with the words "The Queen's Silver Jubilee," and the names of the countries above the animals have been omitted. The back of the rim is embossed with the words "Part of the proceeds from the sale of this souvenir will be donated to the Queen's Silver Jubilee Appeal." The original price was 90p.

The decanter, in the shape of the royal coach, has the words "Royal Jubilee" on the top and "25 year old Pure Malt Whisky" on the front. The cork is in the shape of a royal crown.

Backstamp: A. Red transfer print "Wade England"
B. Red transfer print "Wade Ireland"
C. Raised "Wade England"

No.	Description	Colourways	Size	U.S.$	Can.$	U.K.£
1.	Beer Stein	Dark grey; gold crest	227	90.00	130.00	45.00
2.	Dish	Honey brown	120	18.00	24.00	10.00
3.	Dish	Dark green	120	18.00	24.00	10.00
4.	Dish	Light green	120	18.00	24.00	10.00
5.	Dish	Dark blue	120	18.00	24.00	10.00
6.	Royal Coach Decanter	White; red cork; red/black/gold decoration	165	800.00	1,100.00	475.00
7.	Tankard	Amber; gold band; multi-coloured print	Pint/115	70.00	90.00	35.00
8.	Tankard	White; gold band; multi-coloured print	Pint/115	70.00	90.00	35.00

TAUNTON CIDER LOVING CUPS

A limited edition of 2,500 loving cups was produced by Wade for Taunton Cider for the 1977 Silver Jubilee. Unfortunately the first run of the cups had a mistake in the inscription. It read "Her Royal Highness Queen Elizabeth" instead of the correct title of "Her Majesty Queen Elizabeth II." The cups were immediately recalled and destroyed. Only one cup with the wrong title is known to exist. On the reverse side of the cups is a transfer print of a Taunton Dry Blackthorn Cider label.

Loving Cup, front

Loving Cup, back "Her Royal"

Loving Cup, back "Her Majesty"

No.	Description	Colourways	Size	U.S.$	Can.$	U.K.£
1.	Loving Cup	White; black lettering "Her Royal Highness Queen Elizabeth"	90		Rare	
2.	Loving Cup	White; black lettering "Her Majesty Queen Elizabeth II"	90	40.00	55.00	20.00

LESNEY TRAY QUEEN'S SILVER JUBILEE, 1977

ASHTRAY

Backstamp: Raised "S42/9"

No.	Description	Colourways	Size	U.S.$	Can.$	U.K. .£
1.	Ashtray Coat of Arms (Metal)	Silver; brown tray; black lettering "1953 The Silver Jubilee 1977"	Round/77 x 110	25.00	30.00	15.00

SUNDERLAND FOOTBALL CLUB

CENTENARY TANKARD, 1979

This jug was produced in a limited edition to commemorate the centenary of the Sunderland Football Club.

Backstamp: Green transfer print "Wade England"

No.	Description	Colourways	Size	U.S.$	Can.$	U.K. .£
1.	Tankard	White; purple lustre rim, handle; multi-coloured print	120	250.00	300.00	150.00

ROYAL WEDDING OF PRINCE CHARLES AND LADY DIANA, 1981

To commemorate the marriage of Prince Charles and Lady Diana Spencer on July 29, 1981, George Wade & Son Ltd. produced a quantity of commemorative ware.

Although the backstamp on the "Royal Wedding Candlesticks" only says "Wade," they were produced by Wade Ireland. They are decorated with transfer printed portraits of the couple within a floral garland.

For many years Wade Ceramics has collaborated with Arthur Bell & Sons Ltd. to produce decanters, in the shape of hand bells, to commemorate royal occasions. The first such decanter was created for the royal wedding. The multi-coloured print on this 75-centilitre decanter is of a portrait of Prince Charles and Lady Diana at the time of their engagement. A limited edition of 2,000 miniature "Royal Wedding Decanters" was made to present to the staffs of the George Wade Pottery and Bell's Whisky in commemoration of the event.

The "Royal Wedding Goblet" was produced by Wade Ireland, although the backstamp only says "Wade." It is white on the outside and glazed inside with gold.

The two-handled "Royal Wedding Loving Cup" is decorated on the front with a multi-coloured transfer print of Charles and Diana within two hearts, as well as the royal coat of arms. The miniature version has gold-leaf silhouettes of the heads of the couple facing each other. On the back is the inscription, "To Commemorate the Wedding of H.R.H. Prince Charles and Lady Diana Spencer at St Paul's Cathedral 29th of July 1981." The original price was £1.50.

The "Royal Wedding Napkin Ring" has gold-leaf silhouettes of the heads of the bride and groom facing each other. On the back of the ring is the inscription "To Commemorate the Wedding of H.R.H. Prince Charles and Lady Diana Spencer at St Pauls Cathedral 29th of July 1981." It was manufactured in alumina ceramic, a material usually associated with the electronics and space industries and well known for its durability. The original price for the napkin ring was £1.50.

On the front of the "Royal Wedding Tankard" there is a transfer print of the couple within two hearts, as well as the royal coat of arms. On the back is the Welsh dragon, Scottish thistle, Irish shamrock and English rose. It was produced by Wade Ireland but the backstamp reads" Wade England."

Only a small number of teapots were produced. They had a transfer print of the couple within two hearts and the royal coat of arms on the front.

GIFTWARE

Decanter   Goblet

Backstamp: **A.** Black transfer print "Wade"
B. Black transfer print "Wade—Commemorative Porcelain Decanter From Bell's Scotch Whisky Perth Scotland 75cl Product of Scotland 40% vol"
C. Black transfer print "Wade—Commemorative Porcelain Decanter From Bell's Scotch Whisky Perth Scotland Product of Scotland"
D. Black transfer print "Wade England"
E. Black transfer print "Wade Made in England"
F. Black transfer print "Genuine Wade Porcelain"
G. Red printed "Wade"

Candlestick

Tankard

No.	Description	Colourways	Shape/Size	U.S.$	Can.$	U.K.£
1.	Candlesticks (pair)	White; multi-coloured print	145	80.00	110.00	40.00
2.	Decanter	White; gold rim; multi-coloured print	250	150.00	200.00	100.00
3.	Decanter	White; gold rim; multi-coloured print	Miniature/105	110.00	150.00	80.00
4.	Goblet	White/gold; multi-coloured print	145	100.00	140.00	60.00
5.	Goblet	White/gold; multi-coloured print	114	150.00	200.00	85.00
6.	Goblet Prince of Wales	White outside; gold inside; red dragon; flowers	114	150.00	200.00	85.00
7.	Loving Cup	White; multi-coloured print	85	50.00	70.00	25.00
8.	Loving Cup	White; gold silhouettes	Miniature/50	30.00	35.00	15.00
9.	Napkin Ring	White; gold silhouettes	45	30.00	35.00	15.00
10.	Tankard	White; gold band; multi-coloured print	Pint/95	50.00	70.00	25.00
11.	Teapot	White; multi-coloured print	120	80.00	110.00	40.00

Derivative

Napkin Ring with Base and Lid

A napkin ring has been found positioned on a polished turned-wood stand with a polished wood lid. In this form it resembles a mustard pot, although the ring is not attached to the top or base.

Photograph not available
at press time

Backstamp: Black transfer print "Wade Made in England"

No.	Description	Colourways	Size	U.S.$	Can.$	U.K.£
1.	Napkin Ring	White ring; gold silhouettes; wood base, lid	43	35.00	50.00	15.00

DECORATIVE WARE

The ashtray is square, with a multi-coloured transfer print of Charles and Diana within two hearts and the royal coat of arms in the centre.

Although the "Royal Wedding Bell" was backstamped "Wade," it was produced by Wade Ireland. It is decorated with a gold band around the base and transfer-printed portraits of Charles and Diana within a floral wreath.

The "Royal Wedding Plaque" was produced by Wade Ireland, although the backstamp reads only "Wade." It is white with a transfer print of Prince Charles and Lady Diana Spencer inside a garland. There is a supporting foot on the back. The portrait plaque, produced by Wade Ireland, is from the same mould as one of the Greys Art standing plaques.

In the centre of the heart-shaped trinket box is a transfer print of Charles and Diana within two hearts and the royal coat of arms. The original price was £2.50.

One version of the "Royal Wedding Vase" has a red Welsh dragon over the royal portraits, which are in a yellow circular design. The other version was produced by Wade Ireland, even though the backstamp says "Wade." On the front it has a transfer print of the royal portraits within two hearts and the royal coat of arms.

The mould for the round long necked vase was previously used in 1961 for the Disney "Fantasia" series.

Photograph not available
at press time

Backstamp: **A.** Black transfer print "Wade"
                B. Black transfer print "Wade England"
                C. Raised "Wade Porcelain Made in England"

No.	Description	Colourways	Size	U.S.$	Can.$	U.K.£
1.	Ashtray	White; multi-coloured print	110	15.00	20.00	8.00
2.	Bell	White; multi-coloured print	145	50.00	70.00	25.00
3.	Plaque	White; multi-coloured print	100	50.00	70.00	25.00
4.	Portrait Plaque	White; multi-coloured print	98 x 98	45.00	60.00	30.00
5.	Trinket Box	White; multi-coloured print	40	30.00	35.00	15.00
6.	Heart shaped Trinket Box	White; multui-coloured print	42 x 80	55.00	70.00	30.00
7.	Vase	White; red dragon; multi-coloured print	220	150.00	180.00	50.00
8.	Vase	White; multi-coloured print	220	50.00	70.00	25.00

ROTARY CLUBS OF GREAT BRITAIN 75th ANNIVERSARY, 1980

TANKARD

This Irish Wade pint knurled tankard is unusual in that it is white instead of the normal Irish Wade blue grey colour. Produced to commemorate the 75th Anniversary of the Rotary Club of Great Britain. A list of Rotary Club "landmarks" dating from 1905-1980 is printed on the back.

Backstamp: Printed "No 302 of a Limited Edition of 3,000 by George Wade & Son Ltd Burslem England"

No.	Description	Colourways	Size	U.S.$	Can.$	U.K. £
1.	Tankard	White; black lettering	Pint/162	200.00	250.00	125.00

POPE JOHN PAUL II, 1982

DISH

This square dish was produced to commemorate the visit to England of His Holiness Pope John Paul II on May 28, 1982.

Backstamp: Brown transfer print "Wade England"

No.	Description	Colourways	Size	U.S.$	Can.$	U.K.£
1.	Dish	White; gold rim; multi-coloured print	135	20.00	28.00	8.00

COMPASITE ORDNANCE DEPOT, 1982

TANKARD

The Compasite Ordnance Depot (COD) in Donnington, Shropshire, England, is one of two locations where all British military equipment is stored. This pint-sized traditional tankard, with a rolled rim, was decorated with coats of arms and bears the inscription "To commemorate the Royal Visit of Her Majesty to COD Donnington on the 4th June 1982." The tankards were presented to the staff.

Photograph not available
at press time

Backstamp: Red transfer print "Royal Victoria Pottery Staffordshire Wade England"

No.	Description	Colourways	Size	U.S.$	Can.$	U.K.£
C-66	Tankard	White; multi-coloured prints	Pint/115	25.00	30.00	12.00

PRINCE WILLIAM, 1982

HAND-BELL DECANTER

This decanter was produced in partnership with Bell's Whisky to commemorate June 21, 1982, the birth of the first son of Prince Charles and Princess Diana. The 50-centilitre container is in the shape of a hand-bell and has a porcelain cap. It is decorated with a blue and gold transfer print of a crown, cherubs and ribbons.

| Hand-Bell Decanter, Front | Hand-Bell Decanter, Back |

Backstamp: Black transfer print "Wade—Commemorative Porcelain Decanter From Bells Scotch Whisky Perth Scotland50cl Product of Scotland 40% vol"

No.	Description	Colourways	Size	U.S.$	Can.$	U.K.£
1.	Decanter	White; gold bands; blue/gold print	205	100.00	145.00	55.00

75th ANNIVERSARY OF THE FIRST SCOUT CAMP, 1982

Wade produced a series of porcelain items to celebrate the 75th anniversary of the first Scout camp on Brownsea Island, near Poole, in Dorset, England. They have a portrait of Lord Baden Powell in the centre, encircled by "1907-1982 Celebrates the 75th Anniversary of the First—Camp—Brownsea Island."

Plate

Tankard

Backstamp: **A.** Black transfer print "Wade England"
B. Black transfer print "Produced by Wade Potteries Ltd"
C. Black transfer print "Produced for Commemorative House by Wade Potteries England"

No.	Description	Colourways	Size	U.S.$	Can.$	U.K.£
1.	Dish	White; multi-coloured print	140	30.00	35.00	15.00
2.	Loving Cup	Amber; black print	85	40.00	55.00	20.00
3.	Loving Cup	Amber; multi-coloured print	85	50.00	70.00	25.00
4.	Loving Cup	Amber; two-colour Scout flag print	85	40.00	55.00	20.00
5.	Plate	White; gold rim; multi-coloured print	195	40.00	55.00	20.00
6.	Tankard	Amber; multi-coloured print	Pint/115	50.00	70.00	25.00
7.	Tankard	Amber; black print	Pint/115	40.00	55.00	20.00
8.	Tankard	Amber; multi-coloured print	Pint/115	50.00	70.00	25.00

PRINCE HENRY, 1984

HAND-BELL DECANTER

Bell's Whisky issued this decanter to commemorate the birth of Prince Henry on September 15, 1984, the second son of Prince Charles and Princess Diana.

Backstamp: Black transfer print "Wade—Commemorative Porcelain Decanter From Bell's Scotch Whisky Perth Scotland—50cl Product of Scotland 40% vol"

No.	Description	Colourways	Size	U.S.$	Can.$	U.K.£
1.	Decanter	White; gold bands; red/gold print	200	100.00	145.00	55.00

QUEEN ELIZABETH'S 60th BIRTHDAY, 1986

This decanter was produced by Bell's Whisky to commemorate the 60th birthday of Queen Elizabeth on April 21, 1986.

HAND-BELL DECANTER

Backstamp: Black transfer print "Wade—Commemorative Porcelain Decanter from Bell's Scotch Whisky Perth Scotland—75cl product of Scotland 43% GL"

No.	Description	Colourways	Size	U.S.$	Can.$	U.K.£
1.	Decanter	White; gold bands; multi-coloured print	250	95.00	135.00	50.00

PRINCE ANDREW AND SARAH FERGUSON, 1986

WEDDING HAND-BELL DECANTER

This decanter, shaped like a hand-bell, was issued by Bell's Whisky to commemorate the royal wedding of Prince Andrew and Sarah Ferguson on July 23, 1986.

Backstamp: Black transfer print "Wade—Commemorative Porcelain Decanter from Bell's Scotch Whisky Perth Scotland—75cl product of Scotland 43% GL"

No.	Description	Colourways	Size	U.S.$	Can.$	U.K.£
1.	Decanter	White; gold bands; multi-coloured print	250	95.00	135.00	50.00

PRINCESS BEATRICE, 1988

CHURCH-BELL DECANTER

In 1988 Wade and Bell's Whisky produced this decanter to commemorate the birth of Princess Beatrice on August 8, 1988, the first child of Prince Andrew and the Duchess of York.

Backstamp: Black transfer print "Genuine Wade Porcelain—Commemorative Porcelain Decanter From Bells Scotch Whisky Perth Scotland—50cl Product of Scotland 40% vol"

No.	Description	Colourways	Size	U.S.$	Can.$	U.K.£
1.	Decanter	White; gold/red/blue bands; blue/gold/brown print	200	70.00	90.00	35.00

PRINCESS EUGENIE, 1990

CHURCH-BELL DECANTER

Wade and Bell's Whisky issued this decanter to commemorate the birth of Princess Eugenie on March 23, 1990, the second daughter of Prince Andrew and the Duchess of York.

Backstamp: Black transfer print "Genuine Wade Porcelain—Commemorative Porcelain Decanter From Bell's Scotch Whisky Perth Scotland—50cl Product of Scotland 40% vol"

No.	Description	Colourways	Size	U.S.$	Can.$	U.K.£
1.	Decanter	White; gold/red/blue bands; blue/gold/brown print	200	70.00	90.00	35.00

90th BIRTHDAY OF QUEEN ELIZABETH, THE QUEEN MOTHER, 1990

The "Church-Bell Decanter" was issued by Bell's Whisky to commemorate the Queen Mother's 90th birthday on August 4, 1990. Wade also produced 10,000 circular dishes and 10,000 circular trinket boxes for Ringtons Teas Ltd.

"Church-Bell Decanter"

Dish and Trinket Box

Backstamp: **A.** Black /red/blue transfer print "Genuine Wade Porcelain Commemorative Decanter from Arthur Bell and Son Perth Scotland—Product of Scotland 75cl—43% proof "
B. Red transfer print "Wade Ceramics "
C. Printed "Ringtons Ltd Tea Merchants Algernon Road Newcastle-On-Tyne Manufactured Exclusively for Ringtons by Wade Ceramics"

No.	Description	Colourways	Size	U.S.$	Can.$	U.K.£
1.	Decanter	White; gold/blue bands; multi-coloured print	200	90.00	130.00	45.00
2.	Dish	White; multi-coloured print	110	10.00	15.00	5.00
3.	Trinket Box	White; multi-coloured print	44 x 95	30.00	40.00	25.00

WORLD CUP FINAL ROME, 1990

WORLD CUP 1990 STEIN, MATTHEW BROWN, LION BREWERY, BLACKBURN, ENGLAND

On the front of this stein is printed "World Cup Final Rome 1990" together with a print of Concord and the Lion Brewery Lion logo. On the back is printed "This Commemorative tankard was awarded as a consolation prize in the 1990 Matthew Brown World Cup Competition."

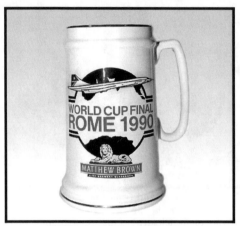

1990 World Cup Final Stein, Front

1990 World Cup Final Stein, Back

Backstamp: Printed circular "Wade P D M" (P D M separated 1984-1990)

No.	Description	Colourways	Size	U.S.$	Can.$	U.K. .£
1.	Stein	White; multi-coloured print	183	70.00	90.00	35.00

MANCHESTER UNITED FOOTBALL CLUB, 1991

EUROPEAN CUP WINNERS CUP, 1991

This beautiful loving cup has the Manchester United Football Team Crest on the front and the winning team members on the back.

European Cup Winners Cup, Front

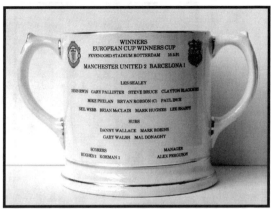

European Cup Winners Cup, Back

Backstamp: Unknown

No.	Description	Colourways	Size	U.S.$	Can.$	U.K. £
1.	European Cup	White; red/gold crests; black lettering "Winners Cup, 1991"	Pint/120	145.00	200.00	95.00

CHEDDAR PARISH COUNCIL, 1995

CHEDDAR PARISH COUNCIL CENTENARY CELEBRATIONS

The limited edition of 1,500 loving cups have the Cheddar coat of arms on the front and "The Market Cross" on the back. They were produced to celebrate Cheddar Parish Council's Centenary. Each Loving Cup came with a numbered and signed certificate.

Cheddar Parish Council Loving Cup, Front

Cheddar Parish Council Loving Cup, Back

Backstamp: Red printed "Wade England" with two lines "No 1255" (each cup was individually numbered).

No.	Description	Colourways	Size	U.S.$	Can.$	U.K. £
1.	Loving Cup	White; black prints/lettering	85	60.00	80.00	40.00

RUGBY WORLD CUP, 1995

RUGBY DECANTER GILBERT MAKER, RUGBY, ENGLAND

A limited edition (1,995) of these decanters were commissioned by Gilbert Maker of Rugby England to commemorate the 1995 Rugby World Cup. The decanter is a replica of the official match ball used for the game.

Rugby World Cup Decanter, Front

Rugby World Cup Decanter, Back

Backstamp: Printed "Genuine Wade Porcelain"

No.	Description	Colourways	Size	U.S.$	Can.$	U.K. .£
1.	Rugby Ball Decanter	White; blue bands; black print/lettering	Unknown	100.00	130.00	65.00

GOLDEN WEDDING ANNIVERSARY OF THE QUEEN AND PRINCE PHILIP, 1997

DECANTER

Bell's produced a 75cl Commemorative "Church-Bell Decanter" to celebrate the Golden Wedding Anniversary of Her Majesty Queen Elizabeth II and Prince Philip.

Backstamp: Gold printed "Extra Special Old Scotch Whiskey Arthur Bell & Sons" "Purple Genuine Wade Porcelain"

No.	Description	Colourways	Size	U.S.$	Can.$	U.K. .£
1.	Decanter	White; gold top, bands & decoration; blue collar; multi-coloured print; red/gold lettering	200	90.00	130.00	45.00

COMMISSIONED PRODUCTS
1940 to the present

ADDIS LTD.

SHAVING MUGS, c.1965-c.1980

These shaving mugs were produced intermittently for Addis Ltd. of England in white and beige. These mugs have four drainage holes as opposed to the Culmak shaving mugs which have only one drainage hole.

Steam Coach by Gurney, 1827 (3)

Bi-Plane, R.A.F. (13)

Backstamp: A. Red transfer print "Wade England"
B. Green transfer print "Wade England"
C. Brown transfer print "Wade England"

No.	Description	Colourways	Size	U.S.$	Can.$	U.K.£
1.	La Mancelle by Bollee, 1878	White; multi -coloured print	90	25.00	30.00	12.00
2.	Steam Car	White; multi-coloured print	90	25.00	35.00	12.00
3.	Steam Coach by Gurney, 1827	White; multi-coloured print	90	25.00	30.00	12.00
4.	Steam Engine	White; multi-coloured print	90	25.00	30.00	12.00
5.	Steam Roller by Aveling, 1893	White; multi-coloured print	90	25.00	30.00	12.00
6.	Rotary Cultivator by Rickett, 1858	White; multi-coloured print	90	25.00	30.00	12.00
7.	Her Majesty by Burrell, 1897	White; multi-coloured print	90	25.00	30.00	12.00
8.	Steam Omnibus by Thornycroft, 1902	White; multi-coloured print	90	25.00	30.00	12.00
9.	Vintage Ford Car	Beige; brown print	90	15.00	20.00	8.00
10.	Convertible Car, 1920	Beige; brown print	90	15.00	20.00	8.00
11.	Bentley Car	Beige; brown print	90	15.00	20.00	8.00
12.	Spitfire Plane, RAF	Beige; brown print	90	15.00	20.00	8.00
13.	Bi-Plane, RAF	Beige; brown print	90	15.00	20.00	8.00

BARNEY LEWIS

VETERAN CAR HUMIDOR / PIPE HOLDER, c.1960S

This large one litre capacity humidor/pipe holder tobacco pot was commissioned by Barney Lewis (no other details known) and exported to the United States in the early 1960s. It is an adaptation of the Veteran Car Traditional tankard with the addition of two rings on one side in which pipe stems could be inserted. It has a decorative domed lid, the rim of which has a cork band to make the lid airtight. On the front of the humidor is a black Veteran Car transfer print with the Veteran Car series No and other information printed on the back.

Veteran Car Tobacco Pot/Humidor

Backstamp: None

No.	Description	Colourways	Shape/size	U.S.$	Can.$	U.K.£
1.	Humidor Ford Model T, 1912	Amber; silver rim & bands; black print & lettering	200	45.00	60.00	30.00
2.	Humidor Oldsmobile, 1904	Amber; silver rim & bands; black print & lettering	200	45.00	60.00	30.00

BOOTS THE CHEMIST

BATHROOM UTENSILS, 1988 -1995

Wade produced many items for British department stores that have houseware departments, and have for a number of years produced gift and housewares exclusively for Boots The Chemist.

Shaving Mug, Bathtub Soap Dish, Toothbrush Holder

Wash Basin and Jug

Backstamp: "Boots The Chemists"

No.	Description	Colourways	Shape/size	U.S.$	Can.$	U.K.£
1.	Shaving Mug	White: blue label	75/190	25.00	30.00	15.00
2.	Bathtub Soap Dish	White	65/155	25.00	30.00	15.00
3.	Toothbrush Holder	White; blue	85	15.00	20.00	10.00
4.	Wash Basin	White	265	25.00	30.00	15.00
5.	Jug	White; blue	205	25.00	30.00	15.00
6.	Wash Basin/Jug (Pair)			50.00	60.00	30.00

BOOKENDS, 1988 -1989

Bookends

Backstamp: Unmarked

No.	Description	Colourways	Size	U.S.$	Can.$	U.K.£
1.	Bookend - Bear Reading	White; black eyes; brown nose; blue jumper	150	30.00	35.00	18.00
2.	Bookend - Bear Waving	White; black eyes; brown nose; blue dungarees	150	30.00	35.00	18.00
	Bookends (Pair)			55.00	60.00	30.00

BOWLS, 1995

Pet Treat Bowls

Backstamp: Red transfer printed "Wade England" between two lines

No.	Description	Colourways	Shape/size	U.S.$	Can.$	U.K.£
1.	Fish Face Dish	White; blue lettering red/white paw print; white lettering	120	15.00	20.00	8.00
2.	H R H Dish	White; blue lettering red/white paw print; white lettering	120	15.00	20.00	8.00

MONEY BOX, 1995

The delivery van money box has an embossed "Boots" on the side and a "Boots 1" number plate. Original price £10.00.

Delivery Van Money Box

Backstamp: None

No.	Description	Colourways	Shape/size	U.S.$	Can.$	U.K.£
1.	Delivery Van	Cobalt Blue	135/210	55.00	75.00	45.00

TEA CADDY AND UTENSIL POT, 1988 - 1995

Tea Caddy

Utensil Pot

Backstamp: None

No.	Description	Colourways	Shape/size	U.S.$	Can.$	U.K.£
1.	Tea Caddy	Honey; black print	153	25.00	30.00	15.00
2.	Utensil Pot	White; black eyes; brown nose; blue jumper	133	40.00	45.00	20.00

BOULDRAY BRASS AND METAL FOUNDRIES

CANDLE HOLDERS, 1963-1965

As with the Bouldray trays, the candle holders, which were formerly used as Wade's 19591960 *First Whimsies Zoo Lights,* had a hole drilled in the base and a miniature metal model was attached with a screw through the bottom. The models are brass, black metal and black metal with some brass. Wade supplied the base only; the metal figure was supplied and attached by Bouldray Brass.

Black Cat (1)

Duck (7)

Backstamp: Raised "Wade Porcelain made in England"

No.	Description	Colourways	Size	U.S.$	Can.$	U.K.£
1.	Black Cat	Black metal/brass cat; yellow holder	50	18.00	24.00	12.00
2.	Cockerel	Black metal/brass cockerel; blue holder	45	18.00	24.00	12.00
3.	Cockerel	Black metal/brass cockerel; pink holder	45	18.00	24.00	12.00
4.	Cockerel	Black metal/brass cockerel; yellow holder	45	18.00	24.00	12.00
5.	Cockerel	Brass cockerel; blue holder	45	18.00	24.00	12.00
6.	Cornish Pixie	Brass pixie; blue holder	50	18.00	24.00	12.00
7.	Duck	Black metal/brass duck; blue holder	45	18.00	24.00	12.00
8.	Duck	Brass duck; blue holder	45	18.00	24.00	12.00
9.	Rearing Horse	Black metal/brass horse; yellow holder	45	18.00	24.00	12.00
10.	Rearing Horse	Brass horse; yellow holder	45	18.00	24.00	12.00

TRAYS, 1958-1965

Bouldray trays were adapted from the base of Wade *Whimtrays*, with the backstamp changed to Bouldray. Models made of brass, black metal or a combination of black metal and brass, produced by Bouldray Brass, were attached to the trays with a screw through a hole in the base of the tray.

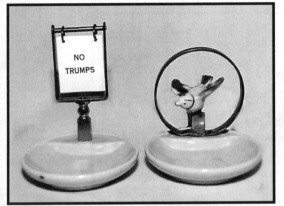

Card Trumps (2), Swallow Ring (15)

Cockerel (4), Stag (14)

Welsh Lady

Backstamp: Raised "Bouldray Wade Porcelain 2 Made in England"

No.	Description	Colourways	Size	U.S.$	Can.$	U.K.£
1.	Alsatian	Brass dog; blue tray	75	18.00	24.00	12.00
2.	Card Trumps	Brass frame; white plastic cards; yellow tray	90	18.00	24.00	12.00
3.	Black Metal Horse	Black horse; yellow tray	65	18.00	24.00	12.00
4.	Cockerel	Black metal/brass cockerel; yellow tray	75	18.00	20.00	12.00
5.	Cockerel	Brass cockerel; yellow tray	75	18.00	24.00	12.00
6.	Cockerel	Brass cockerel; black tray	75	18.00	24.00	12.00
7.	Cornish Pixie on Mushroom	Brass pixie/mushroom; pink tray	60	18.00	24.00	12.00
8.	Crinoline Lady/Rose Bush	Brass figure; black tray	70	18.00	24.00	12.00
9.	Crinoline Lady/Rose Bush	Brass figure; blue tray	70	18.00	24.00	12.00
10.	Crinoline Lady/Rose Bush	Brass figure; pink tray	70	18.00	24.00	12.00
11.	Duck	Black metal duck; blue tray	55	18.00	24.00	12.00
12.	Duck	Brass metal duck; black tray	55	18.00	24.00	12.00
13.	Jenny Lind	Brass figure; yellow tray	75	18.00	24.00	12.00
14.	Stag	Brass stag; yellow tray	75	18.00	24.00	12.00
15.	Swallow Ring	Brass ring; blue/white swallow (from Swallow Posy Bowl); yellow tray	72	18.00	24.00	12.00
16.	Welsh Lady	Brass lady; black tray	75	18.00	24.00	12.00
17.	Welsh Lady	Brass lady; pink tray	75	18.00	24.00	12.00

BOURNE OF HARLESDON

NURSERY AND OTHER DOOR SIGNS, c.1965

These door plaques, which were produced by Wade for Bourne of Harlesdon, London, were sold by Bourne under its own name.

Backstamp: Raised "Bourne of Harlesdon"
Embossed "Bourne of Harlesdon"

No.	Description	Colourways	Size	U.S.$	Can.$	U.K.£
1.	Bedroom	White; multi-coloured print	105 x 57	50.00	70.00	25.00
2.	Boy's Room	White; multi-coloured print	105 x 57	50.00	55.00	25.00
3.	Girl's Room	White; multi-coloured print	105 x 57	50.00	70.00	25.00
4.	Kitchen	White; multi-coloured print	105 x 57	50.00	70.00	25.00
5.	Kitchen	White; multi-coloured print	57 x 105	50.00	55.00	25.00
6.	Lounge	White; multi-coloured print	105 x 57	50.00	70.00	25.00
7.	Nursery	White; multi-coloured print	105 x 57	50.00	70.00	25.00
8.	Linen Cupboard	White; multi-coloured print	105 x 57	50.00	70.00	25.00

CAMPBELL MOTOR EXPORTS LTD.
AUCKLAND, NEW ZEALAND

TIRE DISHES, 1966

Wade produced two tire dishes for the Campbell Motor Group of Auckland, New Zealand. The dishes depict the Peugeot and Rambler cars sold by Campbell Motors and were given as gifts to the purchasers of those cars. Only 500 of each dish were produced. Campbell Motors was sold to the Challenge Corporation in 1975 and ceased business in the early 1980s.

Rambler, 1902

Backstamp: A. Black transfer print "1902 Rambler, Model D. In the first year 1,500 were sold, establishing Rambler as the worlds second massed produced automobile. N.Z. Rambler Distributors, Campbell Motor Exports Ltd Auckland"
B. Unknown

No.	Description	Colourways	Size	U.S.$	Can.$	U.K.£
1.	Peugeot	White; grey rim; black print	125	20.00	30.00	10.00
2.	Rambler, 1902	White; grey rim; black print	125	20.00	30.00	10.00

COLIBRI

CIGARETTE LIGHTERS, c.1965

The Colibri cigarette lighter is mounted inside a Wade Ireland Celtic porcelain pot with an embossed design of Beard Pullers; the design was copied from illustrations made by medieval monks in "The Book of Kells." The design is said to represent the Merchants cast out of the temple by Jesus. The second cigarette ligher has a rounded Raindrop design, which was used on tea and coffee sets. (See *Charlton Standard Catalogue of Wade Volume Three, Tablewares*).

Beard Puller Cigarette Lighter

Raindrop Cigarette Lighter

Backstamp: Embossed "Colibri Irish Porcelain Made in U.K."

No.	Description	Colourways	Shape/Size	U.S.$	Can.$	U.K.£
1.	Beard Puller	Brownish red	To top of lighter/85	50.00	70.00	35.00
2.	Raindrop	Greenish grey/silver	To top of lighter/70	25.00	30.00	15.00

CULMAK LTD.

BARBERS SHOP SHAVING MUG, c.1965

The "Barbers Shop Shaving Mug," with a rolled rim on the top and on the base, is the same style originally used by Victorian barbers.

Backstamp: A. Red transfer prin "Wade England"
B. Printed "Wade England"
C. Black printed "Wade Made in England"

No.	Description	Colourways	Size	U.S.$	Can.$	U.K.£
1.	Shaving Mug	Beige; gold rim; brown print	88	25.00	30.00	12.00
2.	Shaving Mug Duck and duckling	White; gold bands; multi-coloured print	80	25.00	30.00	15.00

SHAVING MUGS, c.1980

These shaving mugs have only one drainage hole in the soap bowl.

Ford

Wolseley

Backstamp: **A.** Black transfer print "Wade Made in England"
B. Green transfer print "Wade England"
C. Red transfer print "Wade England"

Automobiles

No.	Description	Colourways	Size	U.S.$	Can.$	U.K.£
1.	Ford	White; multi-coloured print	80	25.00	30.00	12.00
2.	Rolls-Royce, 1909	White; multi-coloured print	80	25.00	30.00	12.00
3.	Wolseley	White; multi-coloured print	80	25.00	30.00	12.00

Express Trains

No.	Description	Colourways	Size	U.S.$	Can.$	U.K.£
1.	Blue Express Train Signed "David Bown"	White; multi-coloured print	80	25.00	30.00	15.00
2.	Red Express Train Signed "David Bown"	White; multi-coloured print	80	25.00	30.00	15.00

Nelson

No.	Description	Colourways	Size	U.S.$	Can.$	U.K.£
1.	H.M.S Victory	White; black print	80	20.00	30.00	10.00
2.	Nelson	White; black print	80	20.00	30.00	10.00
3.	Nelson's Column	White; black print	80	20.00	30.00	10.00

Steam Engine Trains

Black Steam Train   Steam Engine Train

No.	Description	Colourways	Size	U.S.$	Can.$	U.K.£
1.	Black Steam Train Signed "David Bown"	White; multi-coloured print	80	25.00	30.00	15.00
2.	Steam Engine Train	White; green/black print	80	25.00	30.00	12.00

DEBENHAMS

REX THE RETRIEVER, 1993

This model was commissioned by Debenhams to commemorate the installation of its new computerized retrieval system, which was christened "Rex" by the installers of the system. Only 250 models were produced.

Backstamp: Raised "Wade England"

No.	Description	Colourways	Size	U.S.$	Can.$	U.K.£
1.	Retriever	Fawn	153	290.00	400.00	200.00

DOUGLAS MACMILLAN HOSPICE

DOUGIE MAC TEDDY BEAR MONEY BOX, 1998

A seated model of a teddy bear was chosen by the Douglas MacMillan Hospice as a fund raiser for their Silver Jubilee. The proceeds from the sale of the money box would be used towards the proposed opening of a daycare centre. Order forms for the money box were included in the May and August issues of the Official Wade Collectors Club Magazine and had to be received by the Hospice before September 30th, 1998. The number of orders determined the number of models to be made. The sale of the money boxes was to commence in October 1998. Original cost was £22.50

Photograph not available
at press time

Backstamp: Unknown

No.	Description	Colourways	Shape/size	U.S.$	Can.$	U.K.£
1.	Money box	Brown; black eyes and nose; gold bow; dark brown paw pads	155	35.00	50.00	22.50

DUNBAR CAKE DECORATORS, SCOTLAND

WEDDING CAKE TOPPER, 1992

This model was produced in all white; however, the staff of Dunbar Cakes decorated some with lace and other materials. Less than three thousand of these figures have been made.

Backstamp: Black print "Wade England"

No.	Description	Colourways	Size	U.S.$	Can.$	U.K.£
1.	Bride and Groom	White	100	70.00	90.00	40.00

GARDNER MERCHANT CATERING SERVICES

TRINKET BOX, 1986

The trinket box was commissioned by the British firm of Gardner Merchant Catering Services to commemorate 100 years in business. It was presented to Gardner's employees.

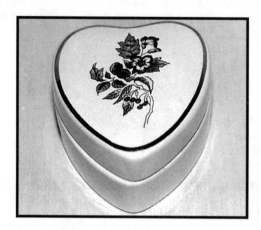

Backstamp: Purple transfer print "Royal Victoria Pottery Wade Staffordshire England," with "Gardner Merchant a century of catering service, 1886-1986" in gold letters

No.	Description	Colourways	Size	U.S.$	Can.$	U.K.£
1.	Trinket Box	White/gold band; purple/green flower, berries	42 x 80	28.00	32.00	16.00

GLAXO LABORATORIES

LIDDED DERMOVATE OINTMENT JAR, LATE 1970s

Glaxo Laboratories of Slough, Berkshire, commissioned these lidded ointment jars in the late 1970s. They were give-aways to general practitioners.

Photograph not available
at press time

Backstamp: Printed "Wade Ireland"

No.	Description	Colourways	Shape/size	U.S.$	Can.$	U.K.£
1.	Dermovate glaxo jar	White; blue print and lettering	177	40.00	25.00	20.00

GRAY FINE ARTS

PLAQUES, c.1988c.1990

Irish Artists Plaques

Wade Ireland produced a large assortment of Picture Plaques for Gray Fine Arts of Belfast, Northern Ireland. The porcelain plaques all have photographs of paintings by famous Irish Artists J. C. Gray and E. McEwen on the front. Produced in four shapes, circular, oval, rectangular and square, with a choice of Banded or Irish Knot rims. The plaques were produced with an applied ring for hanging, a foot on the back for standing, a slotted stand to stand the plaque in and as a circular pintray (Shape No. IP619). These plaques are more often found with no labels.

Oxylis

Primrose

Backstamp: **A.** Yellow paper label "One in a series of Paintings By Irish Artist James Gray All Copyrights Reserved Manufactured by Gray Fine Arts.Belfast.Ireland"
    B. Gold paper label "One of a series of paintings by Irish artist James C. Gray All Copyrights Reserved Manufactured by Gray Fine Arts Belfast. Ireland" with "Gray Fine Art Belfast" logo
    C. Paper insert in box with painting title & story of painting
    D. Embossed "Made in Ireland Irish Porcelain Wade eire tire a dheante IP619" with shamrock and crown in the center (on pintray only)

CIRCULAR

No.	Description	Colourways	Shape/Size	U.S.$	Can.$	U.K.£
1.	Blaze (Horse Head)	Grey green plaque; multi-coloured print	72	18.00	25.00	12.00
2.	Oxylis (Flowers)	Grey green plaque; multi-coloured print	72	18.00	25.00	12.00
3.	Primrose (Flowers)	Grey green plaque; multi-coloured print	72	18.00	25.00	12.00

Christmas Rose

Sunrise

Winter Morning

OVAL

No.	Description	Colourways	Shape/Size	U.S.$	Can.$	U.K.£
1.	Camellia (Flowers)	Grey green plaque; multi-coloured print	105 x 85	35.00	45.00	25.00
2.	Christmas Rose (Flowers)	Grey green plaque; multi-coloured print	105 x 85	35.00	45.00	25.00
3.	Nice Morning (Blacksmith)	Grey green plaque; multi-coloured print	105 x 85	45.00	55.00	35.00
4.	Primrose (flowers)	Blue-grey; yellow flowers	Oval/105	30.00	35.00	15.00
5.	Primula (flowers)	Blue-grey; yellow flowers	Oval/105	30.00	35.00	15.00
6.	Red Clover (flowers)	Blue-grey; pink flowers	Oval/105	30.00	35.00	15.00
7.	Rose (flowers)	Blue-grey; white flowers	Oval/105	30.00	35.00	15.00
8.	Sunrise (Ducks Flying)	Grey green plaque; multi-coloured print	105 x 85	45.00	55.00	35.00
9.	Title unknown (Springer Spaniel & Pheasant in field)	Grey green plaque; multi-coloured print	105 x 85	45.00	55.00	35.00
10.	Winter Morning (Springer Spaniel and Pheasant)	Grey green plaque; multi-coloured print	105 x 85	45.00	55.00	35.00

Red Clover

Thoughts and Surprise

RECTANGULAR

No.	Description	Colourways	Shape/Size	U.S.$	Can.$	U.K.£
1.	Autumn Morning (Tree & Fallen Leaves)	Grey green plaque; multi-coloured print	110 x 90	45.00	55.00	35.00
2.	Camellia (Flowers)	Grey green plaque; multi-coloured print	110 x 90	35.00	45.00	25.00
3.	Christmas Rose (Flowers)	Grey green plaque; multi-coloured print	110 x 90	35.00	45.00	25.00
4.	Lipizzaner Mare (White Horse)	Grey green plaque; multi-coloured print	110 x 90	45.00	55.00	35.00
5.	Mandarin (Ducks)	Grey green plaque; multi-coloured print	110 x 90	45.00	55.00	35.00
6.	Mare & Foal (Mare & Foal walking)	Grey green plaque; multi-coloured print	110 x 90	45.00	55.00	35.00
7.	Nice Morning (Blacksmith)	Grey green plaque; multi-coloured print	110 x 90	45.00	55.00	35.00
8.	Oxylis (Flowers)	Grey green plaque; multi-coloured print	110 x 90	45.00	55.00	35.00
9.	Red Clover (flowers)	Blue-grey; pink flowers	110 x 90	30.00	35.00	15.00
10.	Spring Morning (Springer Spaniel & Pigeon)	Grey green plaque; multi-coloured print	110 x 90	45.00	55.00	35.00
11.	Springer & Woodchuck (Springer Spaniel & Woodchuck)	Grey green plaque; multi-coloured print	110 x 90	45.00	55.00	35.00
12.	Surprise (Irish Setter and Pheasant)	Grey green plaque; multi-coloured print	110 x 90	45.00	55.00	35.00
13.	The Cobbler (Old Man)	Grey green plaque; multi-coloured print	110 x 90	45.00	55.00	35.00
14.	The Farrier (Blacksmith)	Grey green plaque; multi-coloured print	110 x 90	45.00	55.00	35.00
15.	Thoughts (Lady looking out of window)	Grey green plaque; multi-coloured print	110 x 90	45.00	55.00	35.00
16.	Up & Away (Pheasant Flying)	Grey green plaque; multi-coloured print	110 x 90	35.00	45.00	20.00
17.	Winter Morning (Springer Spaniel & Woodchuck)	Grey green plaque; multi-coloured print	110 x 90	45.00	55.00	35.00
18.	Title Unknown (Couple in cart)	Grey green plaque; multi-coloured print	110 x 90	45.00	55.00	35.00
19.	Title Unknown (Couple sitting in field)	Grey green plaque; multi-coloured print	110 x 90	45.00	55.00	35.00
20.	Title Unknown (Huntsman & Hounds)	Grey green plaque; multi-coloured print	110 x 90	45.00	55.00	35.00
21.	Title Unknown (Plough horse & dog in stable)	Grey green plaque; multi-coloured print	110 x 90	45.00	55.00	35.00
22.	Title Unknown (Reaper)	Grey green plaque; multi-coloured print	110 x 90	45.00	55.00	35.00

SQUARE LARGE

Away — Suprise — Spring Morning

No.	Description	Colourways	Shape/size	U.S.$	Can.$	U.K.£
1.	Away	Grey green plaque; multi-coloured print	98 x 98	45.00	55.00	35.00
2.	Blaze (Horse Head)	Grey green plaque; multi-coloured print	98 x 98	45.00	55.00	35.00
3.	Dog Rose (Flowers)	Grey green plaque; multi-coloured print	98 x 98	45.00	55.00	35.00
4.	In The Open (Golden Retriever & Pheasant)	Grey green plaque; multi-coloured print	98 x 98	45.00	55.00	35.00
5.	Mare & Foal	Grey green plaque; multi-coloured print	98 x 98	45.00	55.00	35.00
6.	Nice Morning (Blacksmith)	Grey green plaque; multi-coloured print	98 x 98	45.00	55.00	35.00
7.	Primrose (Flowers)	Grey green plaque; multi-coloured print	98 x 98	35.00	45.00	20.00
8.	Rock Rose (flowers)	Blue-grey; yellow flower	98 x 98	30.00	35.00	15.00
8.	Spring Morning (Springer Spaniel & Pigeon)	Grey green plaque; multi-coloured print	98 x 98	45.00	55.00	35.00
9.	Springer & Woodchuck	Grey green plaque; multi-coloured print	98 x 98	45.00	55.00	35.00
10.	Stepping Out (Horse)	Grey green plaque; multi-coloured print	98 x 98	45.00	55.00	35.00
11.	Sunrise (Ducks Flying)	Grey green plaque; multi-coloured print	98 x 98	45.00	55.00	35.00
12.	Sunset (Tree & Mountains)	Grey green plaque; multi-coloured print	98 x 98	35.00	45.00	20.00
13.	Surprise (Irish Setter & Pheasant)	Grey green plaque; multi-coloured print	98 x 98	45.00	55.00	35.00
14.	Title Unknown (Giants Causeway Portrush Bush Valley railway)	Grey green plaque; multi-coloured print	98 x 98	35.00	45.00	20.00

Blaze

Oxylis

Primrose

SQUARE SMALL

No.	Description	Colourways	Shape/Size	U.S.$	Can.$	U.K.£
1.	Blaze (Horse Head)	Grey green plaque; multi-coloured print	66 x 66	18.00	25.00	12.00
2.	Oxylis (Flowers)	Grey green plaque; multi-coloured print	66 x 66	18.00	25.00	12.00
3.	Primrose (Flowers)	Grey green plaque; multi-coloured print	66 x 66	18.00	25.00	12.00

THE GREAT PRIORY OF ENGLAND AND WALES

KNIGHT TEMPLAR, 1991
Variation One

The "Knight Templar" was commissioned in 1991 by the Great Priory Of England and Wales to commemorate its bicentenary.

Backstamp: Transfer print "Made Exclusively for The Great Priory of England and Wales and its Provinces by Wade Ceramics to Commemorate 1791—The Bicentenary 1991"

No.	Description	Colourways	Size	U.S.$	Can.$	U.K.£
1.	Knight Templar	Silver shield; red hat; white cross; black/brown sword, belt	240	360.00	480.00	245.00

THE INTERNATIONAL FEDERATION OF ESPERANTUS RAILWAYMEN

BROOCH, 1963

Produced for the 1963 Congress of the International Federation of Esperantus Railwaymen, this urn-shaped brooch is decorated with a lariat wreath, open wings and the inscription "Esperanto XV a Kongreso De I.F.E.F. Stoke on Trent Majo 1963." Only one brooch is known.

Photograph not available
at press time

Backstamp: Black transfer "Wade England"

No.	Description	Colourways	Size	U.S.$	Can.$	U.K.£
1.	Brooch	White/green	40		Rare	

KEITH AND HENDERSON

ASHTRAYS, 1969-1984

Photograph not available
at press time

Backstamp: "Wade pdm England"

No.	Description	Colourways	Shape/Size	U.S.$	Can.$	U.K.£
1.	Ashtray	Brown; gold lettering "Keith & Henderson Cloth for a Connoisseur"	Rectangular/205	15.00	20.00	8.00
2.	Ashtray	Brown; white lettering "Keith & Henderson Cloth for a Connoisseur"	Square/140	15.00	20.00	8.00

LESNEY PRODUCTS AND CO. LTD.

GIFT TRAYS, 1961-c.1975

Only the trays of these models were produced by Wade. The metal and/or plastic models were mounted on the backs of the trays by Lesney Products and Co. Ltd., a British company famous for its Matchbox miniature car models. A large variety of Lesney products are found on the trays, but most have a Matchbox car, bus or train on the back rim.

Titled "Gifts By Lesney, Ceramic Tray" on the packaging, the trays are found in six different shapes— kidney, oval, round, square, semi-oval and triangular shapes— and in four colours. Some trays have been found with a silver label on the front edge that names the model.

The kidney- and oval-shaped trays were previously used by Wade in 1957 and 1958 as the "Doggie Dish" (kidney shape) and the "Swallow Dish" (oval shape).

Animals and Fish

Pike (plastic)

Roach (plastic)

Backstamp: Raised "R.K. Product by Wade of England"

No.	Description	Colourways	Shape/Size	U.S.$	Can.$	U.K.£
1.	Hare (metal)	Beige hare; green tray	Semi-oval/90 x 150	25.00	30.00	12.00
2.	Pike (metal)	White fish; green tray	Semi-oval/65 x 150	25.00	30.00	12.00
3.	Pike (metal)	Green fish; honey-brown tray	Semi-oval/65 x 150	25.00	30.00	12.00
4.	Pike (plastic)	White fish; honey-brown tray	Semi-oval/65 x 150	25.00	30.00	10.00
5.	Pike (plastic)	Grey fish; honey-brown tray	Semi-oval/65 x 150	25.00	30.00	10.00
6.	Perch (plastic)	Green fish; honey-brown tray	Semi-oval/65 x 150	25.00	30.00	10.00
7.	Roach (plastic)	Green fish; honey-brown tray	Semi-oval/65 x 150	25.00	30.00	10.00
8.	Squirrel (metal)	Brown squirrel; green tray	Semi-oval/90 x 150	25.00	30.00	12.00

Buildings and Figures

The "Big Ben" kidney-shaped tray has a "Souvenir of London" label. The "Mermaid" pen holder is on a flat porcelain stand.

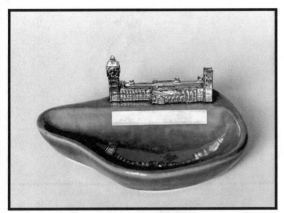

Big Ben & Houses of Parliament

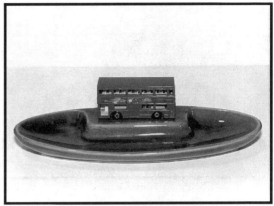

London Tourist Bus "Carnaby Street"

Policeman & St. Paul's Cathedral

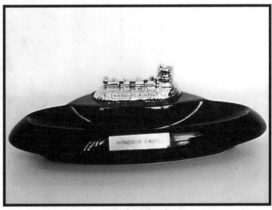

Windsor Castle

Backstamp: A. Impressed "Wade Made In England"
B. Raised "R.K. Product by Wade of England"
C. Raised "S42/9"
D. Raised "S42/10"

No.	Description	Colourways	Shape/Size	U.S.$	Can.$	U.K.£
1.	Big Ben & Houses of Parliament (metal)	Silver Big Ben; green tray	Kidney/40 x 100	25.00	30.00	12.00
2.	Buckingham Palace (plastic)	Silver palace; black tray	Oval/33 x 150	25.00	30.00	12.00
3.	Edinburgh Castle (metal)	Gold model; dark brown tray	Round/77 x 110	25.00	30.00	12.00
4.	London Bridge (metal)	Silver bridge; green tray	Kidney/40 x 100	25.00	30.00	12.00
5.	Policeman and St. Paul's Cathedral (plastic)	Gold policeman; brown tray	Round/80 x 110	25.00	30.00	12.00
6.	Tower Bridge (metal)	Silver bridge; brown tray	Kidney/40 x 100	25.00	30.00	12.00
7.	Windsor Castle (metal)	Silver castle; black tray	Semi-oval/55 x 150	25.00	30.00	12.00
8.	Windsor Castle (plastic)	Silver castle; black tray	Semi-oval/55 x 150	25.00	30.00	12.00

Pub Names

The Cock

The Lion

The Mermaid

Backstamp: A. Raised "S42/9"
             B. Raised "S42/8"

No.	Description	Colourways	Shape/Size	U.S.$	Can.$	U.K.£
1.	The Cock (metal)	Gold cock; brown tray	Round/77 x 111	25.00	30.00	15.00
2.	The Lion (metal)	Silver lion; black tray	Semi oval/77 x 150	25.00	30.00	15.00
3.	The Mermaid (metal)	Gold mermaid; brown tray	Round/77 x 111	25.00	30.00	15.00

Transportation

The "Tourist Bus" is on a new-shaped tray.

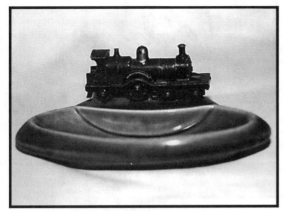

Duke of Connaught Locomotive

B Type Bus "Dewar's"

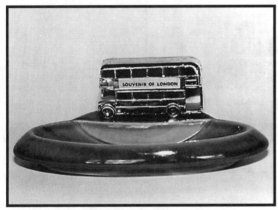

Bus "Souvenir of London"

Horse Drawn Bus "Lipton's Tea"

Backstamp: **A.** Raised "Wade Porcelain Made in England," 1961
B. Raised "R.K. Product by Wade of England"
C. Raised "S42/8"
D. Raised "Made in England Lesney"

No.	Description	Colourways	Shape/Size	U.S.$	Can.$	U.K.£
1.	B Type Bus," Dewar's"	Red metal bus; green tray	Semi-oval/65 x 150	40.00	45.00	20.00
2.	Bus, "Players Please"	Red metal bus; green tray	Semi-oval/55 x 150	40.00	45.00	20.00
3.	Horse Drawn Bus, 1899, "Lipton's Teas"	Red metal bus; green tray	Semi-oval/65 x 150	40.00	45.00	20.00
4.	Bus, "Cliftonville Bus,"	Silver plastic bus; black tray	Semi-oval/55 x 150	25.00	30.00	12.00
		Silver plastic bus; green tray	Semi-oval/55 x 150	25.00	30.00	12.00
5.	"Souvenir of London"					
	Tourist Bus	Red metal bus; green tray	Long-oval/70 x 242	40.00	45.00	20.00
6.	"Carnaby Street"					
7.	Duke of Connaught Locomotive, 1897	Black metal train; honey-brown tray	Semi-oval/65 x 150	40.00	45.00	20.00
8.	Duke of Connaught Locomotive, 1897	Green metal train; beige tray	Semi-oval/65 x 150	40.00	45.00	20.00
9.	Daimler 1911	Silver car; black tray	Square/50 x 130	40.00	45.00	20.00
10.	Ford	Silver metal car; black tray	Triangular/90 x 150	40.00	45.00	20.00

Maxwell Roadster 1911

Mercer Raceabout Sportscar 1913

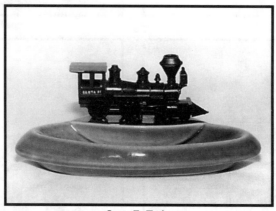

Santa Fe Train

Backstamp: **A.** Raised "Wade Porcelain Made in England"
B. Raised "R.K. Product by Wade of England"
C. Raised "S42/8"
D. Raised "Made in England Lesney"

No.	Description	Colourways	Shape/Size	U.S.$	Can.$	U.K.£
11.	Maxwell Roadster, 1911	Gold metal car; black tray	Square/50 x 130	40.00	45.00	20.00
12.	Mercer Raceabout Sportscar, 1913	Silver metal car; black tray	Triangular/70 x 135	40.00	45.00	20.00
13.	Rolls Royce, 1907	Silver metal car; black tray	Semi-oval/50 x 130	40.00	45.00	20.00
14.	Rolls Royce, 1907	Gold metal car; green tray	Semi-oval/50 x 130	40.00	45.00	20.00
15.	Sailing Ship	White plastic ship; black tray	Semi-oval/90 x 145	25.00	30.00	12.00
16.	Santa Fe 4-4-0 American "General" Locomotive, 1862	Red/silver metal train; honey-brown tray	Semi-oval/65 x 150	40.00	45.00	20.00
17.	Santa Fe 4-4-0 American "General" Locomotive, 1983	Red/green metal train; beige tray	Oval/65 x 150	40.00	45.00	20.00

PEN HOLDER

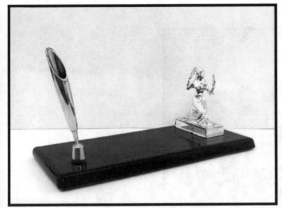

Mermaid Pen Holder

Spitfire Pen Holder

Backstamp: Raised "S42/10"

No.	Description	Colourways	Shape/Size	U.S.$	Can.$	U.K.£
1.	Pen Holder	Gold mermaid and pen holder; dark blue stand	Rectangular/175 x 50	25.00	30.00	15.00
2.	Spitfire Pen Holder	Silver metal plane; black tray	Triangular/100 x 145	25.00	30.00	12.00
3.	Spitfire Pen Holder	Brass metal plane; royal blue tray	Triangular/100 x 145	25.00	30.00	12.00

THE LONDON TEA AND PRODUCE CO. LTD.

TEA CADDY, 1984

Backstamp: Unknown

No.	Description	Colourways	Size	U.S.$	Can.$	U.K.£
1.	Tea Caddy	Off white; brown print	101	30.00	35.00	15.00

LONDON ZOO

150TH ANNIVERSARY CELEBRATION DISH, 1979

150TH ANNIVERSARY CELEBRATION DISH, 1979

This dish was produced to celebrate the 150th anniversary of the London Zoo.

Backstamp: Raised "No 3"

No.	Description	Colourways	Size	U.S.$	Can.$	U.K.£
1.	Dish	Grey blue	120	25.00	30.00	12.00
2.	Dish	Honey brown	120	25.00	30.00	12.00
3.	Dish	Green	120	25.00	30.00	12.00

LYONS TETLEY LTD.

CRUET SET, 1990-1996

The first cruet set was produced 1990-1992. The second set was produced in 1996.

Sidney Pepper Pot, Brew Gaffer Salt Cellar (1st Issue)

Brew Gaffer Pepper Pot, Sidney Salt Cellar (2nd Issue)

Backstamp: **A.** Black transfer print "Wade England"
B. Printed "Wade England © Tetley GB Limited 1996"

No.	Description	Colourways	Size	U.S.$	Can.$	U.K.£
1.	Brew Gaffer Salt Cellar (1st issue)	Light brown hat, slippers; white coat; red tie; blue trousers	90	45.00	60.00	30.00
2.	Sidney Pepper Pot (1st issue)	Light brown hat, slippers; white coat; blue dungarees	100	45.00	60.00	30.00
	Sydney/Gaffer (Pair)			125.00	155.00	65.00
3.	Brew Gaffer Pepper Pot (2nd issue)	Brown hat; white coat; red tie; blue overall; brown/black striped slippers	83	30.00	45.00	22.00
4.	Sydney Salt Cellar (2nd issue)	Brown hat; white coat; blue overall; brown/black striped slippers	102	30.00	45.00	22.00

MONEY BOXES, 1989-1990

The Brew Gaffer Money Box was produced in a limited edition of 10,000 and came with a numbered certificate of authenticity. Produced in 1990, there were 5,000 models of the Lyons Coffee Van.

Brew Gaffer (1st Issue)

Brew Gaffer Holding Cup of Tea (2nd Issue)

Lyons Coffee Delivery Van

Tetley's Teas Delivery Van

Backstamp: A. Black transfer print "Made exclusively for Lyons Tetley by Wade"
B. White transfer print "Manufactured Exclusively for Lyons Tetley Wade Made in England," impressed "Wade"
C. Printed circular "An Original Design for Tetley GB by Wade England ® Tetley GB Limited 1996"

No.	Description	Colourways	Size	U.S.$	Can.$	U.K.£
1.	Brew Gaffer (1st issue)	Brown cap, slippers; white coat, shirt; red tie; blue trousers	140	95.00	125.00	50.00
2.	Brew Gaffer (2nd issue)	Brown hat; white coat; blue overall; brown/black striped slippers	150	45.00	55.00	22.00
3.	Lyons Coffee Delivery Van	Dark green; gold/white lettering "Lyons Coffee Est 1904"	140	70.00	90.00	35.00
4.	Tetley's Teas Delivery Van	Dark blue; gold/white lettering "Tetley's Teas Est 1837"	140	70.00	90.00	35.00

MUGS AND COOKIE JAR, 1990-1996

The coffee mug was issued in 1990 and the cookie jar from 1993 to 1994. There is also a 1996 version of the Gaffer Cookie Jar with bluish-tinted spectacles, but it is not accounted for separately in this edition.

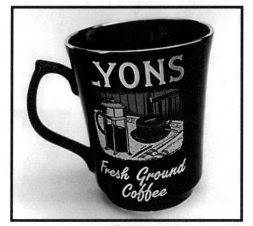

Coffee Mug

Cookie Jar

Hot Chocolate Mug

Backstamp: **A.** Gold transfer "Made exclusively for Lyons Tetley by Wade"
B. White print "An original design for Lyons Tetley by Wade England"
C. Printed "Made exclusively for Lyons Tetley by Wade"

No.	Description	Colourways	Size	U.S.$	Can.$	U.K.£
1.	Coffee mug	Black mug; multi-coloured print; gold lettering "Lyons Fresh Ground Coffee"	90	25.00	30.00	12.00
2.	Cookie Jar/Gaffer	Dark blue; brown hat; white lettering "Cookies"	215	75.00	85.00	35.00
3.	Hot Chocolate Mug	White: multi-coloured print gold and black lettering "Lyons Rich Hot Chocolate Drink"	90	10.00	15.00	8.00

TEAPOTS AND TOAST RACK, 1989-1996

The two-cup teapot was issued in 1989 and the "Sydney Teapot" in 1990. The "Brew Gaffer and Sydney Teapot" and toast rack were offered as mail-in premiums from The Tetley Tea Folk Catalogue in 1996.

Brew Gaffer Teapot

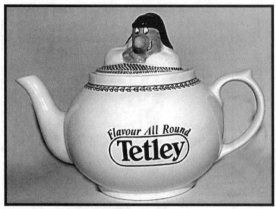

Sidney Teapot

Toast Rack; Brew Gaffer and Sidney Teapot

Two-Cup Teapot

Backstamp: **A.** Black print "Two cup Teapot specially made by Wade Potteries for Lyons Tetley Ltd"
B. Black transfer "Made exclusively for Lyons Tetley by Wade"
C. White print "An original design for Lyons Tetley by Wade England"

No.	Description	Colourways	Size	U.S.$	Can.$	U.K.£
1.	Two-Cup Teapot	Dark blue teapot; white lettering "Tetley"	120	30.00	35.00	15.00
2.	Sydney Teapot	White teapot; brown hat, shoes; white overall; brown/black rope ladder; blue lettering "Flavour All Round Tetley"	135	50.00	70.00	25.00
3.	Brew Gaffer and Sydney Teapot	Dark blue; brown/blue/white print	127	50.00	70.00	25.00
4.	Toast Rack	Dark blue; brown/blue/white print	70	30.00	35.00	15.00
5.	Brew Gaffer Two-Cup Teapot	Dark blue pot; brown hair; bluish glasses; white lettering	140 x 180	40.00	55.00	22.00

LYONS TEA IRELAND LTD.

WORLD CUP FOOTBALL TEAPOT, 1990

This football-shaped teapot, with the knob on the lid depicting a football boot, was produced as a promotional item for Lyons Tea Ireland when Ireland qualified for the 1990 World Cup football competitions.

Backstamp: Unknown

No.	Description	Colourways	Size	U.S.$	Can.$	U.K.£
1.	Football	White; black boot, patches on ball	155	70.00	90.00	35.00

LYONS TETLEY LTD. AND ESSO PETROLEUM

GAFFER AND NEPHEW VAN TEA CADDY, 1994-1995

Lyons Tetley and Esso Petrol stations in Britain joined forces in a promotion that lasted from September 1994 to February 1995. Purchasers of £6 worth of Esso petrol were given a Tiger Token, and 200 of these tokens were needed to obtain the "Gaffer and Nephew Van Tea Caddy." The caddy has moulded figures of the Tetley Tea Gaffer as the driver and his nephew sitting beside him.

Backstamp: White print "An Original Design For Lyons Tetley By Wade England"

No.	Description	Colourways	Size	U.S.$	Can.$	U.K.£
1.	Tea Caddy	Blue; brown/white/blue figures	127	135.00	200.00	65.00

R.H. MACY & CO. INC.

TEAPOT, 1989

The world famous Macy's department store of New York commissioned the Wade pottery to produce a teapot representing its building. Wade used the mould from the *English Life* series "Queen Victoria Pub Teapot" and decorated the teapot with a transfer print of the Macy's store front.

Photograph not available
at press time

Backstamp: Black transfer "Made in England Expressly for R.H. Macy & Co. Inc., New York N.Y. © 10001."

No.	Description	Colourways	Size	U.S.$	Can.$	U.K.£
1.	Teapot	White; red/white/yellow print	145	30.00	35.00	15.00

MARKS AND SPENCER PLC

MONEY BOX

This money box — seated teddy bear, arm raised — was produced for the British department store Marks and Spencer PLC during 1995-1996. He was originally sold filled with milk chocolate coins.

Edward the Teddy Bear Money Box

Backstamp: Unmarked

No.	Description	Colourways	Shape/Size	U.S.$	Can.$	U.K.£
1.	Edward Bear	Honey brown; black eyes and nose	154	25.00	35.00	18.00

MULBERRY GALLERY OF GREAT BRITAIN

MUSTANG P-5 AIRPLANE WALL PLATE, c.1965

A limited edition of 2,500 wall plates was produced for the Mulberry Gallery circa 1965. So far only one plate has been reported.

Photograph not available
at press time

Backstamp: Black transfer print "Wade North American P-5 Mustang by Robert Taylor, one of a Limited Edition of 2,500 Fine English Bone China Plates Created exclusively for the Mulberry Gallery of Great Britain by Wade Potteries PLC"

No.	Description	Colourways	Size	U.S.$	Can.$	U.K.£
1.	Plate	White; multi-coloured print	165	70.00	90.00	35.00

NOTIONS AND NOVELTIES LIMITED OF LONDON

FAMOUS AIRCRAFT TRAYS, 1958-1960

The original price was 3/9d each.

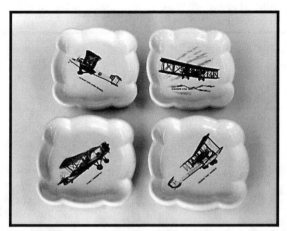

Backstamp: A. Black print a "Moko line by Wade of England Authenticated by Janes All the Worlds Aircraft," with the set and dish number
B. Black print a "Moko line by Wade of England Authenticated by Janes All the Worlds Aircraft," with the set and dish number

No.	Description	Colourways	Size	U.S.$	Can.$	U.K.£
1.	Bleriots Mono Plane 1909	White dish; black/blue print (Set 1)	103	40.00	45.00	20.00
2.	Fairey "Swordfish"	White dish; yellow/black print (Set 2)	103	50.00	70.00	25.00
3.	Handley Page 0/400 Bomber	White dish; yellow/black print (Set 2)	103	50.00	70.00	25.00
4.	Vickers Vimy Bomber	White dish; yellow/black print (Set 2)	103	50.00	70.00	25.00
5.	Vickers Vimy 1919	White dish; black/blue print (Set 1)	103	40.00	45.00	20.00
6.	Wrights Bi-Plane 1903	White dish; black/blue print (Set 1)	103	40.00	45.00	20.00

PEERAGE BRASS

TRAYS, 19581965

Peerage Trays are the same trays used for the Irish Wade *Whimtrays*. With the addition of a hole drilled in the back of the tray, a miniature brass animal or figure, produced by Peerage Brass, was then fixed onto the rim with a screw through the bottom. The client's name was added to the bottom of the tray. They are listed in alphabetical order.

Wire-Haired Terrier; Bear and Staff Warwick

Squirrel with Acorn; Guy De Warwick

Cat & The Fiddle Pub Sign

Long Neck Duck

Backstamp: Raised "Peerage Wade Porcelain Made in England"

No.	Name	Description	Size	U.S.$	Can.$	U.K.£
1.	Bear and Staff Warwick	Brass bear; blue tray	70 x 75	18.00	24.00	12.00
2	Cat & The Fiddle Pub Sign	Brass sign; yellow tray	60 x 75	18.00	24.00	12.00
3.	Cornish Pixie	Brass pixie; yellow tray	50 x 75	18.00	24.00	12.00
4.	Crinoline Lady with Basket	Brass lady; blue tray	60 x 75	18.00	24.00	12.00
5.	Esmeralda	Brass girl; blue tray	70 x 75	18.00	24.00	12.00
6.	Galleon Victory	Brass galleon; yellow tray	70 x 75	18.00	24.00	12.00
7.	Galleon *The Revenge*, 1588	Brass galleon; yellow tray	70 x 75	18.00	24.00	12.00
8.	Guy De Warwick	Brass knight; yellow tray	65 x 75	18.00	24.00	12.00
9.	Long Neck Duck	Brass duck; yellow tray	60 x 75	18.00	24.00	12.00
10.	Pekinese	Brass dog; black tray	55 x 75	18.00	24.00	12.00
11.	Pekinese	Brass dog ; yellow tray	55 x 75	18.00	24.00	12.00
12.	Rearing Horse	Brass horse; yellow tray	65 x 75	18.00	24.00	12.00
13.	Squirrel with Acorn	Brass squirrel; yellow tray	60 x 75	18.00	24.00	12.00
14.	Stag	Brass stag; black tray	70 x 75	18.00	24.00	12.00
15.	Wire-Haired Terrier	Brass dog; black tray	60 x 75	18.00	24.00	12.00

PRICE'S PATENT CANDLE COMPANY LTD.

CANDLE HOLDERS, 1963-1982

Between the middle of 1963 and 1982, Wade was commissioned by Price's Patent Candle Company Ltd. to produce a series of candle holders to sell in gift packages with Price's candles. Only the cube candle holder bears the Wade backstamp; other models listed below are marked with their shape numbers and can be easily recognized by their typical Wade glaze and weight.

Backstamp: **A.** Embossed "Made in England"
B. Embossed "S68/1 Wade England"
C. Embossed "S62/1"

No.	Description	Colourways	Size	U.S.$	Can.$	U.K.£
1.	Bridge	Off white (S2/6)	37 x 137	8.00	10.00	3.00
2.	Cube	Royal blue (S68/1)	49 x 49	8.00	10.00	3.00
3.	Cube	Honey-brown (S68/1)	49 x 49	8.00	10.00	3.00
4.	Daffodil, Small	Brown/grey/blue	19 x 41	6.00	8.00	2.00
5.	Daffodil, Medium	Brown/grey/blue	35 x 64	6.00	8.00	3.00
6.	Daffodil, Large	Brown/grey/blue	35 x 78	8.00	10.00	3.00
7.	Hat, Small	Pale green	20 x 42	6.00	8.00	2.00
8.	Hat, Large	Black (S2/7)	35 x 70	6.00	8.00	2.00
9.	Ink Bottle	Olive green (S2/16)	43 x 73	8.00	10.00	3.00
10.	Ink Bottle	Pale blue (S2/16)	43 x 73	8.00	10.00	3.00
11.	Ink Bottle	White (S2/16)	43 x 73	8.00	10.00	3.00
12.	Leaf	Dark green	35 x 155	8.00	10.00	3.00
13.	Leaf	Light green	35 x 155	8.00	10.00	3.00
14.	Leaf	Dark/light brown	35 x 155	8.00	10.00	3.00
15.	Soap Cake	Off white	19 x 100	8.00	10.00	3.00
16.	Sunflower	Honey-brown/orange-brown	30 x 78	8.00	10.00	3.00
17.	Sunflower	Red-brown/orange-brown	30 x 78	8.00	10.00	3.00
	Star	Yellow	114	8.00	10.00	5.00
18.	Triangle	Pale blue (S62/2)	Unknown	6.00	8.00	2.00
19.	Tulip, Small	Pale blue (S2/18)	43 x 50	6.00	8.00	2.00
20.	Tulip, Small	Maroon (S2/18)	43 x 50	6.00	8.00	2.00
21.	Tulip, Small	Brown (S2/18)	43 x 50	6.00	8.00	2.00
22.	Tulip, Small	White (S2/18)	43 x 50	6.00	8.00	2.00
23.	Tulip, Large	Pale blue	55 x 71	8.00	10.00	3.00
24.	Tulip, Large	Maroon	55 x 71	8.00	10.00	3.00
25.	Water Lily	Mottled brown/blue	24 x 103	8.00	10.00	3.00
26.	Water Lily	Mottled green/brown	24 x 103	8.00	10.00	3.00

PRINCESS HOUSE

OVEN PROOF DISH

This rectangular oven proof dish has a transfer print of oranges on a tree branch.

Backstamp: Impressed "Wade England" and transfer printed "Porcelain Cookware Country Harvest Collection Princess House c.1989 Ltd Microwave, Oven and Dishwasher Safe" with Hay cart logo

No.	Description	Colourways	Shape/size	U.S.$	Can.$	U.K.£
1.	Oven Proof Dish	Off white dish; orange oranges; brown/green branch; yellow green tree/fields	50h x 275w x 225d	26.00	36.00	12.00

PUSSER'S LTD

PERFUME ATOMISERS, 1997

Pusser's Ltd is most famous for the British Navy Rum they distill, but in the mid 1990s they commissioned perfume bottles and an after shave lotion bottle from Wade Ceramics, which were offered for sale in the Pusser's Rum shop in the British Virgin Islands.

Lily Perfume Atomiser

Backstamp: Circular gold printed "Pussers Ltd Tortola British Virgin Islands Pusser's West Indies Finest English Porcelain"

No.	Description	Colourways	Shape/Size	U.S.$	Can.$	U.K.£
1.	After Shave Lotion "West Indian Lim"e	Gold top; green bottle; multi-coloured print; dark green lettering	130	22.00	30.00	15.00
2.	Perfume Atomiser "Gardenia"	Gold top; cream bottle; white flowers; green leaves; blue lettering	130	22.00	30.00	15.00
3.	Perfume Atomiser "Lily"	Gold top; royal blue bottle; white/yellow lilies; green leaves; white lettering	130	22.00	30.00	15.00
4.	Perfume Atomiser "Rose"	Gold lid, royal blue bottle; pink flowers; green leaves; white lettering	130	22.00	30.00	15.00

MINIATURE DECANTERS, SALT & PEPPER

The salt and pepper shakers are scaled down replicas of the Admiral Lord Nelson ship decanters, commissioned by Pusser's and sold in their shop in the British Virgin Islands.

Miniature Decanter Salt and Pepper

No.	Description	Colourways	Shape/Size	U.S.$	Can.$	U.K.£
1.	Salt and Pepper Shakers	Blue top; white body; multi-coloured prints; black lettering "Pusser's West Indies"	130	22.00	30.00	15.00

RINGTONS TEA LTD.

BLUE WILLOW PATTERN TEA AND DINNER SET, 1994-1995

The "Willow Pattern Tea and Dinner Set" items were available direct from Ringtons Tea during Easter of 1994 at the following prices: Set of two beakers £8.99, set of two coasters £4.99, teapot 4-cup £13.99, set of two tea plates £7.50,. set of two cups and saucers £13.25, milk jug and sugar bowl £11.75 the pair. During Easter of 1995 a 6-cup coffee pot £24.99, dinner plates £14.49 set of two and soup/cereal bowls £11.99 set of two were added to the range.

Beaker

Cup and Saucer

Milk Jug, Teapot, Sugar Bowl

Backstamp: **A.** Printed "Especially made for Ringtons a family business Est 1907 Exclusive Willow Pattern Design Specially Commissioned by Ringtons Ltd Produced by Wade Ceramics"
B. Printed "Exclusive Willow Pattern Design Specially Commissioned by Ringtons Ltd Produced by Wade Ceramics" with Ringtons horse drawn van logo

No.	Description	Colourways	Size	U.S.$	Can.$	U.K.£
1.	Beaker	White; blue willow pattern	100	25.00	30.00	12.00
2.	Coaster	White; blue willow pattern	100	24.00	30.00	8.00
3.	Cup/saucer	White; blue willow pattern	70 x 140	45.00	60.00	20.00
4.	Milk jug	White; blue willow pattern	75	48.00	65.00	25.00
5.	Sugar bowl	White; blue willow pattern	75	25.00	30.00	10.00
6.	Tea plate	White: blue willow pattern	170	25.00	30.00	10.00
7.	Teapot 4-cup	White; blue willow pattern	140	45.00	60.00	30.00
8.	Teapot 6-cup	White; blue willow pattern	159	60.00	80.00	35.00
9.	Coffee pot 6-cup	White; blue willow pattern	242	65.00	75.00	38.00
10.	Dinner plate	White: blue willow pattern	225	35.00	45.00	15.00
11.	Soup/cereal bowls	White; blue willow pattern	130	25.00	30.00	10.00

BLUE WILLOW ACCESSORIES

Biscuit barrel, butter dish, egg cups, miniature Maling teapot, toast rack, 1996

The biscuit barrel, butter dish, egg cups and toast rack were additions to the 1994-1995 Tea and Dinner set.

Forty thousand replicas of the 1930s Maling teapot were produced by Wade for Ringtons during Easter of 1996.

Backstamp: **A.** Printed " Exclusive Willow Pattern Design specially commissioned by Ringtons Ltd. Produced by Wade Ceramics"
B. Printed "Ringtons by Wade"
C. Printed "Ringtons Ltd Tea Merchants Algernon Road Newcastle-on-Tyne Produced by Wade Ceramics" based upon an original Maling teapot produced for Ringtons in 1930s. 1996"
D. Printed "Ringtons Ltd by Wade Ceramics"
E. Printed "Ringtons Produced by Wade Ceramics"

No.	Description	Colourways	Size	U.S.$	Can.$	U.K. £
1.	Biscuit barrel	White; blue willow pattern	185	38.00	50.00	22.00
2.	Butter dish	White; blue willow pattern	101 x 210	35.00	45.00	20.00
3.	Egg cup	White; blue willow pattern	50	5.00	7.00	3.00
4.	Maling teapot	White; blue willow pattern	101	50.00	65.00	30.00
5.	Salt and pepper	White: blue willow pattern	88	11.00	15.00	7.00
6.	Toast rack	White; blue willow pattern	76 x 156	18.00	24.00	12.00

BLUE WILLOW ROUND MALING JUG, 1995

A large lidded milk jug was originally produced for Ringtons by Maling Potteries in the 1920s and sold from the delivery vans. In 1995 Wade was commissioned to produce 35,000 miniature replicas of the 1920s lidded jug, and they were available direct from Ringtons at a cost of £14.50

Backstamp: Printed "Ringtons Limited Tea Merchants Newcastle Upon Tyne Produced by Wade Ceramics based upon an original produced for Ringtons in the late 1920s. 1995"

No.	Description	Colourways	Shape/Size	U.S.$	Can.$	U.K.£
1.	Miniature Maling Jug	White; blue willow pattern	150	60.00	80.00	40.00

BLUE WILLOW LIDDED MALING MILK JUG, 1997

This lidded milk jug with a square base was originally produced for Ringtons by Maling Potteries in the 1920s and sold from the delivery vans. In 1997 Wade were commissioned to produce miniature replicas of the 1920s jug, which were available direct from Ringtons at a cost of £14.50.

Backstamp: Printed "Ringtons Ltd Tea Merchants Newcastle-upon-Tyne Produced by Wade Ceramics upon an original Maling jug Produced for Ringtons in the 1920s. 1997"

No.	Description	Colourways	Size	U.S.$	Can.$	U.K.£
1.	Square Willow Pattern Jug	White; blue willow pattern	153	45.00	50.00	27.00

BUNNY MUG, 1996

This one colour rabbit shaped mug was originally produced for Ringtons with an "Especially Made for Ringtons" backstamp. Surplus models were sold in the Wade shop with a "Wade England" backstamp.

Backstamp: Printed "Especially Made for Ringtons"

No.	Description	Colourways	Size	U.S.$	Can.$	U.K.£
1.	Bunny Mug	Cream	105	30.00	40.00	20.00

CARRIAGE CLOCK

This rectangular clock is decorated with an all-over floral design against a white background.

Photograph not available
at press time

Backstamp: Black print "Especially Commissioned by Ringtons Ltd, produced By Wade Ceramics"

No.	Description	Colourways	Size	U.S.$	Can.$	U.K.£
1.	Carriage Clock	White; multi-coloured flowers	162	50.00	70.00	25.00

CARRIAGE CLOCK AND MATCHING VASE, 1992

Produced for Ringtons Teas in 1992, the clock and vase have a Nasturtium floral print on them.

Photograph not available
at press time

Backstamp: Printed "Especially Commissioned by Ringtons Ltd. By Wade Ceramics 1992"

No.	Description	Colourways	Size	U.S.$	Can.$	U.K.£
1.	Clock	Cream; gold highlighting; orange and yellow flowers; green leaves	159 x 127	55.00	75.00	40.00
2.	Vase	Cream; gold highlighting; orange and yellow flowers; green leaves	205 x 133	55.00	75.00	40.00

CATHEDRALS AND CASTLES MALING ROSE BOWL, 1998

This beautiful "Rose Bowl" is a copy of one produced for Ringtons Teas by Maling in the 1920s. The blue transfer prints are of Northern Englands Cathedrals and Castles: York Minster, Selby Abbey, The Castle Newcastle-on-Tyne, Ripon Cathedral, Hexham Abbey and Bamburgh Castle. There is a print of Durham Cathedral in the bottom of the bowl. The original cost direct from Ringtons catalogue was £20.99.

Photgraph not available
at press time

Backstamp: Printed "Ringtons Ltd Tea Merchants Algernon Road Newcastle-on-Tyne Manufactured Exclusively for Ringtons by Wade Ceramics"

No.	Description	Colourways	Size	U.S.$	Can.$	U.K. £
1.	Rose Bowl	White; blue prints	88 x 177	50.00	70.00	25.00

COLLECTOR MUGS, 1995

These heavy mugs which have multi-coloured transfer prints of delivery vehicles and houses around the outside of the mug and a multi-coloured print of a Ringtons delivery vehicle inside the rim. The designs on the mugs match the "Street Scenes Teapots" which were produced from 1993-1994. The mugs were available from Ringtons at a cost of £13.99 per set of two.

Backstamp: A. Printed "1920s Collectors Mug Especially made for Ringtons A Family Business Est 1907 by Wade Ceramics 1995" with Ringtons horse drawn van logo
B. Printed "1950s Collectors Mug Especially made for Ringtons A Family Business Est 1907 by Wade Ceramics 1995" with Ringtons horse drawn van logo
C. Printed "1960s Collectors Mug Especially made for Ringtons A Family Business Est 1907 by Wade Ceramics 1995" with Ringtons horse drawn van logo
D. Printed "1980s Collectors Mug Especially made for Ringtons A Family Business Est 1907 by Wade Ceramics 1995" with Ringtons horse drawn van logo

No.	Description	Colourways	Size	U.S.$	Can.$	U.K.£
1.	1920s Horse Drawn Van	White mug; orange; multi-coloured prints	92	22.00	33.00	18.00
2.	1950s Motor Van	White mug; brown; multi-coloured prints	92	22.00	33.00	18.00
3.	1960s Motor Van	White mug; grey; multi-coloured prints	92	22.00	33.00	18.00
4.	1980s Motor Van	White mug; grey; multi-coloured prints	92	22.00	33.00	18.00

HERITAGE COLLECTION TEA CADDY, 1997

This rectangular tea caddy is from the same mould used for the Boots plain caddy and the wild flowers caddy. Decorated with multi-coloured transfer prints of original teapots in the archives of Ringtons Ltd. Each teapot print is titled; some designs include Maling Autumn Leaves, Maling Chintz, Hunting scene, Floral Trellis, Anniversary and Willow etc. The original cost direct from Ringtons was £13.99.

Photograph not available
at press time

Backstamp: Printed "The Heritage Collection Ringtons a family Business Est 1907 Produced exclusively for Ringtons by Wade Ceramics"

No.	Description	Colourways	Size	U.S.$	Can.$	U.K. £
1.	Heritage Tea Caddy	Cream; multi-coloured print	153	30.00	40.00	20.00

JUG AND BASIN, 1992

Photograph not available
at press time

Backstamp: Printed "Especially Made for Ringtons a Family Business est 1907 By Wade Ceramics 1992"

No.	Description	Colourways	Shape/Size	U.S.$	Can.$	U.K.£
1.	Basin	Unknown	212 dia.	Unknown		
2.	Jug	Unknown	208 dia.	Unknown		

MONEY BOX - DELIVERY VAN, NOVEMBER 1995

This van shaped money box was produced for Ringtons in November 1995 and cost £12.99.

Backstamp: Printed "Exclusive Ringtons Delivery Vehicle specially commissioned by Ringtons Limited Produced by Wade England" backstamp includes the Ringtons Tea Logo

No.	Description	Colourways	Size	U.S.$	Can.$	U.K.£
1.	Delivery Van	Black; yellow and gold crest/lettering	120mm	125.00	150.00	75.00

PHOTO FRAME, 1990

This photo frame has transfer prints of Pinks and Nasturtium flowers in the top and bottom corners.

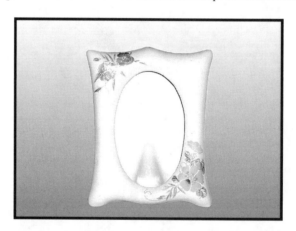

Backstamp: Printed "Especially made for Ringtons Ltd by Wade Potteries 1990"

No.	Description	Colourways	Shape/Size	U.S.$	Can.$	U.K.£
1.	Photo frame	White: pink/grey/yellow flowers; pale green leaves	140 x 95	30.00	35.00	15.00

ROSE BOWL, Pinks and Nasturtiums, 1988

This hexagonal flower bowl has a fitted wire flower holder in the rim, and has transfer prints of Pinks and Nasturtium flowers around the bowl.

Backstamp: Printed "Especially made for Ringtons Ltd by Wade Potteries 1988"

No.	Description	Colourways	Shape/Size	U.S.$	Can.$	U.K.£
1.	Rose Bowl	White; pink/grey/yellow flowers; pale green leaves	101 x 127	50.00	70.00	25.00

TEA CADDIES, 1982-1993

The "Cathedrals and Bridge Tea Caddy" was produced for Ringtons to celebrate its 80th anniversary in 1987. Each panel of the hexagonal jar is ornately decorated with transfer prints of famous Northern landmarks—Durham Cathedral, the Castle and Tyne Bridge in Newcastle-upon-Tyne, Ripon Cathedral, Selby Abby, York Minster—with Windsor Castle on the lid. The design was based on an original caddy that was produced for Ringtons by the Tyneside pottery of C. T. Maling and Sons in 1929 to commemorate the North East Coast Industries Exhibition of that year. The Wade version is smaller and has slightly different transfers than the original Maling tea caddie. Approximately 36,500 Wade caddies were produced, and when they were originally sold in British stores, they were filled with tea. Ringtons commissioned 120 special editions of the caddy to present to the shareholders, directors and suppliers of Ringtons Tea. These editions can be distinguished by an extra gold line in the ornate decoration and are numbered on the bases.

With the success of the "Cathedrals and Bridge Tea Caddy," Ringtons commissioned a larger version in 1989, It was decorated in a similar way, but the transfer prints were changed to Carlisle Cathedral, Hexham Abbey, Newcastle Cathedral, Ripon Cathedral, Selby Abbey and York Minster, with Durham Cathedral on the lid.

The rectangular "Horse -Drawn Van Tea Caddy" was produced in 1982 to celebrate Ringtons 75th anniversary. It has a transfer print on it of a 1907 horse-drawn van with the words "Ringtons Tea 1907-1982."

The "Oriental Jar, Willow Pattern Tea Caddy," produced in 1991, has square sloping sides that are wider at the top than at the base and a round lid. It is decorated with the popular Chinese willow pattern. The design is based upon that of an original 1920s Maling tea caddy, produced for Ringtons, that had a round lid, used as a tea measure. Inside the lid is a copy of the original Ringtons trademark, the monogram *RT* on a blue shield.

The "Pagoda, Willow Pattern Tea Caddy." Produced in 1993, has square sloping sides that are wider at the base than the top and has a square lid. It is also decorated with the popular Chinese willow pattern. The caddy is the same design as a teapot produced by Maling for Ringtons in 1929.

Cathedrals and Bridge Tea Caddy

Oriental Jar Tea Caddy

Pagoda Tea Caddy

Backstamp: **A.** Blue transfer print "Made exclusively for Ringtons Ltd. By Wade Potteries to commemorate Ringtons Est. 1907-80th Anniversary based on an original "Maling" Tea Caddy for Ringtons in the late 1920s"
  B. Blue transfer print "Made exclusively for Ringtons Ltd by Wade Potteries based upon an original 'Maling' Cathedral Jar produced for Ringtons in the late 1920s-1989"
  C. Black print "Specially Commissioned by Ringtons Ltd, produced By Wade Ceramics—Ringtons—Based upon an Original 'Maling' Tea Caddy Produced for Ringtons in the late 1920s"

No.	Description	Colourways	Size	U.S.$	Can.$	U.K.£
1.	Cathedrals/Bridge	Blue/white	100	85.00	110.00	50.00
2.	Cathedrals/Bridge, Gold	Blue/white/gold trim	100		Rare	
3.	Cathedrals and Abbeys	Blue/white	135	35.00	150.00	75.00
4.	Horse-Drawn Van, 75th Anniversary	White; black print	160	70.00	90.00	35.00
5.	Oriental Jar, Willow Pattern	Blue/white	128	75.00	100.00	45.00
6.	Pagoda, Willow Pattern	Blue/white	135	75.00	100.00	45.00

TEAPOTS

Willow Pattern Teapot, 1994

The round four-cup Willow Pattern Teapot was available from Ringtons for £13.99.

No.	Description	Colourways	Size	U.S.$	Can.$	U.K.£
1.	Teapot	White; blue willow print	138	50.00	70.00	25.00

Street Scenes Collector Teapots, 1993-1995

This set of four teapots was all modelled in the shape of a house. They are decorated with transfer prints of street scenes showing Ringtons delivery vans and their progression from the 1920s horse-drawn van to the modern delivery van of the 1980s. They were available from Ringtons for £16.99 each.

The "Horse-Drawn Van Teapot" was made from the same mould as Wade's "Cricketers Teapot," which was first produced in 1991. The transfer print on this teapot is of a Ringtons Tea horse-drawn van, with a driver delivering a box of Ringtons Tea to a lady outside her house.

The "Motor Delivery Van Teapot," 1950 was taken from the same mould as used for Wade's "Wedding Teapot," which was first produced in 1991. The transfer print on this teapot is of a Ringtons Tea delivery van, with the driver delivering a box of Ringtons Tea to a lady outside her house.

Styles 1 and 2 were issued in 1993, styles 3 and 4 in 1995.

| Street Scenes Teapot, 1920s | Street Scenes Teapot, 1950s | Street Scenes Teapot, 1960s |

No.	Description	Colourways	Size	U.S.$	Can.$	U.K.£
1.	Horse-Drawn Van, 1920	White; black/grey roof; beige house; white horse; green/yellow cart	177	50.00	70.00	25.00
2.	Motor Delivery Van, 1950	White; brown house; grey roof; green/yellow van	177	50.00	70.00	25.00
3.	Motor Delivery Van, 1960	White; grey/yellow house; red/white roof; green/yellow van	195	50.00	70.00	25.00
4.	Motor Delivery Van, 1980	White; green/yellow house; green/white roof; green/yellow van	177	50.00	70.00	25.00

TEA SET FLORAL TRELLIS, late 1980s

A teapot, cream jug and sugar bowl were produced for Ringtons Tea Ltd. As part of a promotional line. The teapot shape was originally used for the Prince Charles and Lady Diana wedding in 1981.

Photograph not available
at press time

Backstamp: Printed "Floral Trellis Specially Commissioned for Ringtons Ltd by Wade"

No.	Description	Colourways	Size	U.S.$	Can.$	U.K.£
1.	Cream jug "Floral Trellis"	White; yellow/red/blue flowers; yellow/green leaves/trellis	95	15.00	22.00	10.00
2.	Sugar bowl "Floral Trellis"	White; yellow/red/blue flowers; yellow/green leaves/trellis	70	15.00	22.00	10.00
3.	Teapot "Floral Trellis"	White; yellow/red/blue flowers yellow/green leaves/trellis	165	30.00	40.00	20.00

WALL PLATES

Heritage, 1997

Produced for Ringtons, this decorative wall plate has multi-coloured 1920s - 1990s scenes of Ringtons delivery vehicles set against Durham, Lincoln and York Minster Cathedrals, with the Tyne bridge and Lancashire Moors, all of which are in the North of England.

Backstamp: Printed "The Ringtons Heritage Plate Exclusively commissioned by and produced for Ringtons Ltd by Wade Ceramics For Decorative Use Only" (with Rington's horse drawn delivery van logo)

No.	Description	Colourways	Size	U.S.$	Can.$	U.K.£
1.	Plate	White; multi-coloured print	258	35.00	48.00	22.00

Street Games, 1995

This highly decorative plate has an all over transfer design of children playing games around the rim, and a central design of a 1940s British policeman talking to children in the centre. Original cost direct from Ringtons was £10.99

Backstamp: Printed "Street Games Ringtons a Family business Est 1907 Exclusive Limited Edition Collectors Plate in a design specially Commissioned by Ringtons Produced by Wade Ceramics for decorative use only"

No.	Description	Colourways	Size	U.S.$	Can.$	U.K.£
2.	Plate	White; multi-coloured print	254	35.00	45.00	20.00

ROYAL SOCIETY FOR THE PROTECTION OF BIRDS

TEAPOT, 1989

Produced for the R.S.P.B., this dainty traditional shaped teapot is decorated with flowers.

Photograph not available
at press time

Backstamp: Printed "Wade Potteries R.S.P.B. to celebrate 100 years Made in England"

No.	Description	Colourways	Size	U.S.$	Can.$	U.K.£
1.	Teapot	White: blue finial/handle/spout/flowers	110	40.00	55.00	30.00

RUTHERFORD LABORATORIES

TANKARD, 1985

This tankard was commissioned by Rutherford Laboratories to present to its employees. It bears the inscription, "To commemorate the Inauguration of the Pulsed Spallation Neutron Source ISIS at the Rutherford Appleton Laboratory on 1st October 1985."

Photograph not
available at press time

Backstamp: Black print "Manufacturers of Alumina Ceramic Vacuum Vessels for ISIS. Porcelain Wade No 0507"

No.	Description	Colourways	Size	U.S.$	Can.$	U.K.£
1.	Tankard	White; multi-coloured print	115	75.00	100.00	50.00

SALADA TEA CANADA

TEA CADDY, 1984

This tea caddy was first used in Wades 1982-1983 *Village Stores* series; only the multi-coloured transfer print on the front was changed. Across the front of this caddy is printed "Salon de the Salada Ye olde tearoom." To obtain it the collector had to send in the UPC code from the back of the tea box, plus $13.00 to cover shipping and handling charges.

Backstamp: Transfer print "Village Stores by Wade Staffordshire, England"

No.	Description	Colourways	Size	U.S.$	Can.$	U.K.£
1.	Tea Caddy	White; multi-coloured print	191	50.00	70.00	25.00

SCARBOROUGH BUILDING SOCIETY

BASEBALL MONEY BOX

Note: The baseball money box has been found with his mouth painted a bright red—the red mouth is not original. The Wade pottery has a long history of difficulties using red glazes. It is believed that the red mouth was added after it left the pottery.

Backstamp: Unknown

No.	Description	Colourways	Size	U.S.$	Can.$	U.K.£
1.	Money Box	White ball head; royal blue cap	150	140.00	160.00	90.00
2.	Money Box	White ball head; royal blue cap/red lips	150	85.00	90.00	65.00

SCHERING

APOTHECARY JAR, c.MID 1970s

This dome-lidded jar, produced for Schering, a pharmaceutical company in Canada is from the same mould as a decorative jar produced by Wade in the early mid-1970s.

Backstamp: Brown printed "Wade England" (c.late 1970s-1980s)

No.	Description	Colourways	Size	U.S.$	Can.$	U.K.£
1.	Apothecary Jar	White; gold bands and finial; brown frame and lettering	250	35.00	50.00	25.00

SLIMBRIDGE WILDFOWL TRUST

RUDDY DUCK, 1976

The "Ruddy Duck" is a slip-cast model produced in a bisque porcelain and was commissioned by Sir Peter Scott of the Slimbridge Wildfowl Trust. Only 3,500 models of the "Ruddy Duck" were made. The original price was £1.75.

Backstamp: Unmarked

No.	Description	Colourways	Size	U.S.$	Can.$	U.K.£
1.	Ruddy Duck	Red-brown body; black head, wings; blue bill	35	400.00	500.00	250.00

SMITHS CRISPS

MONSTER MUNCHER MONEY BOX, 1987

Backstamp: Impressed "Wade England"

No.	Description	Colourways	Size	U.S.$	Can.$	U.K.£
1.	Money Box	Bright blue body; red/white/green/blue/ yellow hat; pink feet	170	100.00	145.00	65.00

J. W. THORNTON LTD.

MONEY BOXES, 1984 - 1993

Wade produced five money boxes for J.W. Thornton Ltd. of England, manufacturers of chocolate and toffee: three "Delivery Vans" (1984, 1991 and 1993), "a Letter Box" (1985) and "Peter the Polar Bear" (1989) .The original price for the "Delivery Van" and the "Letter Box" was £3.99 each. The original 1984 "Delivery Van" and the 1993 reissue have solid back doors. A new style of delivery van, with two circular holes in the rear doors, was produced in 1991. The original 1984 "Delivery Van" was reissued for Christmas 1993 in a lighter brown. It was marked "Wade" on the packaging. Printed on the box is "1609 A Wade's Collectable Money Box." The original price from Thornton's was £14.95.

1993 Delivery Van, 1991 Delivery Van

Rear 1984 Van (Solid); Rear 1991 Van (two holes)

Letter Box

Peter the Polar Bear

Backstamp: A. Impressed "Made Exclusively for J. W. Thornton Ltd" on the base and" Thorntons Chocolates 1911" embossed on the side
B. Embossed "Thorntons Estd 1911" on the back

No.	Description	Colourways	Size	U.S.$	Can.$	U.K.£
1.	1984 Delivery Van	Chocolate brown	120	75.00	95.00	40.00
2.	1991 Delivery Van	Royal blue	120	60.00	80.00	30.00
3.	1993 Delivery Van	Light brown	120	50.00	70.00	25.00
4.	1985 Letter Box	Chocolate brown	180	45.00	60.00	30.00
5.	1989 Peter the Polar Bear	Off white; brown eyes, nose; red/green scarf	160	28.00	42.00	20.00

POTS, 1985 AND 1988

The "Father's Day Plant Pot" was produced in 1985 for Father's Day, and the "Special Toffee Pot" was produced in 1988. Printed on the box is "1609 A Wade's Collectable Money Box."

Happy Father's Day

Thornton's Special Toffee

Backstamp: Unmarked

No.	Description	Colourways	Size	U.S.$	Can.$	U.K.£
1.	Father's Day Plant Pot	Dark brown; light brown letters	110	70.00	90.00	35.00
2.	Father's Day	Amber brown	110	70.00	90.00	35.00
3.	Special Toffee Pot	Dark brown; light brown letters	110	70.00	90.00	35.00
4.	Special Toffee Pot	Amber brown	110	70.00	90.00	35.00

TOBY INNS

CRUETS, c.1950–c.1960

Backstamp: Red printed "Wade England"

No.	Description	Colourways	Size	U.S.$	Can.$	U.K.£
1.	Pepper Pot	Beige; red/black print, lettering "The Sign of Good Food"	114	8.00	10.00	3.00
2.	Salt Cellar	Beige; red/black print, lettering "The Sign of Good Food"	114	8.00	10.00	3.00
3.	Pepper Pot	Beige; red/black print, lettering "Welcome Food Award"	114	8.00	10.00	3.00
4.	Salt Cellar	Beige; red/black print, lettering "Welcome Food Award"	114	8.00	10.00	3.00

UNIVERSITY OF ILLINOIS

ILLINI ASHTRAY, EARLY 1980s

Commissioned by the University of Illinois whose logo and mascot is a North American Indian chief; the logo and the term "The Fighting Illinis" is used for all events connected to the University. The ashtray listed has the slogan "The 80s belong to the Illinis" printed around the sides and a print in the centre of a North American Indian wearing a war bonnet.

Photograph not available
at press time

Backstamp: Red Printed "Wade pdm England" (pdm joined 1969-1984)

No.	Description	Colourways	Shape/size	U.S.$	Can.$	U.K.£
1.	Ashtray	Blue tray; multi-coloured Indian head wearing war bonnet	177	20.00	28.00	20.00

UNIVERSITY TREASURES INC.

RAZORBACK PIGS, 1981

These hollow models, produced in biscuit porcelain, depict a North American wild pig called a razorback. They were designed by Alan Maslankowski, who modelled Wades *Survival Animals* series. A limited edition of 500 models was produced for the University of Arkansas, whose football-team mascot is a razorback pig. These models are extremely rare: a collector/dealer in UK was offered £2,000 for one, which was refused.

Backstamp: Black ink stamp "Wade England"

No.	Description	Colourways	Size	U.S.$	Can.$	U.K.£
1.	Razorback	Dark grey	130	700.00	775.00	350.00
2.	Razorback	Red brown	130	700.00	775.00	350.00

WALTER HOLLAND LIMITED

PIE SHAPED POT, c.1960s

This miniature pie shaped pot was produced as a promotional item in the late 1960s for Walter Holland Limited Bakers of Baxenden, Accrington, Lancashire, UK. Fleur de Lys pies was a popular cooked meat pie sold in Lancashire bakeries.

Miniature Pie Pot

Baclstamp of Miniature Pie Pot

Backstamp: Printed "Wade Regicor Made in UK" (c.late 1950s)

No.	Description	Colourways	Size	U.S.$	Can.$	U.K.£
1.	Miniature Pie Pot	Brown; dark blue lettering	38 x 63	145.00	160.00	75.00

WILLIAMSON AND MAGOR TEA DISTRIBUTORS

ELEPHANT TEA CADDIES, 1990-1998

The original 1990 "Elephant Tea Caddies" were issued with a matt finish, and the models were decorated with a red and gold design. In 1993 the "Elephant Tea Caddies" were reissued in high-gloss glazes with a gold decoration.

Elephant Tea Caddy, Earl Grey   Elephant Tea Caddy, English Breakfast

Backstamp: Black print "Handcrafted and Produced Exclusively for Williamson and Magor by Wade Royal Victoria Pottery" and a silhouette of an elephant

No.	Description	Colourways	Size	U.S.$	Can.$	U.K.£
1.	Earl Grey Tea	Grey matt finish; red/blue/gold decoration	185	70.00	90.00	48.00
2.	Earl Grey Tea	Grey gloss finish; gold decoration	185	70.00	90.00	48.00
3.	Earl Grey Tea	Creamy white; maroon; royal blue and gold decoration	185	70.00	90.00	48.00
4.	English Breakfast Tea	Blue matt finish; red/blue/gold decoration	185	70.00	90.00	48.00
5.	English Breakfast Tea	Blue gloss finish; gold decoration	185	70.00	90.00	48.00

MUG

The trunk of this unusual elephant shaped mug forms the handle.

Elephant Tea Caddy and Mug

No.	Description	Colourways	Size	U.S.$	Can.$	U.K.£
1.	Elephant mug	Creamy white; maroon; royal blue and gold decoration	100	35.00	55.00	28.00

MISCELLANEOUS COMMISSIONED, COMMISSIONERS UNKNOWN

APOTHECARY JAR PENCIL POT, LATE 1970s

These black and white jars were produced for an unknown pharmaceutical company and were intended as pencil pots to be given to medical practictioners by sales representatives. The latin name *Unguentum Ultralanum* on the front and back translates to Extra Lanolin Ointment, a cortisone ointment. On the sides is a print of an ointment tube with the words "The ultimate in modern topical corticoid therapy." Some jars are found with a wooden lid; the lids may have been added at a later date.

Backstamp: Printed "Made in Ireland by Wade Co Armagh"

No.	Description	Colourways	Size	U.S.$	Can.$	U.K.£
1.	"Unguentum Ultralanum" no lid	White jar; black print and lettering	110 x 80	25.00	35.00	18.00
2.	"Unguentum Ultralanum" with lid	White jar; black print and lettering	125 x 80	30.00	40.00	20.00

DOOR HANDLES

The large circular door handles produced by Wade Ireland appear to have been used on glass entrance doors and are believed to have come from one of the offices at the Wade Ireland Pottery. For sale at the 1995 June Wade Show at £60.00 the pair.

Door Handle

Side View of Door Handle

Backstamp: None

No.	Description	Colourways	Size	U.S. $	Can.$	U.K.£
1.	Circular Door Handle	Green	diameter 185mm	63.00	86.00	30.00

GLOVE FORMER HANDS

These porcelain hands are produced by Wade for companies making latex gloves for industrial use.

Photograph not available
at press time

Backstamp: Printed "Wade England" between two lines

No.	Description	Colourways	Size	U.S.$	Can.$	U.K.£
1.	Hand	Black	430	25.00	35.00	15.00
2.	Hand	White	430	25.00	35.00	15.00

LABORATORY DISHES, c.LATE 1940s - 1953

At some time between the late 1940s to 1953 Wade produced a number of laboratory dishes and bowls for use in the laboratoies of British pharmaceutical companies. Wade have a reputation for making heat resistant porcelain, a quality needed in laboratory work. The two items found were produced in a an eggshell thin translucent bone china.

Backstamp: **A.** Blue ink stamp on side of pot "Wade England 1"
B. Blue ink stamp on side of dish "Wade England 4"

No.	Description	Colourways	Size	U.S.$	Can.$	U.K.£
1.	Mixing bowl with pouring lip	White; blue tinted edges	55 x 110	35.00	50.00	25.00
2.	Pot	White; blue tinted edges	38	25.00	35.00	18.00

MB UNKNOWN PRIVATE COMMISSION

PEN-AND-INK HOLDER

The pen-and-ink holder has four holes with the letters *MB* and a star in a circle on the front. It was produced circa 1980.

Pen-and-Ink Holder

Backstamp: Unmarked

No.	Description	Colourways	Size	U.S.$	Can.$	U.K.£
1.	Pen-and-Ink Holder	Off white; blue print	35 x 85	25.00	30.00	12.00

MEIN ZAHNARZT (My Dentist)

This teapot is from the same mould that was used for the "Cockleshell Pier Theatre" teapot. The wording on the front roughly translates as "My Dentist," and the colourful transfer print on the front shows a man with a bandaged jaw walking into the dentist's office. The commissioner of this teapot is unknown.

Backstamp: Printed "Wade England"

No.	Description	Colourways	Size	U.S.$	Can.$	U.K.£
1.	Teapot	White; red roof; multi-coloured print	159	30.00	45.00	22.00

PAPER WEIGHTS c.1996 - 1997

These paper weights were produced by Wade PDM sometime during 1996 - 1997. To date the commissioners are unknown. Surplus paperweights were available from the Wade shop in early 1997 for £5.00

Backstamp: None

No.	Description	Colourways	Size	U.S.$	Can.$	U.K.£
1.	Nautical Map	White; multi-coloured print of map	Round/93	38.00	50.00	25.00
2.	Yacht Race America winning the cup Isle of Wight, England 1851	White; multi-coloured print of yacht black lettering	Round/93	38.00	50.00	25.00

POT LID, c.1996 - 1997

This pot lid is similar in design to the nautical paper weight, but in this version the animals are missing from the design.

Photograph not
available at press time

Backstamp: None

No.	Description	Colourways	Size	U.S.$	Can.$	U.K.£
1.	Pot Lid Globe	White; multi-coloured globe print	Round/80	25.00	35.00	12.00

PROFESSIONAL MERCHANDISER TANKARD 1960s

The commissioner is unknown for this traditional tankard; there is a company logo on the reverse side.

Backstamp: Red printed "Wade England"

No.	Description	Colourways	Size	U.S.$	Can.$	U.K.£
1.	Tankard	Black; gold rim, print and lettering	Pint/115	10.00	14.00	5.00

Sunderland Football Club
Centenary Tankard 1879 - 1979

FIGURES

The production of Wade figures began in late 1927. "Pavlova" was the first Wade figure to be produced followed by "Curtsey" and "Romance." In 1930 a talented modeller, Jessie Van Hallen, was employed by the company to increase their production. With her input Wade figures started to appear in large numbers at various trade shows and retail outlets. Original cost of the figures was 10/6d.

All Wade figures are slip cast and therefore hollow, with a circular casting hole in the base. Initially they were glazed with what was at that time a new Scintillite cellulose glaze. In 1939 and again in the late 1940s to the mid 1950s, a number of models were produced in high-gloss glaze. These figures command a much higher price than the cellulose-glazed figures and are considered extremely rare.

The figures are divided into three sections—Cellulose Figures, 1927-1939; High-Gloss Figures, 1939 to the the mid 1950s; Sets and Series, c.1948 to the present. The models are listed alphabetically within the cellulose and high-gloss sections. The sets and series are presented in chronological order.

Care and Handling

The Scintillite glaze easily chips and flakes off models that have been kept in direct sunlight or in damp conditions. Most of these figures now have varying degrees of flaking. On no account should the collector try to touch up these models as it will detract from their value. If models have more white porcelain exposed than glazing, the job of restoration should be done by a professional.

Pricing

The degree of flaking on the cellulose figures will affect the price. Prices in this catalogue are for figures with a moderate degree of flaking. Mint figures with no flaking will command higher prices than those listed here, while figures with excessive flaking will be worth much less.

BACKSTAMPS

Cellulose Figures

The earliest Wade figures were produced with a rarely seen backstamp that included a grey ink-stamped owl. Because some models were reissued once or twice, they can be found with two or three different backstamps on the base. The following backstamps can be found on the cellulose figures:

1927-1930: Paper label "Scintillite Ware," grey ink stamp "BCM/OWL Made in England" and owl's head, with the name of the model hand painted in red

1927-1930: Grey ink stamp of an owl over "British Scintillite REGD" and "Made in England" (or British Make with the name of the model hand painted in red (some include "Red - Ashay" and registration number)

1930-c.1935: Grey ink stamp of an owl over "British Scintillite REGD," black handwritten "Wade Figures," black ink stamp "Made in England" and the name of the model hand painted in black (with and without Jessie Van Hallen's signature hand painted in black)

Mid 1930s: Black hand painted Wade Figures, a red ink stamp of a leaping deer with "Made in England" and the name of the figure handwritten in black

c.1930-c.1939: Black hand painted "Wade," a red ink stamp of a leaping deer over "Made in England" and the name of the figure handwritten in black

1938-1939: 1) Black hand painted "Wade," black ink stamp "Made in England" (may include Great Britain) and the name of the figure handwritten in black
2) Black handwritten "Pageant Made in England" and black handwritten name of the figure

1939: 1) Black hand painted "Wade England" with the name of the figure handwritten in black
2) The name of the figure handwritten in black

Numbers or a letter written in black on the base along with the backstamp do not signify the order in which the models were produced. Instead, they identify the decorator or that it is a second version of the model.

High-Gloss Figures

The following backstamps are found on the high-gloss figures:

1939: 1) Blue handwritten "Wade England 1939" and the figure name
2) Black handwritten "Wade England"

c.1948-c.1952: Blue handwritten "Wade England" and the figure name

c.1948-c.1955: Black or green ink stamp "Wade England" (sometimes includes the name of the figure)

Sets and Series

The figures of the sets and series were backstamped as follows:

c.1945-c.1952: Black ink stamp "Wade England"

1962-1963: Black transfer print "Irish Porcelain Made in Ireland"

1977: Black ink stamp "Made in Ireland"

1977-1986: Black transfer print "Irish Porcelain Made in Ireland" with shamrock or inside Irish-knot wreath

1986: 1) Black transfer print "Irish Porcelain Made in Ireland"
2) Black transfer print "Irish Porcelain Figures Made in Ireland" inside an Irish-knot wreath

1990-1992: Red or grey transfer print "My Fair Ladies, fine porcelain, Wade Made in England" with the figure name

1991: 1) Red transfer print "Wade England"
2) Green ink stamp "Seagoe Ceramics Wade Ireland 1991"

Alfie and Peggy

Anita

Ann

Anton

Argentina, no bracelets

Argentina, with bracelets

No.	Name	Colourways	Size	U.S.$	Can.$	U.K.£
1.	Alfie and Peggy	Grey wall; green shawl; yellow clothes	150	350.00	450.00	225.00
2.	Alfie and Peggy	Green wall, shawl; yellow clothes	150	350.00	450.00	225.00
3.	Alfie and Peggy	Green wall; red shawl; green clothes	150	350.00	450.00	225.00
4.	Anita	Grey ruff; multi-coloured suit; yellow wall	170	275.00	360.00	185.00
5.	Anita	Orange ruff; multi-coloured suit; grey wall	170	275.00	360.00	185.00
6.	Ann	Yellow top; red/brown skirt	145	250.00	300.00	135.00
7.	Anna	Black hair band, tutu, ballet slippers	160		Rare	
8.	Anna	Green hair band; yellow/green/orange tutu; black ballet slippers	160		Rare	
9.	Anton	Black cape; black/yellow/red suit; red hat	135	275.00	360.00	185.00
10.	Anton	Red cape; black/yellow/pink suit; black hat	135	275.00	360.00	185.00
11.	Anton	Red cape, hat; black/yellow/green suit	135	275.00	360.00	185.00
12.	Anton	Green cape; black/yellow/red suit; red hat	135	275.00	360.00	185.00
13.	Argentina, bracelets	Mauve dress; black scarf	240	350.00	450.00	190.00
14.	Argentina, bracelets	Black/red/orange dress; orange scarf	240	350.00	450.00	190.00
15.	Argentina, bracelets	Black/red/green/yellow dress; yellow scarf	240	350.00	450.00	190.00
16.	Argentina, without bracelets	Yellow/red/orange dress; black/yellow scarf	240	350.00	450.00	190.00
17.	Argentina, without bracelets	Red dress; black scarf	240	350.00	450.00	190.00

Note: Condition is important in pricing due to the poor aging of these figurines.

Barbara

Betty, Style One

Betty, Style Two

Betty, Style Three

No.	Name	Colourways	Size	U.S.$	Can.$	U.K.£
18.	Barbara	Pink/yellow bonnet; pink ribbons; yellow/green dress	210	245.00	325.00	150.00
19.	Barbara	Black/pink bonnet; green ribbons, pink/yellow dress	210	245.00	325.00	150.00
20.	Barbara	Orange bonnet; black/orange ribbons, pale orange dress	210	245.00	325.00	150.00
21.	Betty, Style One	Black hair; yellow/orange dress; yellow/black fan	115	215.00	285.00	125.00
22.	Betty, Style Two	Black hair; yellow/maroon dress; yellow flowers	125	215.00	285.00	125.00
23.	Betty, Style Two	Black hair; pink/red dress; pink/yellow flowers	125	215.00	285.00	125.00
24.	Betty, Style Two	Black hair; yellow dress	125	215.00	285.00	125.00
25.	Betty, Style Three	Black hair/cat; grey blue dress; pink/blue flowers	125	225.00	250.00	125.00

Bride

Carmen

Carnival

No.	Name	Colourways	Size	U.S.$	Can.$	U.K.£
26.	Blossoms with Mirror	Black hair; pink shawl	200	450.00	600.00	300.00
27.	Boy Scout	Beige uniform; green base	Unkn.		Rare	
28.	Bride	Cream dress, lilies; pink garland in hair	190	400.00	500.00	250.00
29.	Carmen	Orange dress; red shoes; red/yellow earrings	265	675.00	900.00	450.00
30.	Carmen	Orange dress; black shoes; gold earrings;	265	675.00	900.00	450.00
31.	Carmen	Green/yellow dress; gold earrings	265	675.00	900.00	450.00
32.	Carmen	Red dress, earrings	265	675.00	900.00	450.00
33.	Carmen	Yellow/orange/black dress; yellow earrings	265	675.00	900.00	450.00
34.	Carnival	Maroon bodice; yellow skirt; brown hat, pompon	245	240.00	300.00	150.00
35.	Carnival	Green dress, pompon; black hat	245	240.00	300.00	150.00
36.	Carnival	Orange/black dress; black hat; orange pompon	245	240.00	300.00	150.00

Carole

Cherry

Christina

Claude with Coin

No.	Name	Colourways	Size	U.S.$	Can.$	U.K.£
37.	Carole	Black/red dress; red shoes	215	245.00	325.00	150.00
38.	Carole	Red/yellow dress; red shoes	215	245.00	325.00	150.00
39.	Cherry with Cherries	Red dress; yellow/green sash; black hair	250	245.00	325.00	150.00
40.	Cherry with Cherries	Red/yellow dress; green sash; black hair	250	245.00	325.00	150.00
41.	Choir Boy	White smock; red cassock	190	245.00	325.00	150.00
42.	Christina	Black hair; pink shirt; yellow trousers; yellow dog	275	275.00	360.00	185.00
43.	Christina	Black hair; yellow shirt; brown trousers; black/brown dog	275	275.00	360.00	185.00
44.	Christina	Yellow hair, shirt; gold/brown trousers; grey/yellow dog	275	275.00	360.00	185.00
45.	Claude with Cards	Green coat, trousers; red waistcoat; brown cloak	200	550.00	625.00	300.00
46.	Claude with Coin	Black/brown coat; blond hair; green trousers; maroon/brown cloak	200	550.00	625.00	300.00
47.	Claude with Coin	Black/brown coat; brown hair; yellow trousers; black cloak	200	550.00	625.00	300.00
48.	Claude with Coin	Black coat; pink waistcoat; yellow trousers; green cloak	200	550.00	625.00	300.00
49.	Claude with Coin	Green coat; yellow waistcoat; gold trousers; black cloaks	200	550.00	625.00	300.00

Colorado

Conchita

Curls

Curtsey

Cynthia

Daisette

No.	Name	Colourways	Size	U.S.$	Can.$	U.K.£
50.	Colorado	Man red/black jacket; black trousers Woman red/yellow dress	245	750.00	1,000.00	500.00
51.	Colorado	Man black suit; yellow waistcoat Woman yellow dress	245	750.00	1,000.00	500.00
52.	Colorado	Man black suit; yellow waistcoat Woman red dress	245	750.00	1,000.00	500.00
53.	Conchita	Green/ yellow dress; yellow fan; orange shoes	220	225.00	300.00	150.00
54.	Curls	Dark brown hair, puppy	120	245.00	325.00	150.00
55.	Curls	Pale yellow hair, puppy; pale green nappy	120	245.00	325.00	150.00
56.	Curls	Light brown hair, puppy; blue eyes; yellow/green nappy	120	245.00	325.00	150.00
57.	Curtsey, Style One	Yellow bonnet, ribbon; green/yellow dress	125	165.00	250.00	95.00
58.	Curtsey, Style One	Yellow/red bonnet; yellow ribbon; red/black dress	125	165.00	250.00	95.00
59.	Curtsey, Style One	Black bonnet; yellow ribbon; pink dress	125	165.00	250.00	95.00
60.	Curtsey, Style One	Black/yellow bonnet; yellow ribbon; red/yellow dress	125	165.00	250.00	95.00
61.	Curtsey, Style One	Black bonnet; pink ribbon, dress	125	165.00	250.00	95.00
62.	Curtsey, Style One	Black/green bonnet; yellow ribbon, bodice; maroon dress	125	165.00	250.00	95.00
63.	Curtsey, Style One	Black/pink bonnet; blue dress	125	165.00	250.00	85.00
64.	Curtsey, Style Two	Pale blue bonnet/dress; moulded pink flowers	120	165.00	250.00	95.00
65.	Cynthia	Yellow bonnet; green ribbon; cream dress	110	165.00	250.00	95.00
66.	Cynthia	Green bonnet; red ribbon; cream flowered dress	110	165.00	250.00	95.00
67.	Cynthia	Black bonnet; orange ribbons; cream flowered dress	110	165.00	250.00	95.00
68.	Cynthia	Black/pink bonnet; green ribbons; yellow dress	110 x 45	165.00	250.00	95.00
69.	Cynthia	Pink bonnet; pale green ribbons; pink dress	110 x 45	165.00	250.00	95.00

Dawn, Version One

Dawn, Version Two

Delight

Dolly Varden

Elf

Ginger

No.	Name	Colourways	Size	U.S.$	Can.$	U.K.£
70.	Daisette	Multi-coloured dress; silver petticoat, shoes	250	400.00	500.00	250.00
71.	Dawn, Version One	Green dress, scarf	205	365.00	500.00	200.00
72.	Dawn, Version One	Yellow dress; maroon scarf	205	365.00	500.00	200.00
73.	Dawn, Version One	Yellow dress, scarf	205	365.00	500.00	200.00
74.	Dawn, Version Two	Yellow/red dress, scarf	205	365.00	500.00	200.00
75.	Delight	Yellow hair; multi-coloured flowers; green base	75	400.00	500.00	250.00
76.	Dolly Varden	Maroon hat; yellow/orange dress, bows; green shoes	265	300.00	350.00	175.00
77.	Dolly Varden	Yellow hat, dress, bows; mauve shoes	265	300.00	350.00	175.00
78.	Dolly Varden	Yellow hat, dress; black bows; red shoes	265	300.00	350.00	175.00
79.	Dolly Varden	Brown hat; yellow dress, shoes	260	300.00	350.00	175.00
80.	Dolly Varden	Brown hat; yellow dress, shoes	260	300.00	350.00	175.00
81.	Dora	Nude; black hair; long pink/maroon robe	190	400.00	500.00	250.00
82.	Elf	Dark green butterfly, base	100	300.00	350.00	175.00
83.	Elf	Yellow butterfly; light green base	100	300.00	350.00	175.00
84.	Elf	Blue/red butterfly; pink base	100	300.00	350.00	175.00
85.	Elf	Pink/yellow butterfly; pink base	100	300.00	350.00	175.00
86.	Ginger	Silver hat, shoes; silver/lilac suit	245	600.00	700.00	350.00
87.	Ginger	Black hat, suit, shoes	245	600.00	700.00	350.00
88.	Ginger	Black hat; orange/yellow suit	245	600.00	700.00	350.00

Gloria

Grace, long-stemmed flowers

Grace, short-stemmed flowers

Greta

Harriet with Flowers

Harriet with Fruit

No.	Name	Colourways	Size	U.S.$	Can.$	U.K.£
89.	Gloria, Version One (hand out)	Maroon fan/shawl; yellow/orange skirt	135	215.00	285.00	125.00
90.	Gloria, Version Two (hand on fan)	Yellow/orange fan, skirt; black/maroon shawl	135	215.00	285.00	125.00
91.	Gloria, Version Two (hand on fan)	Maroon fan, shawl; red/yellow dress	135	215.00	285.00	125.00
92.	Gloria, Version Two (hand on fan)	Yellow/red fan; black/yellow shawl; green/orange dress	135	215.00	285.00	125.00
93	Gloria, Version Two (hand on fan)	Maroon fan, shawl; red/black dress	135	215.00	285.00	125.00
94.	Grace, Version One	Pink hat; yellow dress; long-stemmed pink flowers	245	245.00	325.00	150.00
95.	Grace, Version Two	Green hat; yellow dress; short-stemmed orange/yellow flowers	245	245.00	325.00	150.00
96.	Greta	Green dress, shoes	198	450.00	550.00	250.00
97.	Greta	Yellow/green/pink dress; yellow shoes	198	450.00	550.00	250.00
98.	Harriet with Flowers	Black hat; red feather, shawl; yellow blouse, apron; green/yellow skirt	210	400.00	530.00	200.00
99.	Harriet with Flowers	Black hat; yellow feather; green shawl; yellow blouse, apron; green/yellow skirt	210	400.00	530.00	200.00
100.	Harriet with Fruit	Green hat; yellow feather; black shawl; yellow skirt	210	400.00	530.00	200.00
101.	Harriet with Fruit	Black hat; red feather, maroon shawl; yellow skirt	210	400.00	530.00	200.00

Helga

Hille Bobbe

Humoresque

Iris

No.	Name	Colourways	Size	U.S.$	Can.$	U.K£
102.	Helga	Yellow hair; yellow/orange dress; black scarf, shoes	230	425.00	460.00	230.00
103.	Helga	Yellow hair, scarf, shoes; yellow/red dress	230	425.00	460.00	230.00
104.	Helga	Black hair; yellow/green dress, scarf	230	425.00	460.00	230.00
105.	Helga	Black hair; red/black dress; black scarf	230	425.00	460.00	230.00
106.	Hille Bobbe	Green/yellow/black dress; brown table	255	200.00	250.00	125.00
107.	Hille Bobbe	Blue dress; cream collar, apron	255	200.00	250.00	125.00
108.	Hille Bobbe	Brown dress; yellow bonnet	255	200.00	250.00	125.00
109.	Hille Bobbe	Green dress; yellow bonnet	255	200.00	250.00	125.00
110.	Humoresque	Green hat, pompon, shoes, bobbles; yellow/orange dress	200	245.00	325.00	150.00
111.	Humoresque	Black hat, shoes, bobbles; red pompon; red dress	200	245.00	325.00	150.00
112.	Humoresque	Red hat, bobbles; black pompon, shoes; yellow/green dress	200	245.00	325.00	150.00
113.	Humoresque	Black hat, shoes; red pompon, bobbles; black/red dress	200	245.00	325.00	150.00
114.	Iris	Black dress with yellow/green/orange splashes; light brown hair	190	300.00	350.00	175.00

Jean

Jeanette

Jose

Joy

No.	Name	Colourways	Size	U.S.$	Can.$	U.K.£
115.	Jean	Yellow hat; yellow/green dress; black base	170	300.00	350.00	175.00
116.	Jeanette	Yellow flowered dress; yellow gloves; black hat	145	245.00	325.00	150.00
117.	Jeanette	Yellow/orange/black dress; yellow gloves; black hat	145	245.00	325.00	150.00
118.	Jeanette	Green/yellow dress; yellow gloves; black hat	145	245.00	325.00	150.00
119.	Jeanette	Red dress; black hat, gloves	145	245.00	325.00	150.00
120.	Joie Ballerina	Yellow dress, slippers	110	300.00	350.00	175.00
121.	Jose	Pink/yellow/lilac dress	110	125.00	155.00	85.00
122.	Jose	Green/yellow dress	110	125.00	155.00	85.00
123.	Jose	Green/blue dress	110	125.00	155.00	85.00
124.	Jose	Yellow/orange dress	110	125.00	155.00	85.00
125.	Jose	Yellow dress	110	125.00	155.00	85.00
126.	Joy	Yellow/orange dress; orange shoes; floral cap	245	550.00	625.00	300.00
127.	Joy	Yellow/red dress; green shoes; floral cap	245	550.00	625.00	300.00
128.	Joy	Yellow flowered dress; green shoes; floral cap	245	550.00	625.00	300.00

Joyce

June

Lady Gay

Lotus/Anna May Wong

Lupino Lane

Madonna and Child

No.	Name	Colourways	Size	U.S.$	Can.$	U.K.£
129.	Joyce	Yellow/green dress; black hat; red shoes	185	300.00	350.00	175.00
130.	Joyce	Black/yellow dress; multi-coloured hat; green shoes	185	300.00	350.00	175.00
131.	Joyce	Black/gold dress; black hat, shoes	185	300.00	350.00	175.00
132.	June	Yellow hat; maroon suit, shoes	180	245.00	325.00	150.00
133.	June	Yellow/green hat, suit; yellow shoes	180	245.00	325.00	150.00
134.	June	Green hat; yellow suit; red shoes	180	245.00	325.00	150.00
135.	June	Green hat; yellow suit; black shoes	180	245.00	325.00	150.00
136.	June	Yellow hat; red suit; green shoes	180	245.00	325.00	150.00
137.	Lady Gay	Grey hair; brown hat, muff; yellow dress; red stripe	230	400.00	500.00	250.00
138.	Lady Gay	Grey hair; brown hat, muff; red dress; yellow stripe	230	400.00	500.00	250.00
139.	Lady Gay	Brown hair; black/green hat; green dress; yellow/brown muff	230	400.00	500.00	250.00
140.	Lady Gay	Yellow hair; green hat; yellow/green dress, muff	225	400.00	500.00	250.00
141.	Lotus/Anna May Wong	Orange/green brassiere, skirt; orange shoes	245	400.00	500.00	250.00
142.	Lotus/Anna May Wong	Yellow/green brassiere, skirt; yellow shoes	245	400.00	500.00	250.00
143.	Lupino Lane	Red/white crown, cloak	100	175.00	250.00	100.00
144.	Madonna and Child	Cream scarf; green robe	340	400.00	500.00	250.00

Maria Theresa

Midnight

Mimi

Mother and Child

Pavlova

No.	Name	Colourways	Size	U.S.$	Can.$	U.K.£
145.	Maria Theresa	Maroon/orange/green dress	195	400.00	500.00	250.00
146.	Midnight	Grey hair; black and cream tutu;	Unkn.		Rare	
147.	Mimi	Mottled red dress; yellow top; black shoes	190	365.00	500.00	200.00
148.	Mimi	Black dress, shoes	190	365.00	500.00	200.00
149.	Mimi	Red/yellow dress; red shoes	190	365.00	500.00	200.00
150.	Mimi	Green dress; brown shoes	190	365.00	500.00	200.00
151.	Mother and Child	Mother: brown hair; yellow dress	229	350.00	500.00	250.00
152.	Pavlova, Large	Orange/yellow dress; orange hat, shoes	240	300.00	400.00	200.00
153.	Pavlova, Large	Green/yellow dress; yellow hat, shoes	240	300.00	400.00	200.00
154.	Pavlova, Large	Yellow dress; black hat, shoes	240	300.00	400.00	200.00
155.	Pavlova, Large	Red dress; black hat, shoes	240	300.00	400.00	200.00
156.	Pavlova, Large	Pink dress; black hat, shoes	240	300.00	400.00	200.00
157.	Pavlova, Large	Black/orange dress, hat	240	300.00	400.00	200.00
158.	Pavlova, Large	Green dress, hat	240	300.00	400.00	200.00
159.	Pavlova, Large	Red/yellow dress; black hat, shoes	240	300.00	400.00	200.00
160.	Pavlova, Large	Yellow/maroon dress; maroon hat	240	300.00	400.00	200.00
161.	Pavlova, Large	Black/orange hat; yellow/orange dress	240	475.00	630.00	200.00
162.	Pavlova, Large	Black/yellow hat; yellow/turquoise blue dress	240	300.00	400.00	200.00
163.	Pavlova, Small	Red/yellow dress; yellow hat	110	175.00	250.00	100.00

Peggy

Phyllis

Pompadour

Princess Elizabeth

No.	Name	Colourways	Size	U.S.$	Can.$	U.K.£
164.	Pavlova, Small	Green dress; black hat	110	175.00	250.00	100.00
165.	Pavlova, Small	Pink dress; black hat	110	175.00	250.00	100.00
166.	Pavlova, Small	Black dress, hat	110	175.00	250.00	100.00
167.	Pavlova, Small	Blue/yellow/orange dress; black hat	110	175.00	250.00	100.00
168.	Peggy	Yellow/pink dress; black hat, shoes	175	245.00	325.00	150.00
169.	Peggy	Yellow dress; green hat, shoes	175	245.00	325.00	150.00
170.	Peggy	Yellow dress, hat; black shoes	175	245.00	325.00	150.00
171.	Phyllis	Yellow/ orange dress; pink/bustle; black hat, shoes	180	300.00	350.00	175.00
172.	Phyllis	Pink dress; brown bustle; black hat, shoes	180	300.00	350.00	175.00
173.	Pompadour	Yellow/maroon dress; maroon fan	150	245.00	325.00	150.00
174.	Pompadour	Cream/yellow/orange dress; green fan	150	245.00	325.00	150.00
175.	Pompadour	Yellow/maroon dress; red fan	150	245.00	325.00	150.00
176.	Pompadour	Yellow/orange/black dress; orange fan	150	245.00	325.00	150.00
177.	Pompadour	Orange dress; green fan	150	245.00	325.00	150.00
178.	Princess Elizabeth	Yellow/orange dress; grey shoes; black stool	150	300.00	350.00	175.00
179.	Princess Elizabeth	Pink dress; white shoes; brown stool	150	300.00	350.00	175.00
180.	Princess Elizabeth	Green dress; black shoes	150	300.00	350.00	175.00
181.	Princess Elizabeth	Yellow dress; green shoes	150	300.00	350.00	175.00

Queenie

Rhythm

Romance

Sadie

No.	Name	Colourways	Size	U.S.$	Can.$	U.K.£
182.	Queenie	Pink/yellow dress; green hair band; pink/black fan	100	175.00	250.00	100.00
183.	Queenie	Yellow/pink dress; pink hair band; pink fan	100	175.00	250.00	100.00
184.	Queenie	Yellow/red dress; green hair band; green/red fan	100	175.00	250.00	100.00
185.	Rhythm	Red dress; black hair	230	350.00	380.00	190.00
186.	Rhythm	Yellow/green dress; black hair	230	350.00	380.00	190.00
187.	Rhythm	Green mottled dress; black hair	230	350.00	380.00	190.00
188.	Rhythm	Red/black dress; black hair	230	350.00	380.00	190.00
189.	Romance	Yellow/orange/black dress; yellow parasol	165	250.00	350.00	155.00
190.	Romance	Yellow/green dress	165	250.00	350.00	155.00
191.	Romance	Orange dress, parasol	165	250.00	350.00	155.00
192.	Romance	Yellow/green all over	165	250.00	350.00	155.00
193.	Sadie	Yellow wall; maroon hat; orange suit	350	350.00	380.00	190.00
194.	Sadie	Yellow wall, hat; green suit	350	350.00	380.00	190.00
195.	Sadie	Brown wall; red suit	350	350.00	380.00	190.00
196.	Sandra	Green scarf, bolero, skirt	230	300.00	350.00	175.00
197.	Sleepyhead	Yellow pillow; dull yellow all over	140	245.00	325.00	150.00
198.	Sleepyhead	Orange/yellow pillow; green/yellow coat	140	245.00	325.00	150.00

Springtime

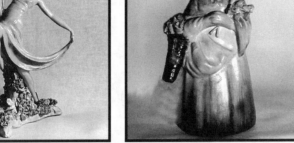

Strawberry Girl

Sunshine

Susan

Sylvia

No.	Name	Colourways	Size	U.S.$	Can.$	U.K.£
199.	Springtime	Red shoes; yellow dress; green base	235	420.00	550.00	275.00
200.	Springtime	Yellow shoes, dress; green base	235	420.00	550.00	275.00
201.	Springtime	Green shoes; yellow dress; green base	235	420.00	550.00	275.00
202.	Strawberry Girl	Red hat; green/yellow dress; brown basket	135	300.00	350.00	175.00
203.	Strawberry Girl	Blue hat; orange dress; brown basket	135	300.00	350.00	175.00
204.	Sunshine	Green/orange jacket, green/yellow dress	165	185.00	245.00	125.00
205.	Sunshine	Black/green jacket; yellow/orange dress	165	185.00	245.00	125.00
206.	Sunshine	Maroon jacket; orange/yellow dress	165	185.00	245.00	125.00
207.	Sunshine	Green dress	165	185.00	245.00	125.00
208.	Sunshine	Yellow jacket; yellow/orange dress	165	185.00	245.00	125.00
209.	Sunshine	Green/yellow jacket; yellow/orange dress	165	185.00	245.00	125.00
210.	Sunshine	Blue and yellow streaked dress	165	185.00	245.00	125.00
211.	Susan	Orange/yellow dress; green belt; yellow daffodils	135	330.00	450.00	225.00
212.	Sylvia	Yellow/green dress; silver sandals	200	300.00	350.00	175.00
213.	Sylvia	Yellow dress; brown sandals	200	300.00	350.00	175.00
214.	Sylvia	Black dress with red/yellow/green patches; silver sandals	200	300.00	350.00	175.00
215.	Sylvia	Red/yellow dress; gold sandals	200	300.00	350.00	175.00
216.	Sylvia	Black dress with red/yellow/green patches; green sandals	200	300.00	350.00	175.00

Tessa

Tony

Trixie

Zena, Large

No.	Name	Colourways	Size	U.S.$	Can.$	U.K.œ
217.	Tessa	Yellow dress; green bow; black shoes	120	215.00	285.00	125.00
218.	Tessa	Green flowered dress; pink bow; black shoes	120	215.00	285.00	125.00
219.	Tessa	Green/yellow dress; pink bow; black shoes	120	215.00	285.00	125.00
220.	Tessa	Pink dress, bow; black shoes; brown bench	120	215.00	285.00	125.00
221.	Tony	Cream suit; black hat, shoes	120	215.00	285.00	125.00
222.	Trixie	Cream/red hat; brown/cream suit; red gloves, shoes	255	365.00	500.00	200.00
223.	Zena, Large	Green hat; yellow/orange dress	220	350.00	380.00	190.00
224.	Zena, Large	Maroon/green hat; red/yellow dress	220	350.00	380.00	190.00
225.	Zena, Large	Black/green hat; black/green/red/yellow dress	220	350.00	380.00	190.00
226.	Zena, Small	Yellow hat; yellow/orange dress; red shoes	105	185.00	245.00	125.00
227.	Zena, Small	Green hat; green/yellow dress	105	185.00	245.00	125.00
228.	Zena, Small	Pink/ yellow hat, dress	105	185.00	245.00	125.00
229.	Zena, Small	Blue/green hat, dress	105	185.00	245.00	125.00

Derivatives

Models on Mirrors, c.1935-1939

Some figures have been found mounted on a base with an oval or round mirror. In the 1938 trade papers, Wade advertised the model "Blossoms" attached to a mirror decorated in porcelain flowers. Mirrors that were not incorporated into the design and had no floral decoration were not produced by Wade. Models found mounted with a plain mirror were attached by another company. Backstamps are unavailable on attached figures. The Pavlova mirror model has a moulded wall, pillar, shrubs and flowers on a three stepped base; Pavlova stands to one side of the circular mirror.

Sunshine and Mirror

No.	Name	Colourways	Size	U.S.$	Can.$	U.K.£
1.	Curtsey	Yellow bonnet, ribbon; green/yellow dress	125	185.00	265.00	100.00
2.	Pavlova	Maroon hat; yellow/maroon dress;	240	400.00	465.00	225.00
3.	Pavlova	Green bonnet; yellow dress and shoes	350	400.00	500.00	250.00
4.	Sunshine	Yellow parasol; yellow/green dress	165	215.00	285.00	125.00

Models on Table Lamps, c.1935-1939

Figures have been found mounted on wooden table lamp bases. The wooden bases are usually black. The model of "Phyllis" is moulded in one piece as a table lamp: the tree stump of the original model has been extended to form the tree trunk lamp holder. Note: There are no moulded flowers on this model.

| Curtsey | Pavlova | Phyllis |

Backstamp: A. Black ink stamped "Made in England" handwritten "Phyllis 3. L" with incised letter *H*
B. Black hand written "Phyllis, 4L"

No.	Name	Colourways	Size	U.S.$	Can.$	U.K. £
1.	Carnival	Black hat; yellow/green balloons, pompon dress	245	250.00	300.00	125.00
2.	Curtsey	Black/yellow bonnet; yellow ribbon; red/yellow dress	125	240.00	290.00	120.00
3.	Curtsey	Yellow bonnet; light orange dress	125	240.00	290.00	120.00
4.	Conchita	Yellow dress	220	240.00	290.00	120.00
5.	Pavlova	Green bonnet; black/yellow/orange dress	240	210.00	320.00	160.00
6.	Phyllis	Black hat; yellow/orange dress; brown tree trunk	177	210.00	320.00	160.00
7.	Phyllis	Black hat; yellow/green dress; brown tree trunk	177	210.00	320.00	160.00
8.	Pompadour	Orange flowered dress; green fan	150	270.00	310.00	135.00
9.	Sunshine	Black/orange bonnet; yellow jacket; yellow/orange dress	165	250.00	300.00	125.00

Models on Bookends and Floral Bases, c.1939

Wade did not attach models to bookends or floral bases; this was done by an outside company marketing such products.

Photograph not available
at press time

No.	Name	Colourways	Size	U.S.$	Can.$	U.K.£
1.	Cynthia	Porcelain floral base; Green/yellow bonnet; green/yellow/brown dress	110	225.00	300.00	150.00
2.	Strawberry Girl	Bookends; Blue hat; orange dress; brown basket	135	240.00	320.00	160.00

PAGEANT FIGURES, 1938-1939

The *Pageant Figures* series is a small set of models based on historical figures, all hand decorated in the cellulose Scintillite glaze. Advertising material suggests that they were produced and offered for sale at the same time as "Barbara," "Zena," "Rhythm," "Daisette" and others created in the late 1930s.

Henry VIII and Elizabeth I

No.	Name	Colourways	Size	U.S.$	Can.$	U.K.£
1.	Henry VIII	Black/white hat, cloak; yellow tunic, shoes	115		Rare	
2.	James I	Yellow cloak; green suit	115		Rare	
3.	Richard the Lionheart	Silver grey chain mail; red cross on white tunic	115		Rare	
4.	Robert the Bruce	Silver grey; dark blue	115		Rare	
5.	Cardinal Wolsey	Red hat, cloak, tunic	115		Rare	
6.	John Knox	Black coat; yellow vest	115		Rare	
7.	Mary, Queen of Scots	White hat; black/white dress	110		Rare	
8.	Elizabeth I	Green/white dress; yellow fan; gold highlights	110		Rare	

Note: Condition is important in pricing.

Table lamp with model of Pavlova

HIGH-GLOSS FIGURES
1939 to the mid 1950s

PINCUSHION DOLLS, 1939

Pincushion dolls are a very popular collectable. They comprise the top half of a lady model, with small holes around the hips with which to attach a dress. The purchaser of the doll sewed, knitted or crocheted a padded dress which formed a pincushion.

The models are hollow and are marked around the rim of the base. Only four varieties of Pincushion dolls have been reported.

Welsh Lady

Backstamp: Green ink stamp "Wade England"

No.	Name	Colourways	Size	U.S.$	Can.$	U.K.£
1.	Gypsy Girl	Black hair, shawl; gold earrings	95	250.00	300.00	150.00
2.	Spanish Lady	Blue dress; pink hair comb	95	250.00	300.00	150.00
3.	Welsh Lady	Black hat; red shawl	95	250.00	300.00	150.00
4.	Welsh Lady	Black hat; green shawl	95	250.00	300.00	150.00
5.	Woman with Bonnet	Yellow bonnet; cream/yellow dress	95	250.00	300.00	150.00

Anita

Betty, Style Two

Curtsey

Cynthia

Hille Bobbe

Iris

No.	Name	Colourways	Size	U.S.$	Can.$	U.K.£
1.	Anita	Black hat/shoes; green ruff; multi-coloured suit; yellow wall	170	485.00	650.00	320.00
2.	Betty, Style Two	White/green/yellow dress; pink flowers	125	340.00	450.00	225.00
3.	Betty, Style Two	Pink dress; yellow/blue garland, flowers	125	340.00	450.00	225.00
4.	Bride	White	190	450.00	600.00	300.00
5.	Choir Boy	White smock; red cassock	205	300.00	350.00	175.00
6.	Curtsey	Cream bonnet, ribbon; green/yellow dress	125	400.00	525.00	265.00
7.	Curtsey	Maroon bonnet, dress; yellow ribbon	125	400.00	525.00	265.00
8.	Curtsey	Grey bonnet; green dress; multi-coloured flowers	125	400.00	525.00	265.00
9.	Curtsey	Black bonnet; pale pink dress; multi-coloured flowers	125	400.00	525.00	265.00
10.	Curtsey	Blue bonnet, dress; pink ribbon	125	400.00	525.00	265.00
11.	Cynthia	Black hat, ribbon; pale pink dress with multi-coloured flowers	110	225.00	300.00	150.00
12.	Cynthia	Black hat; green ribbon; pale pink dress with multi-coloured flowers	110	225.00	300.00	150.00
13.	Cynthia	Yellow hat; pink ribbon; pale pink dress with multi-coloured flowers	110	225.00	300.00	150.00
14.	Harriet with Flowers	Green shawl; white apron; yellow dress	210	340.00	450.00	225.00
15.	Hille Bobbe	White cap/collar/apron/clogs; pastel green blouse; pale blue skirt; mottled blue grey tankard	255	400.00	525.00	300.00
16.	Iris	Pale blue/blue dress; pink/green/gold circles	190	550.00	650.00	325.00
17.	Iris	Pale green/pink dress; gold design	190	550.00	650.00	325.00
18.	Jose	Cream/yellow dress; pink flowers	110	340.00	450.00	225.00

Joy

Juliet

Lady In Armchair

Lady In Armchair with Budgerigar

No.	Name	Colourways	Size	U.S.$	Can.$	U.K.œ
19.	Joy	Pastel green cap, dress, shoes	245	600.00	750.00	380.00
20.	Joy	Pastel blue cap, dress, shoes	245	600.00	750.00	380.00
21.	Juliet	Sage green dress with pink/brown flowers	240	650.00	750.00	400.00
22.	Juliet	White dress with blue/yellow flowers	240	650.00	750.00	400.00
23.	Juliet	Mottled pastel green and blue dress; gold highlights; multi-coloured flowers	240	650.00	750.00	400.00
24.	Lady in Armchair	Pale green dress with flowers	200 x 250	600.00	700.00	350.00
25.	Lady in Armchair with Budgerigar	White dress with flowers	200 x 250	600.00	700.00	350.00
26.	Lady in Armchair with Budgerigar	Multi-coloured dress with flowers	200 x 250	600.00	700.00	350.00
27	Madonna and Child	Cream scarf; green robe	340	400.00	525.00	250.00
28.	Madonna and Child	Cream scarf; pale blue robe	340	375.00	450.00	200.00

Old Nannie

Sunshine

Zena, Large

No.	Description	Colourways	Size	U.S.$	Can.$	U.K.£
29.	Old Nannie	Pale blue dress; white hat, apron	230	400.00	525.00	300.00
30.	Old Nannie	White hat/collar/apron; blue blouse; grey skirt	230	400.00	525.00	300.00
31.	Pavlova, Large	Black hat with multi-coloured flowers; mauve dress	240	290.00	325.00	150.00
32.	Pavlova, Small	Orange hat with multi-coloured flowers; mauve dress	110	180.00	255.00	90.00
33.	Queenie	Cream/pink dress	100	340.00	450.00	225.00
34.	Romance	Pale pink/blue dress; blue parasol; white/yellow sofa	170	225.00	300.00	150.00
35.	Sunshine	Black bonnet; pink feather and dress; pale blue parasol; light green jacket; multi-coloured flowers on dress	165	350.00	465.00	175.00
36.	Sunshine	Black bonnet; pink feather; light grey parasol; maroon jacket; pale blue dress; multi-coloured flowers on dress	165	350.00	465.00	175.00
37.	The Swan Dancer *	Black hair; white hair band, dress	240	450.00	600.00	300.00
38.	Zena, Large	Pastel blue hat; blue/green/pink dress	220	400.00	525.00	300.00
30.	Zena, Large	Grey-blue hat, shoes; dark red dress	220	400.00	525.00	300.00
40.	Zena, Large	Light to dark blue dress; pink bodice/hat/gold highlights	220	400.00	525.00	300.00
41.	Zena, Small	Blue/green hat; lilac dress	100	340.00	450.00	225.00

Notes: **A:** * "The Swan Dancer" is also known as "Pavlova—The Swan."

B: We believe three other models were issued —Amy, Joan and The Lady with Two Greyhounds. We would appreciate any information on these pieces.

1248
Kate

1247
Rachel

1246
Rebecca

1245
Caroline

1241
Marie

1242
Sarah

1244
Lisa

1243
Hannah

My Fair Ladies, 1990 - 1991

SETS AND SERIES
c.1948 to the present

CANTERBURY TALES FIGURES, c.1948-c.1952

These four characters from *The Canterbury Tales* were produced in a limited edition of 100 each. The exact date of production is not known; however the backstamp suggests the period indicated above. A paper label was pasted on the front of the base with a short quote from the poem relating to the model. The label on "The Nun's Priest" reads, "Just look what brawn he has this Gentle Priest." Each figure was produced in two sizes.

The Nun's Priest

No.	Name	Colourways	Size	U.S.$	Can.$	U.K.£
1.	The Nun's Priest	White hat; pale blue cloak; pink robe; beige horse	150		Rare	
2.	The Nun's Priest	Pink hat, robe; grey/blue cloak; beige horse	150		Rare	
3.	The Nun's Priest	White hat; pale blue cloak; pink robe; beige horse	95		Rare	
4.	The Prioress	Dark/light brown habit; grey horse	150		Rare	
5.	The Prioress	Dark/light brown habit; grey horse	95		Rare	
6.	The Reeve	Grey collar; blue robe; white hair; orange-brown horse	150		Rare	
7.	The Reeve	Pink collar; blue robe; white hair; orange-brown horse	150		Rare	
8.	The Reeve	Grey collar; blue robe; white hair; orange-brown horse	95		Rare	
9.	The Squire	Dark blue hat; silver-grey tunic; white hose, horse	150		Rare	
10.	The Squire	Dark blue hat; silver-grey tunic; white hose, horse	95		Rare	

IRISH FOLKLORE CHARACTERS, 1962-1986

This series of figures based on Irish folklore, songs and ballads, were produced in two sizes. The eight small figures (125 to 160 mm) were modelled by William K. Harper, and Phoebe Stabler modelled the three larger (220 - 225 mm) figures.

The backstamps on these models were changed as each model was produced; when models were reissued, different colour variations occured, as well as a difference in the backstamps.

FIRST ISSUE, 1962-63

Dan Murphy

The Irish Emigrant

Little Mickey Mulligan

Backstamps

No.	Name	Colourways	Size	U.S.$	Can.$	U.K.£
11.	Bard of Armagh	Light brown jacket, boots, harp; grey trousers	125	490.00	650.00	325.00
12.	Dan Murphy	Light grey coat, trousers; dark green hat	220	525.00	700.00	360.00
13.	Dan Murphy	Green/brown flecked hat; light grey suit; beige base/green highlights; black shoes	220	525.00	700.00	360.00
14.	Eileen Oge, Style One	Light grey hair; dark blue dress; white apron	225	490.00	650.00	325.00
15.	Irish Emigrant	Light brown suit, hat; blue tie	155	490.00	650.00	325.00
16.	Little Crooked Paddy	Grey suit; beige hat; gold coins	135	490.00	650.00	325.00
17.	Little Mickey Mulligan	Grey/brown coat, trousers	150	490.00	650.00	325.00

Molly Malone, Style One

Phil the Fluter

Star of County Down

Widda Cafferty, Plain Petticoat

Widda Cafferty, Flowered Petticoat

No.	Name	Colourways	Size	U.S.$	Can.$	U.K.£
18.	Molly Malone, Style One	Blue dress; grey cart; pale yellow/blue/pink flowers	150	490.00	650.00	325.00
19.	Mother MacCree, Style One	Light grey shawl, skirt; blue blouse; white apron	225	525.00	700.00	360.00
20.	Phil the Fluter, Style One	White shirt; grey waistcoat; blue trousers; silver flute	160	490.00	650.00	325.00
21.	Star of County Down	Grey dress; white apron; red/yellow comb on chickens	160	490.00	650.00	325.00
22.	Widda Cafferty	Pale blue dress; dark grey shawl, stockings; white apron	160	490.00	650.00	325.00
23.	Widda Cafferty	Grey hair/stockings/dress; brown shawl/boots; white apron; white petticoat with pink flowers	160	500.00	675.00	345.00

SECOND ISSUE, 1977-1986

Some variations in colour were used on these reissues; for example, light grey changed to dark grey and grey-blue changed to blue. Unless the first and second issues are side by side, it is difficult to tell them apart.

Bard of Armagh

Dan Murphy

Eileen Oge, Style One

Little Crooked Paddy

Molly Malone

Mother MacCree, Style One

No.	Description	Colourways	Size	U.S.$	Can.$	U.K.£
24.	Bard of Armagh	Brown jacket; grey trousers; dark brown boots	125	425.00	500.00	250.00
25.	Dan Murphy	Dark brown hat; dark grey trousers	220	490.00	650.00	325.00
26.	Eileen Oge, Style One	Dark grey hair; light blue dress; white apron	225	490.00	650.00	325.00
27.	Irish Emigrant	Brown hat, suit; blue tie	155	425.00	500.00	250.00
28.	Little Crooked Paddy	Grey suit; beige hat; gold coins	135	425.00	500.00	250.00
29.	Little Mickey Mulligan	Brown coat, trousers	150	425.00	500.00	250.00
30.	Molly Malone, Style One	Pale blue dress; beige cart; dark yellow/blue/pink flowers	160	425.00	500.00	250.00
31.	Mother MacCree, Style One	Dark grey shawl, skirt; blue blouse; white apron	225	490.00	650.00	325.00
32.	Phil the Fluter, Style One	White shirt; grey waistcoat; blue trousers; grey flute	160	425.00	500.00	250.00
33.	Star of County Down	Grey blue dress; white apron; yellow comb on chickens	160	425.00	500.00	250.00
34.	Widda Cafferty	Pale blue dress; light grey shawl, stockings; white apron	160	425.00	500.00	250.00

IRISH FOLK-SONG CHARACTERS, 1977-1991

FIRST ISSUE, 1977-1986

This is a set of nine small characters representing well-known Irish folk songs. They were coloured in honey brown and olive-grey glazes. The backstamp washes and wears off easily.

No.	Name	Colourways	Size	U.S.$	Can.$	U.K.£
35.	Danny Boy	Light brown cap, shoes; grey scarf, coat, honey-brown waistcoat/trousers	95	45.00	60.00	30.00
36.	Danny Boy on Marble base	Light brown cap/shoes; grey scarf/coat; honey waistcoat/trousers	117	55.00	75.00	35.00
37.	Eileen Oge, Style Two	Black shawl; blue-grey skirt; honey apron; black shoes	95	40.00	50.00	25.00
38.	Eileen Oge on Marble base	Black shawl; blue grey skirt; honey apron; black shoes; dark grey marble base	117 x 57 x 59	45.00	65.00	35.00
39.	Kathleen	Grey scarf; dark brown fringe on shawl; honey-brown dress	88	40.00	50.00	25.00
40.	Molly Malone, Style Two	Grey scarf; red-brown blouse; grey skirt; honey box of cockles and mussels	88	40.00	50.00	25.00
41	Mother MacCree, Style Two	Honey-brown figure; dark brown shoes; olive-green stool	70	40.00	50.00	25.00

No.	Name	Colourways	Size	U.S.$	Can.$	U.K.£
42.	Paddy McGinty	Honey-brown hat; light brown waistcoat, coat; dark brown boots	90	45.00	60.00	30.00
43.	Paddy Reilly	Olive-grey hat, coat; blue-grey waistcoat; honey trousers; red-brown dog	95	45.00	60.00	30.00
44.	Phil the Fluter, Style Two	Blue waistcoat; olive-grey trousers; dark brown boots	85	45.00	60.00	30.00
45.	Rose of Tralee	Blue-grey bonnet; honey dress	100	45.00	60.00	30.00
46.	Rose of Tralee on Marble base	Blue grey bonnet; honey dress	122	45.00	65.00	35.00

SECOND ISSUE, 1991-1996

The reissued models are in a darker honey glaze and have a different backstamp, although it also washes and wears off easily.

Photograph not available
at press time

No.	Name	Colourways	Size	U.S.$	Can.$	U.K.£
47.	Danny Boy	Dark brown cap, shoes; honey scarf, coat, trousers; grey waistcoat	95	30.00	40.00	20.00
48.	Eileen Oge, Style Two	Dark grey shawl; skirt; dark honey-brown apron; black shoes	95	30.00	40.00	20.00
49.	Kathleen	Grey scarf, shawl; honey-brown dress	88	30.00	40.00	20.00
50.	Molly Malone, Style Two	Grey scarf, skirt; dark honey-brown blouse, box of cockles and mussels	88	30.00	40.00	20.00
51.	Mother MacCree, Style Two	Dark honey-brown figure; grey blouse, honey-brown stool	70	30.00	40.00	20.00
52.	Paddy McGinty	Dark brown hat, coat, boots; light brown waistcoat, trousers	90	45.00	60.00	30.00
53.	Paddy Reilly	Honey-brown hat, coat; grey waistcoat; honey trousers; red-brown dog	95	45.00	60.00	30.00
54.	Phil the Fluter, Style Two	Dark grey waistcoat; dark honey-brown trousers, boots	85	45.00	60.00	30.00
55.	Rose of Tralee	Blue-grey bonnet; dark honey-brown dress	100	40.00	50.00	25.00

Derivatives

Pipe Stands, 1991

No.	Name	Colourways	Size	U.S.$	Can.$	U.K.£
1.	Paddy McGinty	Greenish brown stand; honey-brown figure	95	60.00	80.00	30.00
2.	Phil the Fluter	Greenish brown stand; honey-brown figure	95	60.00	80.00	30.00

THE BABY, 1986

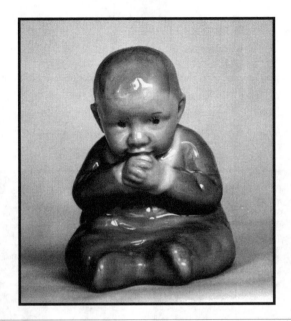

No.	Name	Colourways	Size	U.S.$	Can.$	U.K.£
1.	The Baby	Light brown hair; pale blue suit	110	450.00	600.00	300.00

MY FAIR LADIES, 1990-1991

A series of 16 Victorian-style lady figures was produced in Wade's Royal Victoria Pottery from 1990 to 1991. They were issued in two sets of eight, although only four moulds were used for each set.

A number of these models were also used by Hebrides Scotch Whiskey in late 1992 as decanters. "Natalie" has been found wrongly named "Belinda. "

The grey transfer print backstamp was first used on Set 1 and the red transfer print on Set 2, but because of firing difficulties with the red transfer, the second set was later produced with the grey backstamp.

SET 1, 1990

"Sarah" is from the same mould as "Marie"; "Lisa" is from the same mould as "Hannah"; "Rebecca" is from the same mould as "Caroline" ; "Kate" is from the same mould as "Rachel."

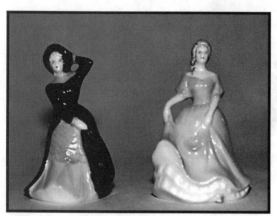

Marie/Sarah and Hannah/Lisa

Caroline/Rebecca and Rachel/Kate

No.	Name	Colourways	Size	U.S.$	Can.$	U.K.œ
1.	Marie	Dark green hat; dark green/grey-green dress	92	25.00	40.00	20.00
2.	Sarah	Greenish grey hat; greenish grey/white dress; pink flowers	92	25.00	40.00	20.00
3.	Hannah	Brown hair; green/grey/white dress	94	40.00	50.00	25.00
4.	Lisa	Brown hair; pastel blue/white dress	94	95.00	120.00	58.00
5.	Caroline	Dark blue hat; yellow flower; dark blue bodice; grey-blue skirt; yellow bow	94	30.00	40.00	20.00
6.	Rebecca	Yellow/beige hat; pink flower; grey bodice; white skirt; pink bow	94	30.00	40.00	20.00
7.	Rachel	White/grey-blue dress; grey-blue hat	96	30.00	40.00	20.00
8.	Kate	Off white/grey/white dress with red roses; grey hat	96	30.00	40.00	20.00

SET 2, 1991

"Amanda" is from the same mould as "Melissa"; "Anita" is from the same mould as "Belinda"; "Natalie" is from the same mould as "Emma"; "Diane" is from the same mould as "Lucy."

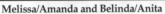

Melissa/Amanda and Belinda/Anita

Emma/Natalie and Lucy/Diane

No.	Name	Colourways	Size	U.S.$	Can.$	U.K.£
9.	Melissa	Light brown hat; dark blue jacket; pale blue skirt; white petticoat	95	95.00	120.00	58.00
10.	Amanda	Dark brown jacket; pink skirt; white petticoat	95	60.00	80.00	35.00
11.	Belinda	Pearl/white/yellow dress	90	45.00	65.00	30.00
12.	Anita	Shell pink dress	90	30.00	40.00	20.00
13.	Emma	White dress; creamy yellow shawl, ribbons, bows	90	40.00	50.00	25.00
14.	Natalie	Pale pink dress; light grey scarf, ribbons, bows	90	45.00	60.00	30.00
15.	Lucy	Grey hat, skirt; dark brown jacket, handbag	90	30.00	40.00	20.00
16.	Diane	Pale blue/white hat, jacket, handbag; off-white skirt	90	30.00	40.00	20.00

SOPHISTICATED LADIES, 1991

This is a limited edition of four hand-decorated lady figures in the style of *My Fair Ladies*. The same four figures were also issued in an all-over, white porcelain glaze.

Some of the first models were mistakenly marked "My Fair Ladies Fine Porcelain Wade England" using a grey transfer print. Later models have a red transfer print which reads "Wade England."

Emily

Felicity

Roxanne

Susannah

No.	Name	Colourways	Size	U.S.$	Can.$	U.K.£
17.	Emily	Blonde hair; pink/white dress; white petticoat	145	150.00	200.00	100.00
18.	Emily	White all over	145	60.00	80.00	40.00
19.	Felicity	Brown hair; dark green jacket; pale yellow skirt	150	150.00	200.00	100.00
20.	Felicity	White all over	150	60.00	80.00	40.00
21.	Roxanne	Blonde hair; pale blue/lilac dress	145	150.00	200.00	100.00
22.	Roxanne	White all over	145	60.00	80.00	40.00
23.	Susannah	Brown hair; orange/yellow dress; white	150	150.00	200.00	100.00
24.	Susannah	White all over	150	60.00	80.00	40.00

JUGS, STEINS
AND TANKARDS
c.1938-1991

Toby jugs are named after an 18th-century drinking character named Toby Philpot. The first toby jug was produced in the early 18th century by the Ralph Wood Pottery of Burslem, Staffordshire. It was modelled after Toby Philpot sitting on a barrel with a glass of ale in his hand and carries his name. The Wadeheath Pottery only produced small quantities of toby jugs, usually in limited numbers of 1,000 of each style. Toby jugs represent the full figure of a person; character jugs depict only the head and shoulders.

Beer steins are replicas of continental-shaped tankards, which are taller and narrower than the British style.

The majority of Wade's tankards were produced in a "traditional shape," which is wider at the base than the top and has a leaf-shaped thumb rest on top of the handle.

Wade Ireland's Ulster Ware tankards are decorated in characteristic mottled blue, green and grey and come in styles completely different from the English tankards. As with the other Wade tankards, these tankards were in almost constant production, and the replacement of worn dies produced tankards in varying sizes (from 105 to 107 millimetres in the half-pint size and from 160 to 162 millimetres in the pint size). Actual sizes are given when known.

BACKSTAMPS

Ink Stamps

Jugs and tankards produced from the late 1940s to the early 1950s are stamped with some variation of "Wade Heath England" or "Wade England."

Reddish brown ink stamp, c.1948-c.1955

Green ink stamp, c.1948-c.1952

Black ink stamp, c.1938, c.1940, c.1952

Impressed and Embossed Backstamps

The Ulster Ware tankards, produced from the early 1950s to the 1980s, all have a variety of impressed or embossed "Wade Ireland" marks. It is difficult to place an accurate date on the early Irish porcelain tankards, as no accurate records were kept. When moulds became worn they were replaced, and sometimes a new backstamp was added.

Impressed, c.1952-c.1962

Impressed, c.1952-c.1980

Some backstamps, especially the embossed types, were incorporated in the mould, and when worn moulds were replaced, the backstamps were not always changed. This resulted in old backstamps being used at the same time as the current one. Some backstamps are found with the letters *A, B, C, E, F, G* or *P* usually incorporated in the centre, under or beside a shamrock leaf. They are the potters mark.

Transfer Prints

From 1953 to the present, most jugs and tankards, except for Ulster Ware, were given transfer-printed backstamps.

Transfer print, 1953-c.1968

Transfer print, 1956-1967

Commissioned pieces issued from the mid 1950s included the name Wade Regicor in the backstamp:

Transfer print, c.1953-c.1958

CHARACTER JUGS

COACHMAN, c.1948

A horse whip forms the handle of this jug.

Backstamp: Black ink stamp "Wade England"

No.	Description	Colourways	Size	U.S.	Can.$	U.K. .£
1.	Coachman	Green	Miniature/80	80.00	100.00	50.00

FISHERMAN, c.1948-c.1953

A fish forms the handle of this jug.

Backstamp: A. Grey ink stamp "Wade England"
           B. Red transfer print "Wade England"

No.	Description	Colourways	Size	U.S.$	Can.$	U.K.£
1.	Fisherman	Beige/pink	Miniature/75	55.00	75.00	40.00
2.	Fisherman	Green	Miniature/75	55.00	75.00	40.00

INDIAN CHIEF, c.1958–c.1962

The "Indian Chief" wears a feathered bonnet.

Photograph not available
at press time

Backstamp: Red transfer print "Wade England"

No.	Description	Colourways	Size	U.S.$	Can.$	U.K.£
1.	Indian Chief	White/brown war bonnet; brown shoulders	Unknown		Rare	

JIM, 1968

This character jug was modelled as the head and shoulders of a smiling man and based on the well-loved British radio and television comedian Jimmy Edwards, famous for his handlebar moustache.

Backstamp: Black ink stamp "Wade Regicor, Hand painted in Staffordshire England" with "Toby Jim Jug" impressed on the back of the collar

No.	Description	Colourways	Size	U.S.$	Can.$	U.K.£
1.	Jim	Black hat; brown moustache; green coat	Large/110	120.00	160.00	85.00

R.C.M.P., c.1958–c.1962

This jug depicts the head and shoulders of an R.C.M.P. officer in uniform with a wide brimmed hat.

Photograph not available
at press time

Backstamp: Red transfer print "Wade England"

No.	Description	Colourways	Size	U.S.$	Can.$	U.K.£
1.	R.C.M.P.	Brown hat; red jacket	Unknown		Rare	

SAILOR, c.1948

This miniature character jug depicts the head of an 18th-century sailor. A plaited rope forms the handle.

Backstamp: Black ink stamp "Wade England"

No.	Description	Colourways	Size	U.S.$	Can.$	U.K.£
1.	Sailor	Green	Miniature/75	55.00	75.00	40.00
2.	Sailor	Honey	Miniature/75	55.00	75.00	40.00
3.	Sailor	Pink	Miniature/75	55.00	75.00	40.00
4.	Sailor	Green/black patterned hat; honey face; brown handle	Miniature/75	55.00	75.00	40.00

BEER STEINS

BEETHOVEN AND MOZART, 1991

These German-style beer steins are decorated with transfer prints of Beethoven or Mozart. The slightly larger size of style No 7 may be due to a new mould.

Backstamp: Gold transfer print "Royal Victoria Pottery Wade England"

No.	Description	Colourways	Size	U.S.$	Can.$	U.K.£
1.	Ludwig van Beethoven	Royal blue; gold portrait, lettering	Small/127	60.00	80.00	30.00
2.	Wolfgang Amadeus Mozart	Royal blue; gold portrait, lettering	Small/127	60.00	80.00	30.00
3.	Ludwig van Beethoven	Royal blue; gold portrait, lettering	Medium/153	60.00	80.00	30.00
4.	Wolfgang Amadeus Mozart	Royal blue; gold portrait, lettering	Medium/153	60.00	80.00	30.00
5.	Ludwig van Beethoven	Royal blue; gold portrait, lettering	Large/177	70.00	95.00	35.00
6.	Wolfgang Amadeus Mozart	Royal blue; gold portrait, lettering	Large/177	70.00	95.00	35.00
7.	Wolfgang Amadeus Mozart	Royal blue; gold portrait, lettering	Large/186	70.00	95.00	35.00

IRISH PORCELAIN STEINS, 1953-c.1980

These steins have two rows of impressed knurls around the rim and two rows of embossed knurls around the base. The print on the "Irish Harp Stein" is of a harp.

Stein, "Plain"

Backstamp: Impressed "Irish Porcelain Made in Ireland" with "Wade" printed across a shamrock
Shape: I.P.3

No.	Description	Colourways	Size	U.S.$	Can.$	U.K.£
1.	Irish Harp Stein	Blue-grey; gold print	½ pint/160	20.00	30.00	10.00
2.	Stein	Grey/blue/brown	½ pint/160	20.00	30.00	12.00

ULSTER WARE STEINS IRISH WADE SHAPE No IP/3

The "Toasts" stein has beer drinking toasts printed around a central shield: "Cheerio" ; "Slainre"; "Chin Chin" etc.

Stein, "Drinking Toasts"

Backstamp: Impressed "Irish Porcelain" (curved over shamrock) "Made in Ireland" (in a straight line underneath shamrock) c.1950s and reissued 1970s

No.	Description	Colourways	Size	U.S.$	Can.$	U.K.£
1.	Stein Leopard heads	Grey blue; yellow/black/gold shield; black lettering	160	30.00	35.00	15.00

THE QUEEN'S MEN, c.1962

The same transfer prints used on the "Queen's Men Tankards" were used on these tall, narrow beer steins, which were produced in a set of four. The transfer prints depict the regiments that guard the Queen's residences and parade through London on ceremonial occasions. Each stein has the legend of the regiment on the back. Some of these tankards have been found in New Zealand with a beige brown rim.

Life Guards

Life Guards Trooper

Backstamp: Black transfer print "By Wade of England"

No.	Description	Colourways	Size	U.S.$	Can.$	U.K.£
1.	The Drum Horse	White; gold rim; multi-coloured print	146	25.00	35.00	12.00
2.	The Life Guards	White; gold rim; multi-coloured print	146	25.00	35.00	12.00
3.	Life Guards Trooper	White; gold rim; multi-coloured print	146	25.00	35.00	12.00
4.	The Scots Guards	White; gold rim; multi-coloured print	146	25.00	35.00	12.00

TOBY JUGS

HIGHWAY MAN, c.1948-c.1955

There were 1,000 "Highway Man Toby Jugs" issued.

Backstamp: A. Brown ink stamp "Wade England" inside an ornate crown
B. Black ink stamp "Wade England Highway Man"

No.	Description	Colourways	Size	U.S.$	Can.$	U.K.£
1.	Highway Man	Black/yellow hat; green coat; black cloak	150	225.00	300.00	135.00
2.	Highway Man	Black hat; green coat; red cloak	150	225.00	300.00	135.00
3.	Highway Man	Copper lustre	150	110.00	150.00	75.00
4.	Highway Man	Gold lustre	150	110.00	150.00	75.00

PIRATE, c.1948-c.1955

There were 750 pirate toby jugs produced.

Backstamp: A. Brown ink stamp" Wade England" inside an ornate crown, with the model name
B. Black ink stamp"Wade England Pirate"

No.	Description	Colourways	Size	U.S.$	Can.$	U.K.£
1.	Pirate	Black/yellow hat; green/yellow coat; purple trousers	150	225.00	300.00	135.00
2.	Pirate	Black hat; green coat; blue trousers	150	225.00	300.00	135.00
3.	Pirate	Copper lustre	150	110.00	150.00	75.00
4.	Pirate	Gold lustre	150	110.00	150.00	75.00

TOBY PHILPOT, c.1953-c.1958

The miniature toby depicts a seated Toby Philpot holding a pint of ale. It has a straight handle. The small and large Toby Philpots are sitting with glass of ale in one hand and a jug in the other.

Photograph not available
at press time

Backstamp: A. Red transfer print "Wade England"
B. Black transfer print "Wade Regicor, Hand painted in Staffordshire, England"

No.	Description	Colourways	Size	U.S.$	Can.$	U.K.£
1.	Toby Philpot	Green coat; black hat, trousers, shoes	Miniature/75	55.00	75.00	40.00
2.	Toby Philpot	Black hat, shoes; white/silver buckles; green coat; red trousers	Small/115	110.00	150.00	75.00
3.	Toby Philpot	Black hat, shoes; white/silver buckles; green coat; red trousers	Large/180	110.00	150.00	75.00

TANKARDS

ANIMALS, c.1955

These traditional tankards all have transfer prints of African animals on them.

Photograph not available
at press time

Backstamp: **A.** Red transfer print "Wade England"
B. Red transfer print "Wade Ireland"

No.	Description	Colourways	Size	U.S.$	Can.$	U.K.£
1.	Eland	Amber; multi-coloured print	Miniature/49	10.00	12.00	8.00
2.	Elephant	Amber; multi-coloured print	Miniature/49	10.00	12.00	8.00
3.	Giraffe	Amber; multi-coloured print	Miniature/49	10.00	12.00	8.00
4.	Lion	Amber; multi-coloured print	Miniature/49	10.00	12.00	8.00
5.	Rhinoceros	Amber; multi-coloured print	Miniature/49	10.00	12.00	8.00
6.	Zebra	Amber; multi-coloured print	Miniature/49	10.00	12.00	8.00

BARBECUE, 1954

These tankards are in the form of a tree trunk with a gnarled-wood pattern. The pint size was produced by Wade England; the half-pint size by Wade Ireland. The original price for the pint tankard was 5/9d.

Backstamp: **A.** Black ink stamp "Wade England"
B. Black ink stamp "Made in Ireland"

No.	Description	Colourways	Size	U.S.$	Can.$	U.K.£
1.	Barbecue	Dark green	½ pint/91	20.00	30.00	10.00
2.	Barbecue	Honey brown	½ pint/91	20.00	30.00	10.00
3.	Barbecue	Dark green	Pint/111	30.00	40.00	20.00
4.	Barbecue	Beige brown	Pint/111	30.00	40.00	20.00
5.	Barbecue	Matt white	Pint/111	30.00	40.00	20.00

BARREL TANKARDS, c.1950c.1962

Barrel Tankards are commonly found in three sizes; however, a fourth—the four-pint size—is very rare. These barrel-shaped tankards were produced in Wade's amber glaze, with four wide silver cross bands and a silver twisted-rope handle.

A miniature tankard bearing a transfer print of the coat of arms of Windsor Castle was produced as a souvenir of England circa 1955. The copper lustre pint barrel tankard was produced circa 1961.

Miniature, 1/2 pint, pint, 4-pint   Windsor Castle

Backstamp: A. Red transfer print "Wade England"
B. Black transfer print "Wade England"

No.	Description	Colourways	Size	U.S.$	Can.$	U.K.£
1.	Barrel	Amber; silver bands, handle	Miniature/49	8.00	10.00	4.00
2.	Windsor Castle	Amber; silver bands, handle; multi-coloured print	Miniature/49	8.00	10.00	4.00
3.	Barrel	Amber; silver bands, handle	½ pint/90	9.00	12.00	4.00
4.	Barrel	Amber; silver bands, handle	Pint/123	10.00	15.00	8.00
5.	Barrel	Copper luster	Pint/123	10.00	15.00	8.00
6.	Barrel	Amber; silver bands, handle	4 pint/190	60.00	80.00	40.00

THE BEERSHIFTER'S TANKARD, c.1965

The poem "The Beershifter's Dream of Paradise" is printed on one side of this traditional tankard, and a print of a hand holding a foaming tankard is on the other.

Backstamp: Gold transfer print "Royal Victoria Pottery Wade England"

No.	Description	Colourways	Size	U.S.$	Can.$	U.K.£
1.	Beershifters	Cream; brown print	Pint/115	10.00	15.00	5.00

THE BURSLEM ASSOCIATION FOR THE PROSECUTION OF FELONS

This pint size traditional tankard was produced for the Burslem Association for the Prosecution of Felons. At one time Colonel George Wade was a president of the association. There is a printed history of the association on the back of this tankard, which states that the association was founded in 1821 with Ralph Wood master potter as president "To assist the forces of justice in pursuing, apprehending and prosecuting felons in Burslem and its surrounding district."

Backstamp: Green printed "Wade England"

No.	Description	Colourways	Size	U.S.$	Can.$	U.K.£
1.	Tankard	Amber; multi-coloured crest; gold lettering	Pint/125	30.00	35.00	20.00

CANADIAN COLLEGES AND UNIVERSITIES

Musical Tankards c.Mid 1970s

Photograph not available
at press time

Backstamp: "Wade Ireland" black ink stamp on rim of base

No.	Description	Colourways	Shape/Size	U.S.$	Can.$	U.K.£
1.	Musical tankard	Blue/grey tankard; gold print	I.P.5	35.00	45.00	30.00

Plymouth Tankards, Late 1950s-early 1960s

Plymouth tankards have "Barrel" plank sides and silver bandingo.

Dalhousie University

Backstamp: "Wade England" in red print

No.	Description	Colourways	Shape/Size	U.S.$	Can.$	U.K.£
1.	Dalhousie University	Amber tankard; red/black crest	Pint/115	18.00	25.00	15.00

Steins, Early-Mid 1980s

There are two types of Wade steins; one has an embossed wreath in the centre on which the crest or logo of the college is printed, the name is printed around the bottom of the stein; the other has a plain centre with the crest or logo of the college—the name is printed around the top rim.

Confederation College

Wilfrid Laurier University

Backstamp: **A.** "Wade England"
             B. "Wade Ireland"

No.	Description	Colourways	Shape/Size	U.S.$	Can.$	U.K.£
1.	Confederation College	Royal blue; gold logo/lettering	153	18.00	25.00	15.00
2.	Lakehead University	White; gold bands/crest/lettering	153	18.00	25.00	15.00
3.	Queens University	Royal blue; gold crest/lettering	153	18.00	25.00	15.00
4.	Ryserson Polytechnic	Royal blue; gold crest/lettering	153	18.00	25.00	15.00
5.	Wilfrid Laurier University	Royal blue; gold crest/lettering	153	18.00	25.00	15.00

Taditional Tankards, Late 1950s-Early 1960s

Traditional tankards have a leaf-shaped thumb rest on the top of the handle.

University of Guelph

Lakehead University

Backstamp: A. Green transfer print "Wade England"
B. Red transfer print "Wade England"

No.	Description	Colourways	Shape/Size	U.S.$	Can.$	U.K.£
1	Dalhousie University	Black; gold print	118	15.00	20.00	12.00
2.	Humber College	Black; gold print	118	15.00	20.00	12.00
3.	Lakehead University	White; gold crest/lettering	Pint/118	18.00	25.00	15.00
4.	Niagara College	Royal blue; gold print	118	15.00	20.00	12.00
5.	McMasters University	Amber; multi-coloured print	½ pint/91	15.00	20.00	12.00
6.	Ryserson Polytechnical Inst.	Black; gold print	118	15.00	20.00	12.00
7.	Ryerson Polytechnical INst.	White; gold print	118	15.00	20.00	12.00
8.	University of Guelph	Royal blue; gold print	118	15.00	20.00	12.00
9.	University of Waterloo	Royal blue; gold print	118	15.00	20.00	12.00
10.	Waterloo Lutheran Univ.	Royal blue; gold print	118	15.00	20.00	12.00

COUNTRYMEN, c.1955-c.1962

The first set of these tankards, produced circa 1955, is glazed in amber; the second set, produced circa 1962, is in white. They were modelled in the traditional shape with a leaf-shaped thumb rest. The same decoration of country scenes, dogs and horses that was used on these tankards was also used on dishes and ashtrays. On the back of the Coaching Inn tankards there is a small print of a coach and horses.

Coaching Inn

Coach House, Bristol

Collie's Head

Poodle's Head

Backstamp: **A.** Red transfer print "Wade England"
B. Red printed "Wade England"

No.	Description	Colourways	Size	U.S.$	Can.$	U.K.£
1.	The Coach House Bristol	Amber; multi-coloured print	Pint/115	35.00	45.00	20.00
2.	The Old Coach House Stratford	Amber; multi-coloured print	Pint/115	35.00	45.00	20.00
3.	Coaching Inn	Amber; multi-coloured print (set 1)	Pint/115	35.00	45.00	20.00
4.	Collie's Head	Amber; multi-coloured print (set 1)	Pint/115	25.00	35.00	12.00
5.	Horse's Head	White; brown print (set 2)	Pint/115	25.00	35.00	12.00
6.	Horse's Heads (two)	Amber; dark brown/brown print (set 1)	Pint/115	25.00	35.00	12.00
7.	Horse's Heads (two)	White; grey/brown print (set 2)	Pint/115	25.00	35.00	12.00
8.	Horse's Heads (two)	Cream; black/brown print (set 2)	½ Pint/91	10.00	15.00	8.00
9.	Huntsmen horses (left)	Amber; multi-coloured print	Pint/115	10.00	15.00	8.00
10.	Huntsmen horses (right)	Amber; multi-coloured print	Pint/115	10.00	15.00	8.00
11.	Poodle	Amber; grey print	Pint/115	10.00	15.00	8.00
12.	Poodle's Head	White; black print (set 2)	Pint/115	25.00	35.00	12.00
13.	Poodle's Head	White; grey print (set 2)	Pint/115	25.00	35.00	12.00
14.	Spaniel's Head	White; black print (set 2)	Pint/115	25.00	35.00	12.00
15.	Spaniel's Head	White; brown print (set 2)	Pint/115	25.00	35.00	12.00

CRANKY, c.1939–c.EARLY 1940s

These half-pint and pint tankards are decorated with prints of cartoon animals on the front and a comic verse about the cartoon on the back. The "Cranky Tankards" produced in the late 1930s are shaped like a traditional tankard, which flares out at the base, except they do not have the leaf-shaped thumb rest typical of this type of tankard. The bulbous tankards, issued in the late 1940s and reissued in the early 1950s, do have the leaf-shaped thumb rest.

Traditional, c.1939

The Snoozle (front)

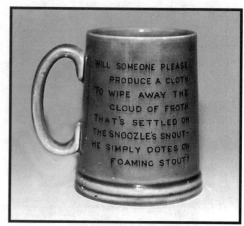
The Snoozle (back)

The Miasma (front)

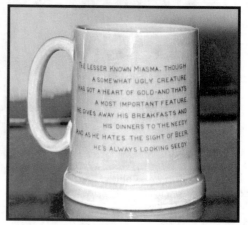
The Miasma (back)

Backstamp: Black ink stamp "Wade Heath England" with "Cranky Tankard" and design number

No.	Description	Colourways	Size	U.S.$	Can.$	U.K.£
1.	The Drumbletum	Amber; black web-footed dog; design 3	½ pint/92	38.00	35.00	15.00
2.	The Floppity	Amber; black horse; design 4	½ pint/92	38.00	35.00	15.00
3.	The Hangovah	Amber; black spotted fly; design 2	½ pint/92	30.00	35.00	15.00
4.	The Hyperfloogie	Amber; black boar; design 5	½ pint/92	30.00	35.00	15.00
5.	The Miasma	Amber; black mule; design 1	½ pint/92	30.00	35.00	15.00
6.	The Snoozle	Amber; black anteater; design 6	½ pint/92	30.00	35.00	15.00
7.	The Drumbletum	Amber; black web-footed dog; design 3	Pint/118	40.00	55.00	20.00
8.	The Floppity	Amber; black horse; design 4	Pint/118	40.00	55.00	20.00
9.	The Hangovah	Amber; black spotted fly; design 2	Pint/118	40.00	55.00	20.00
10.	The Hyperfloogie	Amber; black boar; design 5	Pint/118	40.00	55.00	20.00
11.	The Miasma	Amber; black mule; design 1	Pint/118	40.00	55.00	20.00
12.	The Snoozle	Amber; black anteater; design 6	Pint/118	40.00	55.00	20.00

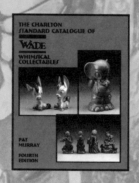

Bear Mug, c.1948-c.1951

Wade's official shape name for these bulbous tankards was Beer Mug.

The Drumbletum

The Hangovah

Backstamp: **A.** Green ink stamp "Harvest Ware Wade England" with "Cranky Tankard" and design number in brown, green or maroon, c.1948

B. Green ink stamp "Wade England" with "Cranky Tankard" and the design number in brown, green or maroon, c.1951

No.	Description	Colourways	Size	U.S.$	Can.$	U.K.£
1.	The Drumbletum	Pinky cream; dark brown web-footed dog; design 3	123	65.00	90.00	45.00
2.	The Drumbletum	Pinky cream; green web-footed dog; design 3	123	65.00	90.00	45.00
3.	The Drumbletum	Pinky cream; maroon web-footed dog; design 3	123	65.00	90.00	45.00
4.	The Floppity	Pinky cream; dark brown horse; design 4	123	65.00	90.00	45.00
5.	The Floppity	Pinky cream; green horse; design 4	123	65.00	90.00	45.00
6.	The Floppity	Pinky cream; maroon horse; design 4	123	65.00	90.00	45.00
7.	The Hangovah	Pinky cream; dark brown spotted fly; design 2	123	65.00	90.00	45.00
8.	The Hangovah	Pinky cream; green spotted fly; design 2	123	65.00	90.00	45.00
9.	The Hangovah	Pinky cream; maroon spotted fly; design 2	123	65.00	90.00	45.00
10.	The Hyperfloogie	Pinky cream; dark brown boar; design 5	123	65.00	90.00	45.00
11.	The Hyperfloogie	Pinky cream; green boar; design 5	123	65.00	90.00	45.00
12.	The Hyperfloogie	Pinky cream; maroon boar; design 5	123	65.00	90.00	45.00
13.	The Miasma	Pinky cream; dark brown mule; design 1	123	65.00	90.00	45.00
14.	The Miasma	Pinky cream; green mule; design 1	123	65.00	90.00	45.00
15.	The Miasma	Pinky cream; maroon mule; design 1	123	65.00	90.00	45.00
16.	The Snoozle	Pinky cream; dark brown anteater; design 6	123	65.00	90.00	45.00
17.	The Snoozle	Pinky cream; green anteater; design 6	123	65.00	90.00	45.00
18.	The Snoozle	Pinky cream; maroon anteater; design 6	123	65.00	90.00	45.00

CRESTS, c.1955–c.1962

These tankards were modelled in the traditional shape with a leaf-shaped thumb rest.

Royal Canadian Air Force

Rugby Football "Lets Have It Back"

Backstamp: **A.** Red transfer print "Wade England"
B. Black transfer print" Royal Victoria Pottery Wade England"

No.	Description	Colourways	Size	U.S.$	Can.$	U.K.£
1.	Beer Drinkers, "The Same Again, Please"	Amber; red/black/white print	½ pint/91	25.00	35.00	12.00
2.	Golfer's Crest	Amber; multi-coloured print	½ pint/91	25.00	35.00	12.00
3.	Rugby Football, "Lets Have It Back"	Amber; pale blue/green/white print	½ pint/91	25.00	35.00	12.00
4.	Beer Drinkers, "The Same Again, Please"	Amber; red/black/white print	Pint/115	25.00	35.00	12.00
5.	Golfers Crest	Amber; multi-coloured print	Pint/115	25.00	35.00	12.00
6.	Royal Canadian Air Force "Per Ardua Ad Astra"	White; multi-coloured print	Pint/115	25.00	35.00	12.00
7.	Rugby Football, "Lets Have It Back"	Amber; pale blue/green/white print	Pint/115	25.00	35.00	12.00
8.	St. George and the Dragon	White; multi-coloured print	Pint/115	25.00	35.00	12.00

EXECUTIVE DEST SET TANKARD, 1993

The half pint traditional tankard was part of an eight-piece executive desk set produced by Wade Ceramics for companies only, and were given as gifts by the company to their business clients. Produced in an all over black glaze with gold edging and a gold "Fleur de Lys" type emblem in the center of each piece.

Photograph not available
at press time

Backstamp: Printed "Wade England"

No.	Description	Colourways	Size	U.S.$	Can.$	U.K.£
1.	Tankard	Black; gold edges and emblem	½ pint/91	10.00	15.00	8.00

THE GALLEON COLLECTION c.late 1940s

These traditional tankards all have multi-coloured prints of galleons on the front. The same designs were later used on "Royal Victoria Pottery" shaving mugs in the 1980s.

Galleon and Small Galleon — Galleon and Dinghy   **Galleon — Galleon and Sailboat**

Backstamp: Ink stamp "Wadeheath Ware England" late 1940s

No.	Description	Colourways	Size	U.S.$	Can.$	U.K.£
1.	Galleon Tankard	White; multi-coloured print	105	25.00	35.00	15.00
2.	Galleon/Dinghy	White; multi-coloured print	105	25.00	35.00	15.00
3.	Galleon/small galleon	White; multi-coloured print	105	25.00	35.00	15.00
4.	Galleon/sailboat	White; multi-coloured print	105	25.00	35.00	15.00

THE GENT'S A GOURMET, c.1958

Backstamp: Red transfer print "Wade England"

No.	Description	Colourways	Size	U.S.$	Can.$	U.K.£
1.	Gent's a Gourmet	White; gold rim; red/blue print	Pint/115	8.00	10.00	5.00

HUMPTY DUMPTY AND RING-O-ROSES MUSICAL TANKARDS, c.1940

This pint tankard has a music box contained in the base. The Swiss musical movement is dated August 26, 1940, and plays "Brahms Lullaby." The transfer print of three children playing "Ri ng-o-Roses" was also used on 1930s-40s Wadeheath toy dishes.

Humpty Dumpty

Ring-O-Roses

Backstamp: Green ink stamp "Wade Heath England"

No.	Description	Colourways	Size	U.S.$	Can.$	U.K.£
1.	Humpty Dumpty	Cream; red line on rim; multi-coloured Humpty Dumpty	Pint/117	100.00	145.00	55.00
2.	Ring-O-Roses	Cream; red line on rim; multi-coloured print No musical movement left	Pint/117	50.00	90.00	55.00

IN THE DOGHOUSE, c.1958-c.1962

The print on this tankard depicts a man lying in a doghouse on the front and a dog asleep in an armchair on the back.

Backstamp: Red transfer print "Wade England"

No.	Description	Colourways	Size	U.S.$	Can.$	U.K.£
1.	Doghouse	Amber; dark brown; black print	Pint/116	25.00	35.00	12.00

MOURNE TANKARDS, 1976

These chunky tankards were produced by Wade Ireland in its Mourne Series. They have a flared base and are completely different in colour and style from previously produced Wade Ireland tankards.

Backstamp: Embossed "Made in Ireland Porcelain Wade eire tira dheanta"

No.	Description	Colourways	Size	U.S.$	Can.$	U.K.£
1.	C.351/Mourne	Mottled browny green; orange flower	½ pint/100	50.00	70.00	25.00
2.	C.351/Mourne	Mottled browny green; yellow flower	½ pint/100	50.00	70.00	25.00
3.	C.352/Mourne	Mottled browny green; orange flower	Pint/124	65.00	85.00	30.00

OLDE WORLDE TAVERN, c.1955–c.1962

A souvenir tankard was issued with a transfer print of Tower Bridge on the front and a print of the coat of arms of the City of London on the back.

Japanese copies of this tankard exist and are slightly larger and lighter in weight. They have "Beer" printed on them, and the decoration on the top band and the moulded decoration are different than the Wade originals.

Tonic, Ale, Bilge   Tower Bridge

Backstamp: A. Red transfer print "Wade England"
B. Black transfer print "Wade England"

No.	Description	Colourways	Size	U.S.$	Can.$	U.K.£
1.	Ale	Amber; silver bands	118	30.00	40.00	18.00
2.	Bilge	Amber; silver bands	125	30.00	40.00	18.00
3.	Gin	Amber; silver bands	125	30.00	40.00	18.00
4.	Tonic	Amber; silver bands	125	30.00	40.00	18.00
5.	Tower Bridge	Amber; silver bands; black bridge; multi-coloured coat of arms	125	30.00	40.00	18.00

PLYMOUTH TANKARDS, C.1955

"Plymouth Tankards" are similar in design to the "Barrel Tankards," but have straight sides tapering in at the top rim. Some of these tankards were issued as souvenirs, with transfer prints depicting various scenes from Canada's Maritime Provinces.

Nova Scotia Shield

Miniature, 1/2 pint, pint

Backstamp: A. Red transfer print "Wade England"
B. Red transfer print "Wade Ireland"

No.	Description	Colourways	Size	U.S.$	Can.$	U.K.£
1.	Plymouth	Amber; siver bands, handle	Miniature/49	6.00	8.00	4.00
2.	St. John	Amber; black lettering	Miniature/49	6.00	8.00	4.00
3.	Lobster From Canada's East Coast	Amber; multi-coloured print	½ pint/90	10.00	15.00	8.00
4.	Maritime Lobster Trap	Amber; multi-coloured print	½ pint/90	10.00	15.00	8.00
5.	New Brunswick Shield	Amber; multi-coloured print	½ pint/90	10.00	15.00	8.00
6.	Nova Scotia Shield	Amber; multi-coloured print	½ pint/90	10.00	15.00	8.00
7.	Plymouth	Amber; silver bands, handle	½ pint/90	10.00	15.00	8.00
8.	Plymouth	Copper Lustre	Pint/115	18.00	25.00	12.00
9.	New Brunswick Shield	Amber; multi-coloured print	Pint/115	18.00	25.00	12.00
10.	Newfoundland Shield	Amber; multi-coloured print	Pint/115	18.00	25.00	12.00
11.	Plymouth	Amber; silver bands, handle	Pint/115	18.00	25.00	12.00
12.	Prince Edward Island Shield	Amber; multi-coloured print	Pint/115	18.00	25.00	12.00
13.	St Thomas Virgin Islands	Amber; black palm tree/lettering	Pint/115	18.00	25.00	12.00

PLYMOUTH TANKARD WITH NO RIBS, c.1960s

This tankard is the same shape as the normal Plymouth tankard but is unusual because it is missing the ribbed design.

Photograph not available
at press time

Backstamp: Red printed "Wade England"

No.	Description	Colourways	Size	U.S.$	Can.$	U.K.£
1.	Plymouth	Copper	Pint/115	12.00	15.00	7.00

PIG CARTOON TANKARDS, c.1958-c.1962

These tankards have been found in two new shapes—bulbous and traditional—and they also have cartoon pig characters on the front. Printed on the back of the "Cricket" and "Punk Pig" tankards is "To commemorate the disappearing wonders of nature this tankard is dedicated to that noble beast—The Chauvinist Pig."

Beer Mug Shape

Cricket Pig

The Punk Pig, Back

Backstamp: Red transfer print "Wade England"

No.	Description	Colourways	Size	U.S.$	Can.$	U.K. £
1.	Cricket Pig	Beige pink; white/red/yellow/ black print/lettering; silver rim	Bulbous/Pint/138	40.00	60.00	30.00
2.	Punk Pig	Beige pink; white/red/yellow/ black print/lettering; silver rim	Bulbous/Pint/138	40.00	60.00	30.00
3.	Punk Pig	Honey-brown; multi-coloured print	Pint/112	25.00	35.00	18.00

Traditional Shape

Hermann Boaring

Backstamp: Red transfer print "Wade England"

No.	Description	Colourways	Size	U.S.$	Can.$	U.K. £
1.	Hermann Boaring	White; dark green/yellow/ black print/lettering	Traditional/Pint/115	40.00	60.00	30.00

THE QUEEN'S MEN TANKARDS, c.1955-c.1962

These traditional tankards are decorated with transfer prints depicting the regiments that guard the Queen's residences and parade through London on ceremonial occasions. Each tankard has the legend of the regiment on the back.

Photograph not available
at press time

Backstamp: **A.** Black transfer print "By Wade of England"
B. Red transfer print "Wade England"

No.	Description	Colourways	Size	U.S.$	Can.$	U.K.£
1.	The Drum Major	White; gold rim; multi-coloured print	Pint/117	25.00	35.00	12.00
2.	The Drum Major	Grey; gold rim; multi-coloured print	Pint/117	25.00	35.00	12.00
3.	Life Guard	Amber; black/red/white print	Pint/117	25.00	35.00	12.00
4.	The Life Guards	White; gold rim; silver breast plate, multi-coloured print	Pint/117	25.00	35.00	12.00
5.	Life Guards Trooper	White; gold rim; red cloak; multi-coloured print	Pint/117	25.00	35.00	12.00
6.	The Scots Guards	White; gold rim; multi-coloured print	Pint/117	25.00	35.00	12.00

REGIMENTAL TANKARDS

Ulster 1972-1974 Traditional Tankard Shape

The first two Traditional tankards listed have military crests on them of British Army units that served in Ulster in the early 1970s. The Gordon Highlanders motto is "Stand Fast," the Highlanders nickname is "The Gay Gordons," and their regimental march is "Cock-of-the-North"

Royal Tank Regiment's motto is "Fear Nought." This tankard produced by Wade Ireland is an unusual traditional tankard shape with two rows of knurls.

I have no information on the "Tactical Fighter Wing" tankard and would welcome any feedback from collectors.

| **Gordon Highlanders** | **Royal Tank Regiment** | **81st Tactical Fighter Wing** |

Backstamp: **A.** Printed" Wade England"
B. Printed "Wade Regicor London England" in laurel leaf frame, large size (1953-1962)
C. Impressed "Irish Porcelain made in Ireland" with letter *E* in shamrock

No.	Description	Colourways	Size	U.S.$	Can.$	U.K. £
1.	Gordon Highlanders Ulster 1972	White; green/gold stag crest; black lettering	Pint/115	30.00	40.00	20.00
2.	Royal Tank Regiment Ulster 1973-74	Honey brown/grey blue edging; red/grey Tank crest; gold ribbon; black lettering	Pint/120	30.00	40.00	20.00
3.	81st Tactical Fighter Wing	Cream; multi-coloured print; grey blue lettering	Pint/115	30.00	40.00	20.00

ROLL OUT THE BARREL, c.1940

Two styles of "Roll Out the Barrel" tankards were produced by Wade during World War II. One handle is made from a moulded British "tommy" (soldier) and the other is a moulded figure of Winston Churchill.

Tommy — Churchill

Backstamp: Black ink stamp "Wade Heath England"

No.	Description	Colourways	Size	U.S.$	Can.$	U.K.£
1.	Churchill	Amber; dark brown letters	145	75.00	95.00	48.00
2.	Churchill	Light green; greeny white figure	145	90.00	110.00	55.00
3.	Tommy	Amber; dark brown letters	145	75.00	95.00	48.00

SILVER LUSTRE TANKARD, c.1953

This all-over, one-colour tankard has no transfer print decoration.

Photograph not available
at press time

Backstamp: Red transfer print "Wade England"

No.	Description	Colourways	Size	U.S.$	Can.$	U.K.£
1.	Silver Lustre	Silver	½ pint/91	20.00	25.00	12.00
2.	Silver Lustre	Silver	Pint/146	20.00	25.00	12.00

SOUVENIR TRADITIONAL TANKARDS

Souvenir of the Bahamas, c.1955-c.1962

Straw Market, Nassua, Bahamas

Backstamp: Red transfer print "Wade England"

No.	Description	Colourways	Size	U.S.$	Can.$	U.K. £
1.	Island of New Providence, Nassau, Bahamas	Amber; multi-coloured print	½ pint/91	10.00	12.00	5.00
2.	Straw Market Nassau, Bahamas	Amber; multi-coloured print	½ Pint/91	10.00	12.00	5.00
3.	Bahamian Constable	White; multi-coloured print	Pint/120	25.00	30.00	15.00
4.	Bahamian Constable	Amber; multi-coloured print	Pint/118	25.00	30.00	15.00
5.	Grand Bahama Map	Amber; multi-coloured print	Pint/117	15.00	12.00	10.00
6.	Nassau, Horse and Landau	Amber; multi-coloured print	Pint/117	15.00	12.00	10.00

Souvenir of Canada, c.1955-1973

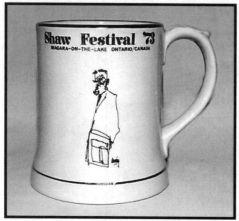

Shaw Festival '73 | British Columbia Canada'a Evergreen Playground

Backstamp: Red transfer print "Wade England"

No.	Description	Colourways	Size	U.S.$	Can.$	U.K.£
1.	Nova Scotia Shield	Amber; multi-coloured print	Miniature/53	8.00	10.00	5.00
2.	Nova Scotia Shield	White; multi-coloured print	Miniature/53	8.00	10.00	5.00
3.	Maritime Lobster and Trap	Cream; red/brown print	½ pint/91	10.00	12.00	5.00
4.	New Brunswick Map	White; multi-coloured print	½ pint/91	10.00	12.00	5.00
5.	Nova Scotia Piper	White; blue/red kilt	½ pint/91	10.00	12.00	5.00
6.	Nova Scotia Shield	White; multi-coloured print	½ pint/91	10.00	12.00	5.00
7.	Blue Nose II, Nova Scotia	Amber; brown yacht	½ pint/91	10.00	12.00	5.00
8.	Blue Nose II, Nova Scotia	White; multi-coloured print	Pint/115	35.00	20.00	18.00
9.	British Columbia, Arms	White; multi-coloured print	Pint/117	35.00	20.00	18.00
10.	British Columbia "Canada's Evergreen Playground"	White; multi-coloured print	Pint/117	35.00	20.00	18.00
11.	"Ontario, Canada" crest	White; multi-coloured print	Pint/117	35.00	20.00	18.00
12.	St John Newfoundland Shield/Plymouth Tankard	Amber; multi-coloured print; black lettering	Pint/115	35.00	20.00	18.00
13.	Shaw Festival/73	White; gold print	Pint/115	35.00	20.00	18.00

Souvenir of England, c.1955-c.1962

The miniature traditional tankards were produced in the mid 1950s and the half-pint size from the mid 1950s to the early 1960s. The size variation is due to replaced moulds.

Balmoral Castle (No. 11)

Giants Causeway (No. 8)

Guernsey (No. 1)

Windsor Castle (No. 6)

Backstamp: A. Red transfer print "Wade England"
B. Black transfer print "A Dee Cee Souvenir by Wade"
C. Black transfer print "Souvenirs of England by Wade England"
D. Gold printed circular "Royal Victoria Pottery Wade England"

No.	Description	Colourways	0Size	U.S.$	Can.$	U.K.£
1.	Guernsey	Amber; black print	Miniature/49	6.00	8.00	5.00
2.	Isle of Wight Pennant	Cream; red pennant	Miniature/55	6.00	8.00	5.00
3.	Shakespeare's Head	Amber; multi-coloured portrait	Miniature/49	6.00	8.00	5.00
4.	Southend	Silver/light grey; metal-coloured crest	Miniature/49	6.00	8.00	5.00
5.	Windemere	Cream; black print	Miniature/49	6.00	8.00	5.00
6.	Windsor Castle	Pale yellow; multi-coloured print	Miniature/55	6.00	8.00	5.00
7.	Brightlingsea	Cream; red pennant; black lettering	Miniature/49	6.00	8.00	5.00
8.	Giants Causeway	White; blue/grey print; black lettering	Miniature/49	6.00	8.00	5.00
9.	Guernsey Shield	Yellow; red/green shield	½ pint/91	12.00	15.00	8.00
10.	Widdecombe Fair	Amber; black print, verse	½ pint/91	12.00	15.00	8.00
11.	Balmoral Castle	White; gold rim; multi-coloured print	Pint/117	22.00	28.00	15.00

Channel Islands

Sark "Cows"

Backstamp: Printed "A Dee Cee Souvenir by Wade" (Dee Cee stood for Desmond Cooper)

No.	Description	Colourways	Size	U.S.$	Can.$	U.K.£
1.	Guernsey Arms	Cream; gold rim; red/yellow/green coat of arms; green lettering	½ pint/91	12.00	15.00	8.00
2.	Sark Cows	Cream; gold rim; multi-coloured print	½ pint/91	12.00	15.00	8.00

Souvenir of Kenya, c.1955

The print on this traditional tankard depicts the Treetops Hotel in the Nyeri Game Reserve.

Photograph not available
at press time

Backstamp: Red transfer print "Wade England"

No.	Description	Colourways	Size	U.S.$	Can.$	U.K.£
1.	Kenya	White; black print	Pint/117	15.00	20.00	8.00

Souvenir of London, c.1955-c.1965

A series of tankards produced for the tourist trade with transfer prints of London landmarks.

| Buckingham Palace | Houses of Parliament and Big Ben | London |

Backstamp: **A.** Red transfer print "Wade England"
B. Black transfer print "Souvenirs of London by Wade England"
C. Red transfer print "Wade Regicor England, Reginald Corfield, Redhill, Surrey"
D. Black transfer print "Souvenir by Wade"
E. Red transfer print "Wade Ireland"
F. Red transfer print "Wade Regicor England, Reginald Corfield, Redhill, Surrey 1955-1965"
G. Printed "A Dee Cee Souvenir by Wade"
H. Printed "Souvenir of England by Wade"

No.	Description	Colourways	Size	U.S.$	Can.$	U.K.£
1.	Big Ben	Yellow; black print	Miniature/49	8.00	10.00	4.00
2.	Big Ben	Cream; black/blue print	Miniature/49	8.00	10.00	4.00
3.	Big Ben	Cream; black print	Miniature/49	8.00	10.00	4.00
4.	Big Ben	Amber; black/blue print	Miniature/49	8.00	10.00	4.00
5.	Eros, Piccadilly Circus	Yellow; black print	Miniature/49	8.00	10.00	4.00
6.	Eros, Piccadilly Circus	Cream; black/blue print	Miniature/49	8.00	10.00	4.00
7.	Piccadilly Circus	White/yellow; black print	Miniature/55	8.00	10.00	4.00
8.	Piccadilly Circus	Amber; black print	Miniature/55	8.00	10.00	4.00
9.	Tower Bridge	White/yellow; black/blue print	Miniature/55	8.00	10.00	4.00
10.	Tower Bridge	Yellow; black print	Miniature/49	8.00	10.00	4.00
11.	Tower Bridge	Cream; black/blue print	Miniature/49	8.00	10.00	4.00
12.	Trafalgar Square	Amber; black/blue print	Miniature/49	8.00	10.00	4.00
13.	Trafalgar Square	White/yellow tankard; black print	Miniature/55	8.00	10.00	4.00
14.	Beefeater Yeoman of the Guard	Amber; black/blue print	½ pint/91	10.00	15.00	4.00
15.	Big Ben	Amber; multi-coloured print	½ pint/91	13.00	18.00	5.00
16.	Big Ben	Amber; black print	½ pint/91	13.00	18.00	5.00
17.	Buckingham Palace	Amber; multi-coloured print	½ pint/91	13.00	18.00	5.00
18.	Buckingham Palace	White; multi-coloured print	½ pint/91	13.00	18.00	5.00
19.	Eros, Piccadilly Circus	White; multi-coloured print	½ pint/91	13.00	18.00	5.00
20.	Houses of Parliament	Amber; multi-coloured print	½ pint/91	13.00	18.00	5.00
21.	St. Pauls Cathedral	Amber; multi-coloured print	½ pint/91	13.00	18.00	5.00
22.	Tower Bridge	Amber; multi-coloured print	½ pint/91	13.00	18.00	5.00
23.	Tower Bridge	White; black/blue print	½ pint/91	10.00	15.00	5.00
24.	Trafalgar Square	Amber; multi-coloured print	½ pint/91	13.00	18.00	5.00
25.	Big Ben	Amber; multi-coloured print	Pint/117	25.00	30.00	12.00
26.	Big Ben	Cream; multi-coloured print	Pint/117	15.00	20.00	12.00
27.	Big Ben	Cream; sepia brown print	Pint/117	15.00	20.00	12.00
28.	Buckingham Palace	White; multi-coloured print	Pint/117	15.00	20.00	12.00
29.	Buckingham Palace	Amber; multi-coloured print	Pint/117	15.00	20.00	12.00

Tower Bridge

Tower Bridge

Trafalgar Square

No.	Description	Colourways	Size	U.S.$	Can.$	U.K.£
30.	Eros, Piccadilly Circus	White; black print	Pint/117	15.00	20.00	12.00
31.	Eros, Piccadilly Circus	Black; white print	Pint/117	15.00	20.00	12.00
32.	Great Britain	White; multi-coloured flags	Pint/117	15.00	20.00	12.00
33.	Houses of Parliament	Amber; multi-coloured print	Pint/117	15.00	20.00	12.00
34.	London, Multiple Scenes	White; multi-coloured print	Pint/117	15.00	20.00	12.00
35.	Nelsons Column,	Amber; multi-coloured print	Pint/114	15.00	20.00	12.00
36.	St. Paul's Cathedral	Amber; multi-coloured print	Pint/117	15.00	20.00	12.00
37.	Tower Bridge	Amber; multi-coloured print	Pint/117	15.00	20.00	12.00
38.	Tower Bridge	White; multi-coloured print	Pint/117	15.00	20.00	12.00
39.	Tower Bridge	Cream; black/blue print	Pint/117	15.00	20.00	12.00
40.	Trafalgar Square	Amber; black print	Pint/117	15.00	20.00	12.00

Souvenir of Tortola

Tortola is the largest of thirty-six islands that make up the British Virgin Islands; it is part of the island chain that continues as the Virgin Islands of U.S.A.

Photograph not available at press time

Backstamp: Red printed "Wade England" (late 1960s)

No.	Description	Colourways	Size	U.S.$	Can.$	U.K. £
1.	Tortola Map showing Francis Drake Channel	Amber; multi-coloured print	Pint/117	30.00	35.00	15.00

SPORTS, c.1955-c.1962

Man Playing Bowls

Backstamp: **A.** Red transfer print "Wade England"
B. Black transfer print "Wade England"

No.	Description	Colourways	Size	U.S.$	Can.$	U.K. £
1.	Man Playing Bowls	Cream; gold rim; black print	½ pint/91	13.00	18.00	5.00
2.	Man Playing Golf	Amber; multi-coloured print	½ pint/91	13.00	18.00	5.00

TOASTS, c.1958

Backstamp: Red transfer print "Wade England"

No.	Description	Colourways	Size	U.S.$	Can.$	U.K.£
1.	Toasts	Amber; black prints	Pint/117	10.00	15.00	5.00

VETERAN CAR SERIES, 19561967

For over ten years Wade Heath produced an almost constant series of tankards, water jugs, dishes, plates, cigarette boxes, miniature oil jugs and miniature oil funnels with transfer prints of veteran cars on them. At the time this was the only series on veteran cars that was authenticated by the Veteran Car Club and by the Vintage Sports Car Club of Great Britain. Not only were the illustrations completely accurate, each piece was numbered in its set and series and had interesting information about the car on the back or base of the product. At the time of production, all the cars depicted were still in existence.

The Veteran Car Series tankards were produced in miniature, half-pint and pint sizes. All are coloured in an amber glaze and have a leaf-shaped thumb rest on the handle, with a silver band around the rim.

At some time during the mid 1960s, the production of the tankards was moved from England to Wade Ireland. Due to the replacement of moulds, some of the Irish tankards are slightly larger and heavier than those from Wade England.

In December 1957 a British car magazine advertised the ½ pint tankards for 7/9d and pint tankards for 10/9d.

Series 1 to 4 are decorated with black transfer prints of cars; series 5 to 9 have coloured transfer prints.

Each tankard is marked on the back with the series number followed by the car number in parentheses. These are indicated in the colourways columns below.

Darracq

Backstamp:
A. "A Moko Product by Wade England - Design authenticated by the Veteran Car Club of Great Britain"
B. "A Moko Product by Wade Design authenticated by the Veteran Car Club of Great Britain" and printed "Made in Ireland"
C. "A Moko Line by Wade England - Design authenticated by the Vintage Sports Car Club of Great Britain"
D. "A Moko Line by Wade Design authenticated by the Veteran Car Club of Great Britain"
E. "A Moko Line by Wade of England Design authenticated by the Veteran Car Club of Great Britain"
F. "A Moko Line by Wade of Ireland Design authenticated by the Veteran Car Club of Great Britain"
G. "A Moko Product by Wade Made in Ireland"
H. "An Rk Product by Wade of England"
I. "An Rk Product by Wade of Ireland - Design authenticated by the Vintage Sports Car Club of Great Britain"
J. "An Rk Product by Wade of England Illustration by Courtesy of Profile Publications Ltd"
K. "An Rk Product by Wade of England Design authenticated by the Veteran Car Club of Great Britain"
L. "An Rk Product by Wade of England Design authenticated by the Vintage Sports Car Club of Great Britain"
M. "An Rk Product by Wade of Ireland"
N. "An Rk Product by Wade" and printed "Made in Ireland"
O. "An Rk Peoduct by Wade of Ireland Design authenticated by the Veteran Car Club of Great Britain"
P. "An Rk Product by Wade of Ireland illustration by courtesy of Profile Publications Ltd"
Q. "An Rk Product by Wade Illustration by courtesy of Profile Publications Ltd" and red printed "Wade England"
R. "Made by the Wolseley Sheep Shearing Machine Company" and a red transfer print "Wade England"

Series 1

No.	Description	Colourways	Size	U.S.$	Can.$	U.K.£
1.	Benz, 1899	Amber; silver rim; black print (1-1)	Miniature/49	8.00	10.00	3.00
2.	Darracq, 1904	Amber; silver rim; black print (1-3)	Miniature/49	8.00	10.00	3.00
3.	Ford, 1912	Amber; silver rim; black print (1-2)	Miniature/49	8.00	10.00	3.00
4.	Benz, 1899	Amber; silver rim; black print (1-1)	½ pint/91	15.00	20.00	8.00
5.	Darracq, 1904	Amber; silver rim; black print (1-3)	½ pint/91	15.00	20.00	8.00
6.	Ford, 1912	Amber; silver rim; black print (1-2)	½ pint/91	15.00	20.00	8.00
7.	Benz, 1899	Amber; silver rim; black print (1-1)	Pint/115	20.00	25.00	12.00
8.	Darracq, 1904	Amber; silver rim; black print (1-3)	Pint/115	20.00	25.00	12.00
9.	Ford, 1912	Amber; silver rim; black print (1-2)	Pint/115	20.00	25.00	12.00

Series 2

Baby Peugeot "Frae Aberdeen"

No.	Description	Colourways	Size	U.S.$	Can.$	U.K.£
1.	Baby Peugeot, 1902,	Amber; silver rim; black print (2-6)	Miniature/49	8.00	10.00	3.00
2.	Baby Peugeot, 1902, Frae Aberdeen	Amber; silver rim; black print; (2-6) black/gold label	Miniature/49	8.00	10.00	3.00
3.	Rolls-Royce, 1907	Amber; silver rim; black print (2-5)	Miniature/49	8.00	10.00	3.00
4.	Sunbeam, 1904	Amber; silver rim; black print (2-4)	Miniature/49	8.00	10.00	3.00
5.	Baby Peugeot, 1902	Amber; silver rim; black print (2-6)	½ pint/91	15.00	20.00	8.00
6.	Rolls-Royce, 1907	Amber; silver rim; black print (2-5)	½ pint/91	15.00	20.00	8.00
7.	Sunbeam, 1904	Amber; silver rim; black print (2-4)	½ pint/91	15.00	20.00	8.00
8.	Baby Peugeot, 1902	Amber; silver rim; black print (2-6)	Pint/115	25.00	35.00	12.00
9.	Rolls-Royce, 1907	Amber; silver rim; black print (2-5)	Pint/115	25.00	35.00	12.00
10.	Sunbeam, 1904	Amber; silver rim; black print (2-4)	Pint/115	25.00	35.00	12.00

Series 3

Photograph not available
at press time

No.	Description	Colourways	Size	U.S.$	Can.$	U.K.£
1.	De Dion Bouton, 1904	Amber; silver rim; black print (3-7)	Miniature/49	8.00	10.00	3.00
2.	Lanchester, 1903	Amber; silver rim; black print (3-9)	Miniature/49	8.00	10.00	3.00
3.	Spyker, 1905	Amber; silver rim; black print (3-8)	Miniature/49	8.00	10.00	3.00
4.	De Dion Bouton, 1904	Amber; silver rim; black print (3-7)	½ pint/91	15.00	20.00	8.00
5.	Lanchester, 1903	Amber; silver rim; black print (3-9)	½ pint/91	15.00	20.00	8.00
6.	Spyker, 1905	Amber; silver rim; black print (3-8)	½ pint/91	15.00	20.00	8.00
7.	De Dion Bouton, 1904	Amber; silver rim; black print (3-7)	Pint/115	25.00	35.00	12.00
8.	Lanchester, 1903	Amber; silver rim; black print (3-9)	Pint/115	25.00	35.00	12.00
9.	Spyker, 1905	Amber; silver rim; black print (3-8)	Pint/115	25.00	35.00	12.00

Series 4

White Steam Car

Itala

No.	Description	Colourways	Size	U.S.$	Can.$	U.K.œ
1.	Cadillac, 1903	Amber; silver rim; black print (4-11)	Miniature/49	8.00	10.00	3.00
2.	Oldsmobile, 1904	Amber; silver rim; black print (4-10)	Miniature/49	8.00	10.00	3.00
J3.	White Steam Car, 1903	Amber; silver rim; black print (4-12)	Miniature/49	8.00	10.00	3.00
4.	Cadillac, 1903	Amber; silver rim; black print (4-11)	½ pint/91	15.00	20.00	8.00
5.	Oldsmobile, 1904	Amber; silver rim; black print (4-10)	½ pint/91	15.00	20.00	8.00
6.	White Steam Car, 1903	Amber; silver rim; black print (4-12)	½ pint/91	15.00	20.00	8.00
7.	Cadillac, 1903	Amber; silver rim; black print (4-11)	Pint/115	25.00	35.00	12.00
8.	Oldsmobile, 1904	Amber; silver rim; black print (4-10)	Pint/115	25.00	35.00	12.00
9.	White Steam Car, 1903	Amber; silver rim; black print (4-12)	Pint/115	25.00	35.00	12.00

Series 5

No.	Description	Colourways	Size	U.S.$	Can.$	U.K.œ
1.	Bugatti, 1913	Amber; silver rim; black/blue/ brown print (5-14)	Miniature/49	8.00	10.00	3.00
2.	Itala, 1908	Amber; silver rim; red/black/blue print (5-13)	Miniature/49	8.00	10.00	3.00
3.	Sunbeam, 1914	Amber; silver rim; green/black/brown/ blue print (5-15)	Miniature/49	8.00	10.00	3.00
4.	Bugatti, 1913	Amber; silver rim; black/blue/brown print (5-14)	½ pint/91	15.00	20.00	8.00
5.b	Itala, 1908	Amber; silver rim; red/black/blue print (5-13)	½ pint/91	15.00	20.00	8.00
6.	Sunbeam, 1914	Amber; silver rim; green/black/brown/ blue print (5-15)	½ pint/91	15.00	20.00	8.00
7.	Bugatti, 1913	Amber; silver rim; black/blue/brown print (5-14)	Pint/115	25.00	35.00	12.00
8.	Itala, 1908	Amber; silver rim; red/black/blue print (5-13)	Pint/115	25.00	35.00	12.00
9.	Sunbeam, 1914	Amber; silver rim; green/black/brown print (5-15)	Pint/115	25.00	35.00	12.00

Series 6

Bugatti

No.	Description	Colourways	Size	U.S.$	Can.$	U.K.£
1.	Alfa Romeo, 1924	Amber; silver rim; red car (6-16)	Miniature/49	8.00	10.00	3.00
2.	Bentley, 1929	Amber; silver rim; green/black/blue car (6-18)	Miniature/49	8.00	10.00	3.00
3.	Bugatti, 1927	Amber; silver rim; blue car (6-17)	Miniature/49	8.00	10.00	3.00
4.	Alfa Romeo, 1924	Amber; silver rim; red/black/blue print (6-16)	½ pint/91	15.00	20.00	8.00
5.	Bentley, 1929	Amber; silver rim; green/black/blue print (6-18)	½ pint/91	15.00	20.00	8.00
6.	Bugatti, 1927	Amber; silver rim; blue/black/brown print (6-17)	½ pint/91	15.00	20.00	8.00
7.	Alfa Romeo, 1924	Amber; silver rim; red/black/blue print (6-16)	Pint/115	25.00	35.00	12.00
8.	Bentley, 1929	Amber; silver rim; green/black/blue print (6-18)	Pint/115	25.00	35.00	12.00
9.	Bugatti, 1927	Amber; silver rim; blue/black/brown print (6-17)	Pint/115	25.00	35.00	12.00

Series 7, Veteran, Vintage and Competition Cars

Vauxhall — MG — Fiat

No.	Description	Colourways	Size	U.S.$	Can.$	U.K.£
1.	Fiat F2, 1907	Amber; silver rim; red/yellow print (7-21)	½ pint/91	13.00	18.00	8.00
2.	MG, 1925	Amber; silver rim; green/black print (7-20)	½ pint/91	13.00	18.00	8.00
3.	Vauxhall, 1913	Amber; silver rim; blue/black/cream print (7-19)	½ pint/91	13.00	18.00	8.00
4.	Fiat F2, 1907	Amber; silver rim; red/yellow print (7-21)	Pint/115-120	25.00	30.00	12.00
5.	MG, 1925	Amber; silver rim; green/black print (7-20)	Pint/115-120	25.00	30.00	12.00
6.	Vauxhall, 1913	Amber; silver rim; blue/black/cream print (7-19)	Pint/115	25.00	30.00	12.00

Series 8, Competition Cars

No.	Description	Colourways	Size	U.S.$	Can.$	U.K.£
1.	Dusenberg, 1933	Amber; silver rim; black/pale blue print (8-22)	½ pint/91	13.00	18.00	8.00
2.	Hispano Suiza	Amber; silver rim; green/grey print (8-24)	½ pint/91	13.00	18.00	8.00
3.	Mercedes GP, 1908	Amber; silver rim; grey/black print (8-23)	½ pint/91	13.00	18.00	8.00
4.	Dusenberg, 1933	Amber; silver rim; black/pale blue print (8-22)	Pint/115-120	25.00	30.00	12.00
5.	Hispano Suiza	Amber; green/grey print (8-24)	Pint/115-120	25.00	30.00	12.00
J6.	Mercedes GP, 1908	Amber; silver rim; grey/black print (8-23)	Pint/120	25.00	30.00	12.00

Series 9, Competition Cars

Austin Seven, 1926

Wolseley

No.	Description	Colourways	Size	U.S.$	Can.$	U.K.£
1.	Austin Seven, 1926	Amber; silver rim; red/black print (9-26)	½ pint/91	13.00	18.00	8.00
2.	Model T Ford, 1915	Amber; silver rim; black print (9-27)	½ pint/91	13.00	18.00	8.00
3.	Wolseley 6hp, 1904	Amber; silver rim; red/black/cream print (9-25)	½ pint/91	13.00	18.00	8.00
4.	Austin Seven, 1926	Amber; silver rim; red/black print (9-26)	Pint/120	25.00	30.00	12.00
5.	Model T Ford, 1915	Amber; silver rim; black car (9-27)	Pint/120	25.00	30.00	12.00
6.	Wolseley 6hp, 1904	Amber; silver rim; red/black/cream print (9-25)	Pint/120	25.00	30.00	12.00

VICTORY, 1942

The two handles of this tankard represent Winston Churchill (right) and President Roosevelt (left).

Backstamp: A. Black ink stamp "Wade Heath England"
   B. Black ink stamp "Wade England"

No.	Description	Colourways	Size	U.S.$	Can.$	U.K.£
1.	Victory	Amber; dark brown/black coastlines, planes, ships	150	200.00	260.00	130.00
2.	Victory	Amber; dark brown/black coastlines, planes/ships; gold rims/highlights	150	200.00	260.00	130.00

WADE APPRENTICE MUGS/TANKARDS

These extra large size mugs/tankards are from the same mould used for the "Vaux" Beer Mugs and the 1977 Taunton Cider Mug. They are so called because the decorations on them are applied by apprentices in the pottery, learning how to apply transfer prints to ceramics. Because they are decorated by apprentices no two tankards are exactly alike; one may have a bird with a decorative frame or a bird with grasses etc. The style of decoration was left to the appentice. The mugs and tankards were sold in the Wade Pottery shop, and also sold at the Trentham Gardens 1997 Wade show.

Birds, Two Frames

Flowers and Frames

Backstamp: A. Gold printed "Wade England" Wade between two lines (1997-1998)
B. Black printed "Genuine wade Porcelain"

No.	Description	Colourways	Size	U.S.$	Can.$	U.K. £
1.	Bird/Grasses	White; gold bands; multi-coloured print	101 x 105	8.00	10.00	3.00
2.	Bird/Two frames	White; gold bands; multi-coloured print	101 x 105	8.00	10.00	3.00
3.	Bird/Three frames	White; gold bands; multi-coloured print	101 x 105	8.00	10.00	3.00
4.	Flowers and Butterfly Scroll inside rim	White; multi-coloured print	101 x 105	8.00	10.00	3.00
5.	Frames and flowers	White; multi-coloured print	101 x 105	8.00	10.00	3.00
6.	Pink Flowers	White; pink flowers; black leaves	101 x 105	8.00	10.00	3.00

WEDDING AND ANNIVERSARY MUGS AND TANKARDS, 1998

These are the same shape mug/tankard as the "Apprentice Mugs" above but have a raised shield on the front and back. The shields are decorated with wedding and anniversary prints. Some tankards have a smaller print on the inside back rim.

Wedding Anniversary

Silver Anniversary

Backstamp: Red printed "Wade England" Wade between two lines

No.	Description	Colourways	Size	U.S.$	Can.$	U.K. £
1.	Congratulations	White; gold bands; multi-coloured print	101 x 108	6.00	10.00	3.00
2.	Good Luck	White: gold bands; black cat on chimney	101 x 108	6.00	10.00	3.00
3.	Wedding	White; gold bands; multi-coloured print	101 x 108	6.00	10.00	3.00
4.	Wedding Anniversary	White; gold bands; yellow flowers; white love birds print	101 x 108	6.00	10.00	3.00
5.	Silver Anniversary	White; gold bands; multi-coloured print	101 x 108	6.00	10.00	3.00

ULSTER WARE TANKARDS

KNURLED, c.1950–c.1980

An initial letter can be seen in the backstamps of many of the Irish Wade pieces: this letter is the code letter of the potter of the piece. Information recently found in a c.1970s advertising brochure lists the code letter and names of some of the potters in the Wade Ireland Pottery as listed below:

Code Letter	Potter
C	Molly Morrow
D	Bernadette Devlin
H	Mary McAtamney
N	Kathleen Winters
P	Patricia Lyness
S	Sheila ODonnell
U	Teresa McAtamney
V	Joe Mallon

Although the initials do not seem to have any connection to the maker's name (except for *D*: "Devlin"), when the moulds were first produced it is likely that the initial matched the potter's name, but with the changes in staff it would have been, of course, uneconomical to renew moulds and their backstamps. The initials on the backstamps remained the same but the decorator changed.

The "Knurled Tankard" has four rows of impressed knurls, shamrock leaves, raised dots and raised knurls on it.

Backstamp: Impressed "Irish Porcelain" curved around a shamrock with "Made in Ireland" in a straight line underneath
Shape: I.P.6

No.	Description	Colourways	Size	U.S.$	Can.$	U.K. £
1.	Knurled	Blue/grey	105	25.00	30.00	12.00

TYRONE, c.1958-c.1980

These slender tankards can be easily recognised by their handles, which resemble one side of an Irish harp. Most of the "Tyrone Tankards" have two or three rows of knurls ans shamrocks on them. Others have knurls with a central design of overlapping linked rings, another has an all over design of linked rings.

Tyrone, Blue/Green

Tyrone, All Over Linked Rings

Backstamp: A. Impressed "Irish Porcelain" curved around a shamrock and "Made in Ireland" in a straight line underneath
B. Circular ink stamp "Seagoe Ceramics - Wade 91 Ireland"
Shape: Miniature — I.P.9; ½ pint — I.P.8; Pint — I.P.10

No.	Description	Colourways	Size	U.S.$	Can.$	U.K.£
1.	Tyrone	Blue/green	Miniature/75	8.00	10.00	3.00
	Tyrone embossed knurls	Blue/grey	Miniature/75	10.00	15.00	5.00
2.	and linked rings					
3.	Tyrone	Blue/green	½ pint/140	10.00	15.00	5.00
4.	Tyrone all over linked rings	Blue/grey	½ pint/140	15.00	20.00	8.00
5.	Tyrone	Blue/green/brown	Pint/164	15.00	20.00	8.00
6.	Tyrone	Blue/green/brown	Pint/164	15.00	20.00	8.00

CHILDREN'S TANKARDS, c.1950-c.1980

Although they were described in an Irish Wade catalogue as childrens tankards, the Leprechauns and Toadstools Tankard is the only one that has a child-like theme. They all have an embossed row of shamrock leaves around the base.

Irish Colleen Carrying Peat

Leprechauns and Toadstools

Backstamp: Embossed circular"Made in Ireland Eire tir a dheanta," "Irish Porcelain" curved over a shamrock crown and "Wade" underneath

Shape: I.P. 4

No.	Description	Colourways	Size	U.S.$	Can.$	U.K.£
1.	Bermuda Map	Blue/grey; black print	74	18.00	22.00	10.00
2.	Fisherman in River	Blue/grey; multi-coloured print	74	18.00	22.00	10.00
3.	Fisherman Walking	Blue/grey; multi-coloured print	74	18.00	22.00	10.00
4.	Flying Ducks	Blue/grey; multi-coloured print	74	18.00	22.00	10.00
5.	Flying Pheasants	Blue/grey; multi-coloured print	74	18.00	22.00	10.00
6.	The Giant Finn McCaul	Blue/grey; multi-coloured print	74	18.00	22.00	10.00
7.	Irish Colleen Carrying Peat	Blue/grey; multi-coloured print	74	18.00	22.00	10.00
8.	Leprechauns and Toadstools	Blue/grey; multi-coloured print	74	18.00	22.00	10.00
9.	Stags Head	Blue/grey; brown print	74	18.00	22.00	10.00

MUSICAL TANKARDS, c.1950-c.1980

The lower quarter of these tankards is hollow and a Swiss musical movement is held in place inside the base by a wooden disc and metal rivets. There is a key for winding and a metal "brake" on the base, which allows the music to play when the tankard is lifted and switches it off when the tankard is put down. The music boxes play a variety of Irish tunes, the names of which are printed on paper labels glued onto the base. Information recently found in a c.1970s advertising brochure lists the tunes available on the Musical tankards as follows: "Galway Bay, Killarney, Mother Machree, My Wild Irish Rose, Rose of Tralee, That's an Irish Lullaby, The Mountains of Mourne, When Irish Eyes are Smiling."

Backstamp: Black ink stamp "Made in Ireland" on the rim of the base
Shape: I.P.5

No.	Description	Colourways	Size	U.S.$	Can.$	U.K.£
1.	Air Force Crest (My Wild Irish Rose)	Blue/grey; gold print	132	70.00	90.00	40.00
2.	Drinking Toasts (Irish Lullaby)	Blue/grey; black prints	132	70.00	90.00	40.00
3.	Finn McCaul (Rose of Tralee)	Blue/grey; multi-coloured print	132	70.00	90.00	40.00
4.	Flying Ducks (Mother Machree)	Blue/grey; multi-coloured print	132	70.00	90.00	40.00
5.	Irish Coach (My Wild Irish Rose)	Blue/grey; multi-coloured print	132	70.00	90.00	40.00
6.	Irish Colleen (Irish Lullaby)	Blue/grey; multi-coloured print	132	70.00	90.00	40.00
7.	Irish Kitchen (Galway Bay)	Blue/grey; multi-coloured print	132	70.00	90.00	40.00
8.	Jaunting Car (Killarney)	Blue/grey; multi-coloured print	132	70.00	90.00	40.00
9.	Duck Hunter (Irish Lullaby)	Blue/grey; multi-coloured print	132	70.00	90.00	40.00
10.	Irish Colleen Carrying Peat (Mother Machree)	Blue/grey; multi-coloured print	132	70.00	90.00	40.00
11.	Irish Colleen Carrying Peat (When Irish Eyes are Smiling)	Blue/grey; multi-coloured print	132	70.00	90.00	40.00
12.	Flying Pheasants (The Mountains of Mourne)	Blue/grey; multi-coloured print	132	70.00	90.00	40.00

ULSTER WARE TANKARDS, c.1952-1977

The only decoration on the miniature tankards is the transfer prints; they do not have a knurled design on them like the larger sizes. They were produced from the 1950s to 1977.

The half-pint size, issued from the early 1950s to the 1970s, has one row of embossed knurls around the base. The "Paddy McGredy, Roses Tankard" has a print of roses on the front, and on the back is the inscription "Paddy McGredy, Florabunda. Raised by Paddy McGredy From Spartan x Tzigane. Awarded Gold Medal National Rose Society, Award of Merit Royal Horticultural Society."

The pint tankards, produced from the early 1950s to the early 1960s, have a double row of impressed knurls around the rim and a double row of embossed knurls around the base. The "Drinkers Toasts" version is covered with toasts from around the World; *L'Chaim, Saludos, Prosit, Bottoms Up, Chin Chin*, etc.

Flying Ducks

The Giant Finn MacCaul

Backstamp: **A.** Impressed "Irish Porcelain" curved over a shamrock with "Made in Ireland" in a straight line underneath
B. Impressed "Irish Porcelain" curved over a shamrock
C. Impressed "Irish Porcelain" slanted across a shamrock with "Wade Co. Armagh" in a straight line underneath
D. Impressed "Irish Porcelain" curved around a shamrock with A, B, E, F or G in the centre, "Made in Ireland" in a straight line underneath (with and without C below shamrock)
E. Impressed "Irish Porcelain" curved around a shamrock with "Made in Ireland by Wade Co. Armagh" in a straight line underneath

Shape: Miniature — I.P.614; ½ pint — I.P.1; Pint — I.P.2

No.	Description	Colourways	Size	U.S.$	Can.$	U.K. £
1.	Flying Ducks	Blue/grey; multi-coloured print	Miniature/52	10.00	12.00	5.00
2.	The Giant Finn MacCaul	Blue/grey; multi-coloured print	Miniature/52	10.00	12.00	5.00
3.	Irish Colleen Carrying Peat	Blue/grey; multi-coloured print	Miniature/52	10.00	12.00	5.00
4.	Irish Jaunting Car	Blue/grey; multi-coloured print	Miniature/52	10.00	12.00	5.00
5.	Irish Kitchen	Blue/grey; multi-coloured print	Miniature/52	10.00	12.00	5.00
6.	My Fair Lady	Blue/grey; multi-coloured print	Miniature/52	10.00	12.00	5.00
7.	North Wales Mountain Cottage	Blue/grey; multi-coloured print	Miniature/52	10.00	12.00	5.00
8.	Red Dragon	Blue/grey; red print	Miniature/52	10.00	12.00	5.00
9.	Stagecoach	Blue/grey; multi-coloured print	Miniature/52	10.00	12.00	5.00

Fishermen on Riverbank   **Houses of Parliament and Big Ben**   **Royal Air Force Crest**

No.	Description	Colourways	Size	U.S.$	Can.$	U.K.£
10.	City Hall Belfast	Blue/grey; black print	Miniature/52	10.00	12.00	5.00
11.	Cymru Am Byth	Blue/grey; multi-coloured print	½ pint/105	25.00	30.00	8.00
12.	Duck Hunter Two Dogs	Blue/grey; multi-coloured print	½ pint/105	25.00	30.00	8.00
13.	Fishermen on Riverbank	Blue/grey; multi-coloured print	½ pint/105	25.00	30.00	8.00
14.	Flying Pheasants	Blue/grey; multi-coloured print	½ pint/105	25.00	30.00	8.00
15.	Fox Hunter Hat on Head	Blue/grey; multi-coloured print	½ pint/105	25.00	30.00	8.00
16.	The Giant Finn MacCaul	Blue/grey; multi-coloured print	½ pint/105	25.00	30.00	8.00
17.	Irish Colleen Carrying Peat	Blue/grey; multi-coloured print	½ pint/105	25.00	30.00	8.00
18.	Irish Huntsman	Blue/grey; multi-coloured print	½ pint/105	25.00	30.00	8.00
19.	My Fair Lady	Blue/grey; multi-coloured print	½ pint/105	25.00	30.00	8.00
20.	Old Coach House, York	White; gold handle; multi-coloured print	½ pint/105	25.00	30.00	8.00
21.	Paddy McGredy Roses	Blue/grey; multi-coloured print	½ pint/105	25.00	30.00	8.00
22.	Stagecoach	Blue/grey; multi-coloured print	½ pint/105	25.00	30.00	8.00
23.	Stag's Head Crest	Blue/grey; multi-coloured print	½ pint/105	25.00	30.00	8.00
	Shield with Three Lions	Grey; multi-coloured print	½ pint/105	25.00	30.00	8.00
24.	Drinker's Toasts	Blue/grey; black prints	Pint/162	30.00	35.00	15.00
25.	Fishermen on Riverbank	Blue/grey; multi-coloured print	Pint/162	30.00	35.00	15.00
26.	The Giant Finn MacCaul	Blue/grey; multi-coloured print	Pint/162	30.00	35.00	15.00
27.	Houses of Parliament and Big Ben	Blue/grey; multi-coloured print	Pint/162	30.00	35.00	15.00
28.	Irish Colleen Carrying Peat	Blue/grey; multi-coloured print	Pint/162	30.00	35.00	15.00
29.	Irish Jaunting Car	Blue/grey; multi-coloured print	Pint/162	30.00	35.00	15.00
30.	Royal Air Force Crest	Blue/grey; gold print	Pint/162	30.00	35.00	15.00
31.	Stagecoach	Blue/grey; multi-coloured print	Pint/162	30.00	35.00	15.00
32.	Bermuda Flag	Grey/blue; red/white/blue flag; black lettering	Pint/162	30.00	35.00	15.00
33.	Crest Shield with Three Lions	Grey; multi-coloured print	Pint/162	25.00	30.00	15.00
34.	Duck Hunter Two Dogs	Blue/grey; multi-coloured print	Pint/162	30.00	35.00	15.00
35.	Eros Piccadilly Circus	Blue/grey; multi-coloured print	Pint/162	30.00	35.00	15.00
36.	Foxhunter Hat in Hand	Blue/grey; multi-coloured print	Pint/162	30.00	35.00	15.00

HALF PINT TANKARD WITH TWO ROWS OF KNURLS AROUND BASE

A new shape in a half pint size tankard has been found. The tankards have two rows of knurls along the bottom rim. Only two tankards have been found to date, which suggests they may have been produced towards the end of Wade Irelands production.

Tankard, Lions Shield and Drinking Toasts

Wales Dragon

Backstamp: Impressed "Made in Ireland"

No.	Description	Colourways	Size	U.S.$	Can.$	U.K. £
1.	Tankard Lions Shield and drinking toasts	Grey/blue; red shield/yellow lions black lettering	½ pint/105	30.00	38.00	15.00
2.	Wales Dragon	Grey/blue; red dragon print; black lettering	½ pint/105	30.00	38.00	15.00

MONEY BOXES

Wade did not produce many money boxes. Those listed in this section were produced as giftware items. Others, such as the "National Westminster Bank Piggies," "Monster Muncher" and "Fried Green Tomatoes" money boxes, can be found either in Advertising or Commissioned Products.

BACKSTAMPS

Transfer Prints

Most of these money boxes are backstamped "Wade England" with either a blue, red or black transfer print.

Transfer print, c.1955-c.1960

Impressed Backstamps

Some are marked with an impressed "Wade England."

Impressed, 1994

CAT AND DOG MONEY BOXES, 1998

The "Cat, seated" and "Scottie Dog" shaped money boxes were first seen at the Ripley Teddy Bears Picnic; they were later on sale at the Wade Shop, Arundel Swap Meet and Buffalo show. The cats were hand decorated therefore no two cats are identical. The original price was £15.00 for the cat and £10.00 for the dog.

Cat Money Box

Scottie Dog Money Box

Backstamp: Embossed "Wade"

No.	Description	Colourways	Size	U.S.$	Can.$	U.K.£
1.	Cat, seated	White; black markings	160	30.00	35.00	18.00
2.	Scottie Dog	Black	160	16.00	20.00	10.00
3.	Scottie Dog	White	160	18.00	24.00	12.00

COMIC ANIMAL MONEY BOXES, 1994

In mid summer 1994, Wade introduced a set of four smiling-animal money boxes, produced in all-over, one-colour glazes. The original price direct from the Wade Pottery was £4.

Backstamp: Impressed "Wade England"

No.	Description	Colourways	Size	U.S.$	Can.$	U.K.£
1.	Bob the Frog	Green	120	25.00	35.00	18.00
2.	Gertie the Jersey	Orange brown	150	25.00	35.00	18.00
3.	Lucky the Rabbit	Grey	173	25.00	35.00	18.00
4.	Priscilla the Pig	Pink	112	25.00	35.00	18.00

ELEPHANT MONEY BOX, c.1960

Photograph not available
at press time

Backstamp: Black transfer print "Wade England"

No.	Description	Colourways	Size	U.S.$	Can.$	U.K.£
1.	Elephant	Dark grey; blue blanket	115	90.00	130.00	45.00

FESTIVE VAN MONEY BOX, NOVEMBER 1997

The "Festive Van" money box is from the same mould as the Lyons "Tetley Tea" and "Coffee Van" money boxes. Decorated with Christmas garlands, teddy bears and Christmas presents in the windows, it was produced in a limited edition of 225. Original price at the Extravaganza was £25.00

Festive Van Money Box

Backstamp: Red printed "Wade England"

No.	Description	Colourways	Size	U.S.$	Can. $	U.K.£
1.	Festive Van	Black; multi-coloured prints; gold lettering/highlights	140	130.00	190.00	85.00

NOEL THE TEDDY BEAR MONEY BOX, NOVEMBER 1997

The mould for this teddy bear money box was originally used for the British department store Marks and Spencer's "Edward Bear" during 1995-1996. The Christmas Extravaganza "Noel" version is in a white glaze with holly motifs on the soles of his feet. It was produced in a limited edition of 1,500 for the first Wade Christmas Extravaganza held on November 29th 1997 at Trentham Gardens, Stoke-on-Trent. The Bears were sold on a first-come first-served basis.

Backstamp: Black printed circular "Christmas Teddy Extravaganza Special 1997 Wade"

No.	Description	Colourways	Size	U.S.$	Can.$	U.K.£
1.	Noel Teddy Bear Money Box	Matt white; black eyes/nose; green/red holly motif on feet	155	50.00	70.00	35.00

PAWS AT THE KERB PIG MONEY BOX, c.1955

The "Paws at the Kerb" pig shaped money box has on it a transfer print of a puppy sitting at a curb and the words "Paws at the Kerb" on one side and a schoolboy, a Belisha Beacon and the words "Look Right—Look Left—Look Right Again" on the other. The print was taken from the winning poster designed by an 11-year-old schoolgirl in a mid-1950s competition to promote British road safety.

Photograph not available
at press time

Backstamp: Blue transfer print "Wade England"

No.	Description	Colourways	Size	U.S.$	Can.$	U.K.£
1.	Pig Money Box	White; black transfers	115 x 160	65.00	80.00	38.00

SMILING PIG MONEY BOXES, 1955-c.1960

This novelty line of money boxes is found with various multi-coloured transfer prints of flowers, parasols and stars. The roses and violets designs were originally used on the "Flair Tablewares" of the mid 1950s and early 1960s, which were produced by the Wade Heath Royal Victoria Pottery. The parasols and shooting-stars designs were used on a series of vases and bowls, called Harmony Wares, made in the late 1950s to early 1960s. These money boxes are sometimes found with no backstamp.

Spring Flowers

Backstamp: **A**. Blue transfer print "Wade England"
　　　　　　　 B. Unmarked

No.	Description	Colourways	Size	U.S.$	Can.$	U.K.£
1.	Galaxy	White; gold inside ears; blue eyes; black stars	115	65.00	80.00	38.00
2.	Galaxy	Yellow; black eyes, stars	115	65.00	80.00	38.00
3.	Parasols	White; gold inside ears; blue eyes; red/yellow/blue parasols	115	65.00	80.00	38.00
4.	Shooting Stars	White; blue eyes, nostrils; pink/green/black stars	115	65.00	80.00	38.00
5.	Spring Flowers	White; gold inside ears; blue eyes, nostrils, flowers	115	65.00	80.00	38.00
6.	Summer Rose	White; gold inside ears; blue eyes; pink roses	115	65.00	80.00	38.00
7.	Summer Rose	White; gold inside ears; blue eyes; yellow roses	115	65.00	80.00	38.00
8.	Summer Rose	Yellow; blue eyes; orange roses	115	65.00	80.00	38.00
9.	Violets	White; gold inside ears; blue eyes; violet flowers	115	65.00	80.00	38.00

TEDDY BEAR MONEY BOXES: RIPLEY TEDDY BEARS PICNIC, ARUNDEL, BUFFALO AND WADE SHOP, 1998

This "Teddy Bear" money box is from the same mould used to produce the Marks and Spencer's "Edward Bear" and the Christmas Extravaganza "Noel." It was reissued in new colours for the Ripley Teddy Bears Picnic, the Arundel Swap Meet and Buffalo combined Jim Beam/Wade Show (blue and pink), and the Wade shop (white). Original price was £10.00.

Backstamp: A. Red printed "Wade England" between two lines
B. Black printed circular "Genuine Wade Porcelain"

No.	Description	Colourways	Size	U.S.$	Can.$	U.K.£
1.	Teddy Bear Money Box	Blue; black eyes/nose	155	22.00	30.00	12.00
2.	Teddy Bear Money Box	Pink; black eyes/nose	155	22.00	30.00	12.00
3.	Teddy Bear Money Box	White; black eyes/nose	155	30.00	40.00	15.00

TIGER MONEY BOX, NOVEMBER 1997

The "Tiger" money box was offered for sale at the Wade Christmas Extravaganza held on November 29th 1997. Originally produced for an Esso Petroleum order that was not fulfilled, only seventy five sample models were made. The date of production is unclear as they were found in a Wade Ceramics store room during an office move. Fifty models were sold on a first-come first-served basis at the Wade Extravaganza and twenty! models (Noted in Newsletter that 5 models were broken when a box was dropped) were held over for the July 1998 Buffalo combined Wade/Jim Beam Collectors show. Produced in an unusual biscuit glaze which had been used on the 1970s *Survival Animals* based on a series with a similar name produced by Anglia Television. The money boxes were offered for sale at the Extravaganza by Wade Ceramics at £200.00 each.

Photograph not available
at press time

Backstamp: Printed "Genuine Wade Porcelain"

No.	Description	Colourways	Size	U.S.$	Can.$	U.K.£
1.	Tiger money box	White; orange; black stripes	190 x 95	400.00	500.00	250.00

VAN MONEY BOXES, 1997

The plain one colour "Van Money Box" is from the same mould used for the 1995 Ringtsons Tea Van, and the 1996 IAJBBSC Van Money Box. Surplus undecorated vans were sold in the Wade Shop in 1997.

Backstamp: Unknown

No.	Description	Colourways	Size	U.S.$	Can.$	U.K.£
1.	Van Money Box	Blue	133 x 205	20.00	30.00	15.00
2.	Van Money Box	Cream	133 x 205	20.00	30.00	15.00

SHAVING MUGS
c.mid-late 1970s - 1985

BACKSTAMPS

This small series of shaving mugs was produced at the Royal Victoria Pottery in 1985. There is one hole in the top of the mugs. These models are more dainty and more rounded than the Addis and Culmak mugs, which are listed in Advertising and Commissioned Products sections.

The following backstamp is found on the Royal Victoria Shavings Mugs.

Red transfer print, 1985

ROYAL VICTORIA POTTERY SHAVING MUGS 1970s-1985

GALLEON COLLECTION

The decoration on these mugs is from a series called the *Galleon Collection*.

Galleon and Dinghy

Galleon and Sailboat

Backstamp: **A.** Red transfer print "Royal Victoria Pottery Wade England"
B. Red printed semicircular "Royal Victoria Pottery Staffordshire Wade England"

No.	Description	Colourways	Size	U.S.$	Can.$	U.K.£
1.	Galleon and Dinghy	White mug; brown sails, hull, dingy	85	25.00	30.00	12.00
2.	Galleon and Sailboat	White mug; yellow sails; brown hull	85	25.00	30.00	12.00

SPORTS AND RECREATION

The decoration on these shaving mugs is from a series called *Sports and Recreation*.

Cricketer

Fisherman

Backstamp: **A.** Red transfer print "Royal Victoria Pottery Wade England"
B. Red printed semicircular "Royal Victoria Pottery Staffordshire Wade England"

No.	Description	Colourways	Size	U.S.$	Can.$	U.K.£
1.	Cricketer	White mug; brown batsman and background	85	25.00	30.00	12.00
2.	Duck Hunter	White mug; multi-coloured print	85	25.00	30.00	12.00
3.	Fisherman	White mug; multi-coloured print	85	25.00	30.00	12.00
4.	Golfer	White mug; yellow/brown golfer; blue sky	85	25.00	30.00	12.00

VINTAGE CARS, 1970s

The multi-coloured prints on these Royal Victoria Pottery shaving mugs are from a series called vintage cars.

Backstamp: Black printed "Wade Made In England" (c.mid-late 1970s)

No.	Description	Colourways	Size	U.S.$	Can.$	U.K.£
1.	Cadillac 1906	White; multi-coloured print	85	25.00	30.00	12.00
2.	Daimler 1905	White; multi-coloured print	85	25.00	30.00	12.00
3.	Dion Bouton 1903	White; multi-coloured print	85	25.00	30.00	12.00
4.	Model T Ford 1908	White; multi-coloured print	85	25.00	30.00	12.00

INDEX

H

I

J

K

U

V

W

Y

Z

335